TEXTUAL
ESCAP(E)ADES

Recent Titles in
Contributions in Women's Studies

Women's Lives and Public Policy: The International Experience
Meredeth Turshen and Briavel Holcomb, editors

Sex, Abortion and Unmarried Women
Paul Sachdev

Mules and Dragons: Popular Culture Images in the Selected Writings of
African-American and Chinese-American Women Writers
Mary E. Young

Women, Community, and the Hormel Strike of 1985–86
Neala J. Schleuning

Edith Wharton's Prisoners of Consciousness: A Study of Theme and Technique
in the Tales
Evelyn E. Fracasso

Mothers and Work in Popular American Magazines
Kathryn Keller

Ideals in Feminine Beauty: Philosophical, Social, and Cultural Dimensions
Karen A. Callaghan, editor

The Stone and the Scorpion: The Female Subject of Desire in the Novels of
Charlotte Brontë, George Eliot, and Thomas Hardy
Judith Mitchell

The Several Worlds of Pearl S. Buck: Essays Presented at a Centennial
Symposium, Randolph-Macon Woman's College, March 26–28, 1992
Elizabeth J. Lipscomb, Frances E. Webb, and Peter Conn, editors

Hear Me Patiently: The Reform Speeches of Amelia Jenks Bloomer
Anne C. Coon, editor

Nineteenth-Century American Women Theatre Managers
Jane Kathleen Curry

TEXTUAL ESCAP(E)ADES

Mobility, Maternity, and Textuality in Contemporary Fiction by Women

Lindsey Tucker

Contributions in Women's Studies, Number 146

GREENWOOD PRESS
Westport, Connecticut • London

PS
374
.F45
T83
1994

Library of Congress Cataloging-in-Publication Data

Tucker, Lindsey.
    Textual escap(e)ades : mobility, maternity, and texuality in
contemporary fiction by women / Lindsey Tucker.
        p. cm. — (Contributions in women's studies, ISSN 0147–104X ;
no. 146)
    Includes bibliographical references and index.
    ISBN 0–313–29156–X
    1. American fiction—Women authors—History and criticism.
2. Feminism and literature—United States—History—20th century.
3. Women and literature—United States—History—20th century.
4. American fiction—20th century—History and criticism.
5. Atwood, Margaret Eleanor, 1939– —Characters—Women. 6. Sex
role in literature. I. Title. II. Series.
PS374.F45T83   1994
813′ .54099287—dc20   94–16130

British Library Cataloguing in Publication Data is available.

Library of Congress Catalog Card Number: 94–16130
ISBN: 0–313–29156–X
ISSN: 0147–104X

First published in 1994

Greenwood Press, 88 Post Road West, Westport, CT 06881
An imprint of Greenwood Publishing Group, Inc.

Printed in the United States of America

The paper used in this book complies with the
Permanent Paper Standard issued by the National
Information Standards Organization (Z39.48–1984).

10 9 8 7 6 5 4 3 2 1

8895

For my mother,
Arline Walker Evans

Contents

Introduction

Woman must put herself into the text—as into the world and into history—by her own movement.

Hélène Cixous
"The Laugh of the Medusa"

When you stir, you disturb their order.

Luce Irigaray
This Sex Which Is Not One

To conceive of women and mobility in the same space has been difficult in historical as well as literary terms. Male-authored texts have represented women as occupying domestic spaces—hearths, kitchens, bedrooms, and even attics and towers—while in a more subtle fixing process, women are transformed into Woman-as-Image, where they exist only within the parameters of their mirrors and function as the reflectors of male desire. In contrast, the street has always meant trouble for women. While much scholarship, some of it feminist, has documented the attitudes of Western patriarchy that have historically contributed to the immobilization of women—their use as exchange objects, their reification in much of Western art and literature—women writers have themselves demonstrated an ambivalence about female mobility and its consequences.

A sampling of some of the better-known fictions by nineteenth-century women reveals a pervasive sense of containment, even claustrophobia, along with an implicit indictment of their causes. One has only to think of Jane Eyre's red room, her insistence that human beings, including women, "must have action," that "they will make it if they cannot find it" (Chap. 12).

Because her thoughts on the subject are accompanied by a relentless pacing along her third-floor corridor just below the room where that" strange wild animal," the maddened Bertha Mason, paces in *her* closed space, the reader, certainly the female reader, is hard put to miss the import of her words. Dorothea Brooke of *Middlemarch* envisions marriage to Causaubon as a voyage, but is fated instead to remain "lost among small closets and winding stairs" (Chap. 20). The nameless narrator of "The Yellow Wallpaper," victim of the medical institutionalizing of female immobility known as the Weir Mitchell Rest Cure, finds action in the projection of her repressed energies onto a wallpaper pattern whose initially unreadable text discloses at last the story of her own imprisonment.[1] Indeed, as Sandra Gilbert and Susan Gubar argue in *The Madwoman in the Attic*, "dramatizations of imprisonment and escape are so all pervasive in the nineteenth-century literature by women that we believe that they represent a uniquely feminine tradition of the period."[2] Nonetheless, escape for most protagonists and their authors remained a problematic achievement.

Late-twentieth-century writing by women continues to reflect concerns about female mobility. For example, Gayle Greene has noted the number of "mad housewife" novels that appeared in America in the 1960s and 1970s, with their proliferation of images of "nets, webs, cages, bonds, and traps."[3] Once again, characters were not the only victims, for, as Greene observes, while the authors of such novels represented a female world in different ways than their nineteenth-century foremothers, they also failed to offer up any "alternative or oppositional energy" that might have freed themselves, their writing, or their subject matter (Greene, 60).

Of course, the aforementioned subgenre is a limited one, and I am not suggesting that either its concerns or the limitations of its narrative conventions completely describe an ongoing problem. I would argue, however, that the problem remains a challenging textual one for a number of women writers who do possess and implement what Greene refers to as alternative or oppositional energy, who manage to create what I call in this study *textual escap(e)ades*. Playing upon the rather frivolous word *escapade*, which suggests a "reckless proceeding," or a "wild prank"—activities not always associated with women—I also allow for the insertion of an *e* to represent eruptive, subversive material that undermines and sometimes transforms patriarchally derived literary models and that signifies discourses that serve the ends of a thematic and stylistic emancipation.

Because for male writers mobility and the condition of stasis against which it defines itself point to process and suggest the ambiguous and hence dangerous powers associated with materiality—both inside and outside the body—artistic and literary productions have over time employed a number of fixing strategies—idealization, abstraction, and categorization—again to protect the human subject (male) from the threatening world of contingency, whose qualities it unconsciously assigns to women.

In a number of places in her writing Luce Irigaray remarks on the tendency of the male subject to valorize volume, to establish fixing and freezing in order to maintain the fiction of his own subjectivity; by creating woman as Other, she argues, the male subject is able to separate Woman, to fix her through "reduction, division, containment, circumspection and reflection."[4] This desire explains, at least in part, the continuous entrapment of Woman-as-Image and also suggests her limited function in conventional plot structures.

For women writers, such plot structures have often proved immobilizing, as Rachel Blau DuPlessis has shown in *Writing Beyond the Ending*. For it can be argued that the manner in which mobility informs the very construction of narrative points to issues of gender, especially if, as some critics have suggested, narrative patterning always possesses an oedipal trajectory. This structure, linear in form, is constituted of the desire to know both origins and endings and revolves around the father, the patriarchal family configuration and its accompanying prohibitions.[5] However, the female figures inscribed in these narratives (the Sphinx and Jocasta, for example) are dispossessed of their own stories and exist instead in the story of the other. Here, as Teresa de Lauretis has observed, they serve as "markers of positions—places and topoi—through which the hero and his story move to their destination and to accomplish meaning."[6]

DeLauretis's observation closely matches the plot typology that appears in the work of Russian semiologist Jurij Lotman, who argues that the novels—what he calls plot-texts (linear structures consisting of a series of discrete events) and myths (texts that are cyclical and non-discrete)—constitute plot spaces that contain the following character types: "those who are mobile, who enjoy freedom with regard to plot space, who can change their place in the structure of the artistic world and cross the frontier, the basic tropological feature of this space, and those who are immobile, who represent, in fact, a function of this space."[7]

Although the issue of gender is not important to Lotman, his plot typology strongly suggests that it is the male figure who moves and the females who, immobilized, become obstacles against which the male quester/hero struggles. Lotman continues: "the mobile character is split into a paradigm-cluster of different characters on the same plane, and the obstacle (boundary) also multiplying in quantity, gives out a sub-group of personified obstacles—immobile enemy-characters fixed at particular points in the plot-space" (167). While this description of plot typology fits nicely with the story of Oedipus, or what Freud called the family romance, it offers a dubious legacy to the woman novelist when she attempts to create female characters who can act in plot space as movers, rather than as obstacles.

Another more subtle bind for some contemporary women writers involves the tendency of both writers and critics to align women writers with the realist tradition, with the result that when their subject matter is tagged as domestic, it can also be judged as trivial, narrow in focus, circumscribed in its range of action, and not the stuff of high art. Molly Hite has argued that feminist critics, with the best of intentions, too often privilege the autobiographical or focus on buried texts and muted voices, thereby succumbing to what she describes as "an exaggerated theory of mimesis in which authors are simply mirrored in their own texts."[8] Hite suggests further that two literary models—the "biographically mimetic" work and the "anxiety of authorship" model noted by Gilbert and Gubar[9]—have been particularly problematic for women because both models encourage masculinist readings, allowing women's writing to be explained as "closer" to women's experience than men's. Thus, when women's writing *is* perceived to be different, that difference "tends to be attributed to [women's] perspective, to their situation in society, to their temperament, or . . . to nature," and never "to conscious intent" (Hite, 14). It seems that when the "other side" is the focus, it is only the masculinist perception of what that other side is that has mattered.

Thus, the *Bildungsroman*, one of the more realistic of narrative forms, offers paradigms that have not proved particularly useful to women writers, especially in the area of mobility. For while the male novel of development depicts the protagonist as entering the world as a mobile being, the female protagonist is precluded from entering the world at all.[10] Indeed, Sigmund Freud's pronouncement that women were "finished" by puberty[11] seems unarguable when examining mimetic novels, especially novels of female development, which, at least in the nineteenth and early twentieth centuries, seem a contradiction in terms. Thus, as DuPlessis has observed, the works of twentieth-century women writers evidence a number of tensions in relation to such paradigms, and these writers have been forced to invent "narrative strategies, especially involving sequence, character, and relationship, that neutralize, minimize, or transcend any oversimplified oedipal drama."[12]

I would argue that when women do write subversive texts, when they do manage escapes from imprisoning, male-identified narrative models, from genre, even from mimesis itself, their discourses often have as a central concern the problem of movement. Hélène Cixous has remarked that cultural containment translates into linguistic imprisonment and that women had to first escape the discourse of men.[13] That escape has been mapped within the discussions that constituted *l'écriture féminine*, and despite some extravagant claims for writing the body feminine, and the essentialist elements that have troubled many feminists, *l'écriture* makes important statements relative to female mobility, statements that can direct our understanding of what it is in women's experimental writing that is different. The tendency of both Cixous and Irigaray to draw upon spatial metaphors that have their origins in the body is one way in which the connection between what is perceived to be "feminine" writing and textual mobility can be demonstrated.

Irigaray, for example, often discusses woman as place, but not, however, as the obstacle of the Jocasta/Sphinx oedipal plot or as the "other" place constructed by the male subject. For Irigaray, Woman is non-localized place, better explained by that untranslatable word *jouissance* (diffused energy or, for Irigaray, an "indefinite flood").[14] Irigaray also prefers to destablize the term *woman* by affixing both definite and indefinite pronouns, the/a, suggesting woman herself as definite and indefinite, sometimes not even a "who," but a "what"—"what cannot be defined, enumerated, formulated or *formalized* (*Speculum*, 230). As this Woman claims her sexual multiplicity, she becomes for Irigaray process—"neither open nor closed. *She is indefinite, in-finite, form is never complete in her*" (*Speculum*, 229).

Cixous, when she is not casting doubt on women as having any place at all, remarks that women have too often served as "labyrinths, ladders, trampled spaces."[15] Instead, Cixous expresses a preference for images of the female body in movement, movement that has everything to do with writing. For her, the female imaginary is "the site . . . of identification of an ego no longer given over to an image defined by the masculine," but now capable of inventing forms of women "on the march," women "in flight" ("Castration," 52). Cixous has had much to say about the women who *do not* write as women, who perpetuate what is for her the most representative of women's tales, namely, the tale of Sleeping Beauty, where woman is "in bed and asleep 'laid out,' " whose only movement or trajectory has been "from bed to bed, one bed to another, where she can dream" ("Castration," 42).

Yet Cixous also claims that writing belongs to women because "for a man it is much more difficult to let himself be traversed by the other."[16] Woman, she says, is open and can be "possessed," that is, "dispossessed of herself," because "women admit the existence of the other." The result is that rather than inscribing the fixity of sexual difference, women's writing can be marked by exchanges: "Writing is in me the passing through, entering, going out, staying, of the other who is me and not me, who I cannot be, but who I feel pass through" ("Sorties," 158).

The fluid rendering of the female subject that seems implicit in some arguments relative to *l'écriture feminine* suggests not only an important recognition of the unstable and alienated nature of the subject (acknowledged by many women writers who may or may not have become familiar with the ideas of Jacques Lacan), but also the importance of the role of space to a number of contemporary women writers. Bounded and unbounded, empty and filled, spaces can be defined as "distance without limit in all directions" or as areas between things. Contexts for movement, spaces are useful metaphors where the problems of the subject and the Other can be projected. But as suggested earlier, plot space has been problematized for the women writer because of the conventions that place women as obstacles within plot space. Thus, when women do construct a female quest narrative, that is, when a female character can be constituted as a mover within plot space, she, like the male protagonist, appears to be confronted with female-as-obstacle, namely, the maternal presence, a presence that, as both her and not-her, gives women writers their special interest in space. Nancy Chodorow and others have shown how problematic the maternal presence is for the daughter, especially in the area of mergence and separation. Because the boundaries between mother and daughter are less decisively determined for a longer period of time (the longer pre-oedipal period for girls), the daughter tends to experience herself as possessing "more flexible or permeable ego boundaries."[17] As a consequence, the difficulty that the daughter appears to experience in separating self from (m)Other marks the daughter's writing in a different way, often metaphorizing the maternal presence in terms of spatial constructs such as the labyrinth and the mirror.

A historically rich symbol, the labyrinth derives its popularity from its representation of both erected and dissolving boundaries. While labyrinths can be inanimate architectural structures consisting of winding, often subterranean passages, they can also be botanical and animate structures, employing intricate networks of pathways whose twists and turns are obscured by thick vegetation. But these later, fixed forms were preceded by a different form, a dance ordered and patterned by floor inscriptions that imitate the dance of birds. There is much scholarly evidence to suggest that the labyrinth never lost its association with the feminine.[18] That the labyrinth has always had an attraction for women writers can be seen in the continuing popularity of gothic fiction, which is typically both written and read by women. As Claire Kahane has suggested, the labyrinth is a crucial configuration for women, who must not simply preside over it, but also use it imaginatively to explore the limits of their own identities, their mergence with and separation from the mothers.[19]

The mirror is another, and far more complex, spatial construct that a number of women writers appear attracted to, mainly because it is a space in which concerns regarding the female subject, the double, and the gaze can be critiqued and subverted. Given women's longstanding cultural associations with the mirror and the privileging of the visual in Western culture, this interest in what has come to represent another form of entrapment is not surprising. Feminist and psychoanalytic theories have also explored the visual and its relationship to signifying practices, focusing also on its role in the creation of sexual difference. Some critics have noted, for example, that the visual is privileged because it is by means of this sensory function that the subject's separation from the other can be established. The visual also allows the subject a distancing from the object and hence a "domain of mastery" whereby s/he has access to the object, but is not endangered by contact with it.[20] The visual is also the producer of the totalized image of the body and, most important, is responsible for the perception of sexual difference defined by lack.

While art often represented the mirror as an attribute of Woman, a symbol of her vanity and narcissism, critics in both feminist and film theory have argued instead that women's apparent narcissism is better explained as a double consciousness whereby they watch themselves *and* watch themselves being watched. Mirrors, therefore, represent the ways in which women become fixed as objects of the male gaze and reflections of male desire. Thus, as metaphors for containment and fixity, mirrors provide important spaces in which to question the nature and condition of female subjectivity. Textual mobility comes to involve, for some women writers, an escape from the dominance of the visual.

Lacan's mirror-stage theories suggest in more elaborate ways the relationship of the mirroring process to mobility. The infant's prematurity and inadequate motor coordination guarantee the pleasure it derives from the introjection of its own image, an image that is stabilizing, yet permanently alienating. Forgoing any simplistic concept of the divided self, Lacan argues instead that any stabilized or unified self must be understood as an ongoing interaction of an imaginary or identificatory (and early) register with a symbolic or substitutive (later) system of language. The infant's acquisition of the image of a totalized self (between the ages of six and eighteen months) helps it to gain a tenuous sense of mastery of a body over which it previously had little control, even as it becomes dependent on vision for wholeness and stability. The mirror, offering the infant a gestalt, a fixed, albeit external, form, supplies it with a comforting contrast to the "turbulent movements that the subject feels are animating him."[21] According to Lacan, while this first gestalt "symbolizes the mental permanence of the *I*," at the same time it "prefigures its alienating destination" (2). In other words, while the child's image is the source of identification, it is also simultaneously an other.

The infant's visual capture of itself is thus, paradoxically, the moment when it loses itself.[22] However, it is around this splitting that all the energies and organization of passions will be situated. The child is thereafter constructed with vacillating attitudes and mobilized by its identification with a specular image that compels it to seek for an original wholeness that can only be reconstituted by hindsight. Important in reference to the Lacanian split subject is that s/he is not thereby immobilized, but is condemned to movement through the intersections of unconscious content with the imaginary and symbolic orders. Yet through the negotiation of these registers, the imaginary *moi* constantly seeks a stasis.

Irigaray, however, implicated the mother more fully in the specular immobilizing of the daughter. For example, by crossing linguistic boundaries Irigaray evokes a *"mer du glace,"* thereby suggesting that the homophonic linkage of mother/sea/liquid (*mere/mer*) with ice/mirror comments unfavorably on the mother who fixes and freezes, the mother of the mirror.[23]

In "And the One Doesn't Stir Without the Other," Irigaray further develops the negative effects of the mirror in terms of the mother-daughter relationship: "You look at yourself in the mirror. And already you see your own mother there. And soon your daughter, a mother. Between the two, what are you? What space is yours alone?" (63).

While the Lacanian imaginary posits the play of mirror images as a means of masking intersubjectivity, Irigaray's use of mirrors suggests the veiling of intersubjectivity by the maternal. Although she expresses hope for a different relationship—"I would like us to play together at being the same and different. You/I exchanging selves endlessly and each staying herself. Living mirrors" (61)—the conditional tense suggests the situation as only a possibility. The final passage reads more like a lament: "And the one doesn't stir without the other. But we do not move together. When the one of us comes into the world, the other goes underground. When the one carries life, the other dies" (67).[24] Nevertheless, Irigaray's textual escap(e)ade succeeds in asking questions about this relationship and in critiquing the Freudian script of female psychosexual development, even as she moves from the realm of theoretical discursivity into the realm of the poetic.

While not exclusively the domain of the woman writer, boundary concerns are relative to both mobility and the spatial constructs mentioned above. This interest points once again to problems of separation and mergence arising from the infantile situation—divisions between self and other, between container and contained, inside and outside.[25] As Roberta Rubenstein has noted, even the term *boundary* is a fluid one: "in the most general sense, it indicates the figurative line that divides, defines, distinguishes two or more contiguous areas. When these areas are conceived as metaphorical rather than literal, the possibilities of meaning extend into diverse aspects of experience" (8).

I would make such an extension by going beyond only spatial constructs in order to discuss boundary violations in a temporal sense. For it would appear that boundary confusions are especially interesting to some writers when they involve the interpenetration of past and present, living and dead, when they suggest beyond the self as a past and present construction, a concurrence of the two, a presence of absence that is best discussed by recalling some of Freud's observations about the uncanny.

Freud noted the importance of the temporal component of the uncanny when he stressed the fact that time was the ingredient that often determined an object's uncanniness.[26] Freud's insight that what was originally a benign manifestation, but becomes at a later time "a thing of terror," suggests an important way in which past invades present, especially given the fact that, in one instance at least, this invasion points to the presence of the mother's body:[27]

To some people the idea of being buried alive by mistake is the most uncanny thing of all. And yet psychoanalysis has taught us that this terrifying phantasy is only a transformation of another phantasy which had originally nothing terrifying about it at all, but was qualified by a certain lasciviousness—the phantasy, I mean, of intra-uterine existence. (*SE*, 17:244)

Freud's recognition of the uncanniness of conditions that evoke infantile relationships to the mother's body also acknowledges the essentially threatening aspects of that relationship, aspects that bear in important ways on gothic material, especially as metaphorized in the labyrinth. But some of the writers I discuss here seem attracted to another image that is spatial in a more complex way, namely, the spiral or vortex. I would argue that writers employ such images in conjunction with different narrative strategies, but that the *appeal* of such images derives from the fantasies we carry forward from early infancy. This time period, described in Lacanian theory as the pre-mirror stage, emphasizes the infant's relationship to its bodily territories, a relationship that is not a conceptual one, but exists instead below the level of language and reinforces the state of fragmentation and rupture that characterizes the constitution of the human subject. Thus, even before sexual differentiation is perceived, before oedipalization, the infant is already marked by castration.[28] As the subject carries with it a consciousness of body "misrecognized as whole, it unconsciously experiences its body as an uncoordinated aggregate, a series of parts, zones, sensations, needs, and impulses," engendering a condition that Ellie Ragland-Sullivan described as follows: "underlying any sense of symmetry through identification with the human totem there flows a piecemeal system, a network of fragments and part objects which first served to symbolize a void during the pre-mirror stage."[29]

I would argue that the images of vortexes and spirals, which are so frequently found in some women's writing, point to a gender-specific relationship of the subject to castration. As feminist critics working in film and suture theory have demonstrated,[30] male writers and directors create works that are noted for their fetishistic quality, for their disinclination to textualize absence, and for their reliance on woman to stand for lack.[31] Reasons for this inclination are offered by Lacanian theorists like Ragland-Sullivan, who argue that women experience the separation trauma differently and that because the daughter's bond with the mother renders her more susceptible to boundary invasions, the female imaginary may be differently constituted; while males experience castration as fear-producing, females experience it as loss.[32] Thus, presence of absence can be a way of talking about repressed infantile material derived from the perceptual flow that structures pre-conscious awareness, "mnemic traces" of which remain unconscious, but reveal themselves symptomatically in images and metaphors and in disruptions and discontinuities in language.

I hope to show in the following chapters that women writers are drawn to material that represents mobility, to material that is fluid in both spatial and temporal terms because such fluidity both opposes patriarchal reification of Woman-as-Image and offers ways of textualizing their critique of patriarchal containment. Such critiques involve the creation of narratives that are both confrontational *and* playful, venturesome and subversive, that utilize mobility as both a condition and a metaphor in the constitution of their own particular form of postmodern textuality.

The writers whose texts I have chosen to discuss here are, with the exception of one or two, well known and frequently studied. Because these writers are familiar and because most have continued to produce interesting and imaginative work, I felt that a study on a more narrow area of their works could be useful. I do not intend that the novels discussed here would constitute a totalizing statement about mobility, maternity, and their textual implications, but rather that they would be useful in opening up the discussion so that questions of class, race, and sexual orientation would be raised in relation to the subject of female mobility. To that end, it was important to have a grouping of novels in which the mother-daughter relationship figured, as well as novels in which the journey or quest was considered an aesthetic, social, and ultimately even a psychosexual problem. These considerations resulted in the selection of a group of novels that are perhaps more noteworthy for their differences. If there is any schematizing to be found here, it resides perhaps in the trajectory of my discussion, my own movement from the more realistic *Bildungsroman* of Sylvia Plath's *The Bell Jar* to the more experimental fictions of E. M. Broner (*Her Mothers*) and Monique Wittig (*Les Guérillères*). I was especially interested in exploring textual escapes not only from a more realistic mode, but also from genre and myth, and the maternal presence. Other forms of textual mobility—decentering and destabalizing strategies and stylistics, critiques of representation, and the use of multiple subject positions—provide further useful points of departure.

Plath's *The Bell Jar* is the subject of Chapter 2. It can no longer be considered "contemporary," of course, but I feel it introduces the problems of textual and thematic mobility while at the same time it negotiates escape less successfully than any other work I discuss. Indeed, its *Bildungsroman* quality and its essentially mimetic mode appear as symptoms of a stunted psychosexual development.

No writer is more concerned with specular selfhood and the contingent nature of both self and boundaries than Margaret Atwood and her protagonist Joan Foster. In Atwood's 1976 novel *Lady Oracle*—the subject of Chapter 3—Joan resists containment and fixing by a mother intent on turning her into product. A conscious boundary violator early in life, Joan also finds gothic fiction an ideal genre for her because it offers her a conventional representation of female entrapment as well as an escape from *it*—*from the mirror imagos* that are so crucial to the form and, finally, from the genre itself.

Chapter 4 treats E. M. Broner's experimental novel *Her Mothers* (1975). Like the preceding work, this novel is all tangents, and it, too, offers escape from genre. Broner's central journey, however, is a textual one that moves through literary history and out of it reconstructs a new, collectively authored female text that tells the story of female entrapment in male projections.

For African American women writers the journey is historical and personal; yet because their legacy of mobility includes both the fugitive slave journey—the women's slave narrative in particular—and the horrors of the Middle Passage, mobility remains potent as a metaphor that is always more collective than individual. Nonetheless, the novels of Alice Walker and Toni Morrison treat women's mobility in different ways, both formally and thematically. In Chapter 5 I examine the proliferating manifestations of mobility—problematic and otherwise—in Walker's novel *Meridian*. More than any other African American woman writer perhaps, Walker seems to find the issue of mobility crucial to her as a literary legacy and as a thematic concern. Chapter 6 offers a discussion of Morrison's representation of mobility in both *Sula* and *Beloved*. Morrison's textual mobility derives from her centrifugally constructed narratives, which serve to mirror the original diaspora, as well as the fragile subjectivity of her female characters.

In an examination of lesbian writing, Chapter 7 turns from the relationship of mobility to race to focus on the possibility of an escape from gender. Freud argues that the lesbian has avoided the "wave of passivity" that incapacitates the so-called normal woman and has kept for herself a larger degree of mobility. But more than salvaging her so-called masculine activity, the lesbian writer and the lesbian text would appear to offer an extensive rewriting and demythologizing of narratives as ways out of the gender bind. To explore this question further, I examine textual (and sexual) mobility in Irigaray's "When Our Lips Speak Together" and Wittig's *Les Guérillères* and *The Lesbian Body*.

While I have intended no exclusive methodology, I have chosen to bring psychoanalytic theory to bear upon some of my discussions because of my view that social and textual mobility points to questions regarding the body, the speaking subject, and the oedipal relationship, whether women writers assume that configuration or write against it. To this end, Freudian and Lacanian views have been useful because of the insights they have brought to bear on the female subject and the otherness that instigates male escape through the domestication of women.

NOTES

1. There have been some interesting studies done on the Rest Cure. See especially Ellen L. Bassuk, "The Rest Cure: Repetition or Resolution of Victorian

Women's Conflicts?" in *The Female Body in Western Culture*, ed. Susan Rubin Suleiman (Cambridge: Harvard University Press, 1986), 139–51; see also Suzanne Poirier, "The Weir Mitchell Rest Cure: Doctor and Patients," *Women's Studies* 10 (1983): 15–40. As a response to the cult of hypochondria, Mitchell's codification of female passivity went as follows: "I do not permit the patient to sit up or to sew or write or read, or to use the hands in any active way. . . . I arranged to have the bowels and water passed while lying down" (Bassuk, 141). Such practices not only kept women immobilized, but also, as Bassuk has shown, had a punitive aspect to them as well, since their ultimate goal was to convince certain difficult cases that domestic duties were a less unpleasant alternative.

2. Sandra Gilbert and Susan Gubar, *The Madwomen in the Attic: The Woman Writer and the Nineteenth-Century Literary Imagination* (New Haven, Conn.: Yale University Press, 1979), 85.

3. Gayle Greene, *Changing the Story: Feminist Fiction and the Tradition* (Bloomington: Indiana University Press, 1991), 59.

4. Luce Irigaray, *This Sex Which Is Not One*, trans. Catherine Porter (Ithaca, N.Y.: Cornell University Press, 1985), 106–18 (hereafter cited in the text as *This Sex*).

5. Roland Barthes, *The Pleasure of the Text*, trans. Richard Miller (New York: Hill and Wang, 1975), 10, discusses the oedipal plot as follows: "The pleasure of the text is . . . an Oedipal pleasure (to denude, to know, to learn the origin and the end), if it is true that every narrative (every unveiling of the truth) is a staging of the (absent, hidden, or hypostatized) father—which would explain the solidity of narrative forms, of family structures, and of prohibitions of nudity."

6. Teresa deLauretis, *Alice Doesn't: Feminism, Semiotics, Cinema* (Bloomington: Indiana University Press, 1984), 109.

7. Jurij M. Lotman, "The Origin of Plot in the Light of Typology," trans. Julian Graffy, *Poetics Today* 1, nos. 1–2 (Autumn 1979): 167.

8. Molly Hite, *The Other Side of the Story: Structures and Strategies of Contemporary Women's Narratives* (Ithaca, N.Y.: Cornell University Press, 1989), 13.

9. The phrase "anxiety of authorship" refers to Harold Bloom's anxiety of influence theory, which argues that every new author fears his literary forefathers' ability to vanquish his creative powers. The paradigm is, as Gilbert and Gubar have observed, both oedipal and patriarchal. They also observe that the anxiety of influence experienced by a male poet is also felt by a female poet as an even more primary anxiety of authorship—a "radical fear that she can never create; that because she can never become a 'precursor,' the act of writing will isolate or destroy her" (Gilbert and Gubar, 47–48).

10. See Elizabeth Abel, Marianne Hirsch, and Elizabeth Langland, *The Voyage In: Fictions of Female Development* (Hanover, NH: University Press of New England, 1983), 3–19. Abel, Hirsch, and Langland suggest that women writers, limited by male-constructed paradigms, transform the novel of development in essentially two different ways. The first involves the retention of a basically linear and chronological narrative treating apprenticeship, while the second constructs a delayed development, an awakening process. There is, however, a second plot or subtext, which stands opposed to the more conventional plot, that becomes the source of tensions.

11. Freud's charting of female psychosexual development is marked by numerous references to the girl's increasing passivity. In "Female Sexuality," for exam-

ple, Freud speaks of the "struggle" undergone with the girl's change of object (the turning away from the mother) as characterized by a "marked lowering of the active sexual impulses and a rise of the passive ones"(*The Standard Edition of the Complete Psychological Works of Sigmund Freud*, ed. James Strachey [London: Hogarth Press, 1953–74], 21:239 [hereafter cited in the text as *SE*]). He also describes the girl's entry into the oedipal situation as a kind of last phase, "a haven of refuge" ("Femininity," *SE*, 22:129). Finally, he says of the girl's development that "the decisive turning points will have already been prepared for or completed before puberty" ("Femininity," *SE*, 22:118).

12. Rachel Blau DuPlessis, *Writing Beyond the Ending: Narrative Strategies of Twentieth-Century Women Writers* (Bloomington: Indiana University Press, 1985), 37.

13. Hélène Cixous, "Castration or Decapitation?" trans. Annette Kuhn, *Signs* 7, no. 1 (Autumn 1981): 42 (hereafter cited in the text as "Castration").

14. Luce Irigaray, *Speculum of the Other Woman*, trans. Gillian C. Gill (Ithaca, N.Y.: Cornell University Press, 1985), 228 (hereafter cited in the text as *Speculum*).

15. Hélène Cixous, "The Laugh of the Medusa," trans. Keith Cohen and Paula Cohen, *Signs* 1, no. 4 (Summer 1976): 878 (hereafter cited in the text as "Laugh").

16. Hélène Cixous, "Sorties," in *The Newly Born Woman*, eds. Hélène Cixous and Catherine Clémont, trans. Betsy Wing (Minneapolis: University of Minnesota Press, 1986), 158. See also Trinh T. Minh-ha, "L'Innécriture: Un-writing/Inmost Writing," in *When the Moon Waxes Red: Representation, Gender and Cultural Politics* (New York: Routledge, 1991), 119–45.

17. Nancy Chodorow, *The Reproduction of Mothering: Psychoanalysis and the Sociology of Gender* (Berkeley: University of California Press, 1978), 169. Chodorow has her critics. Judith Lorber accuses Chodorow of ignoring "significant structural variables" and of "emphasizing psychoanalytic interpretations at the expense of social and behavioral analysis." See Judith Lorber, Rose Laub Coser, Alice S. Rossi, and Nancy Chodorow, "On *The Reproduction of Mothering*: A Methodological Debate," *Signs* 6, no. 3 (1981): 482.

18. Erich Neumann, *The Great Mother*, trans. Ralph Manheim (Princeton, N.J.: Princeton University Press, 1963), 175–76, saw labyrinths and their rituals as symbolizing the negative alimentary character of the Great Mother. Such dances were, in any case, presided over by women and walked through by men.

19. Claire Kahane, "The Gothic Mirror," in *The (M)other Tongue: Essays in Feminist Psychoanalytic Interpretation*, ed. Shirley Nelson Garner, Claire Kahane, and Madelon Sprengnether (Ithaca, N.Y.: Cornell University Press, 1985), 337.

20. See John Berger, *Ways of Seeing* (New York: Viking, 1973), 45–64; discussion of the gaze begins with Laura Mulvey, "Visual Pleasure and Narrative Cinema," *Screen* 16, no. 3 (1975): 8–18, reprinted in *Visual and Other Pleasures* (Bloomington: Indiana University Press, 1989), 14–26; Christian Metz, *The Imaginary Signifier*, trans. Ben Brewster (Bloomington: Indiana University Press, 1981), 58–66.

21. Jacques Lacan, "The Mirror Stage as Formative of the Function of the I as Revealed in Psychoanalytic Experience," in *Écrits: A Selection*, trans. Alan Sheridan (New York: W. W. Norton, 1977), 2.

22. Elizabeth Grosz, *Jacques Lacan: A Feminist Introduction* (New York: Routledge, 1990), 41. See also Kaja Silverman, *The Subject of Semiotics* (New York: Oxford University Press, 1983); for Lacan, the infant's self-recognition is always a

misrecognition; the infant knows itself only by means of a fictional construct. Thus, the mirror stage becomes "one of those crises of alienation around which the Lacanian subject is organized, since to know oneself through an external image is to be defined through self-alienation" (158).

23. In her short essay, "And the One Doesn't Stir Without the Other," trans. Hélène Vivienne Wenzel, *Signs* 7, no. 1 (Autumn 1981): 60–67, Irigaray illustrates the daughter's paralysis in terms of images of freezing, as the opening lines demonstrate: "With your milk, Mother, I swallowed ice. And here I am now, my insides frozen. And I walk with even more difficulty than you do, and I move even less" (60).

24. Translator Wenzel notes that the original French reads *mais ce n'est ensemble que nous mouvons*, rendering the phrase purposefully ambiguous so that "we do not move together" can also mean "it is only together that we can move" (67).

25. See especially Roberta Rubenstein's helpful discussion of boundaries and their relationship both to the self and to questions involving cultural and ethnic identity in the novels of contemporary women writers (*Boundaries of the Self: Gender, Culture, Fiction* [Urbana: University of the Illinois Press, 1987]).

26. In his essay on "The Uncanny," Freud defines it as that which excites fear, even "repulsion and distress." He includes in his cataloguing of uncanny ingredients fears related to the visual, such as the evil eye and the child's fear of eye loss. He also mentions the double and the power of inanimate objects and dismembered parts to evoke this kind of horror. While he considered the double an important example of the uncanny, he also observed that it received "fresh meaning from later stages of the ego's development," here it becomes a "special agency" that "stands over the rest of the ego" (*SE*, 17:235). Originally a feature of primary narcissism, the later manifestation of the double resides in the watching part of the ego and, dissociated from it, treats the ego "like an object" (*SE*, 17:235). Frued concludes that the uncanniness of the double derives from its being "a creation dating back to a very early mental stage" where it appears in a friendly form" (*SE*, 17:236).

27. What is particularly fascinating about Freud's discussion is his recognition of the slippage that characterizes the nature of the uncanny within the two definitions of the word *heimlich*, whose original meaning is "homey" or "familiar," but which has come to mean its opposite, *unheimlich*, as it metamorphoses into that which is unfamiliar, that which is secret, or that which has been concealed, but recently revealed (*SE*, 17:222–24).

28. According to Lacan, the pre-specular infant, by means of a complex process of identification, assimilates its world in a hallucinatory and fragmented manner. These fragments are constituted not so much from the mother's body as such as from the infant's relationship to it. That is, the infant first perceives the mother's bodily territories as its own. Thus, besides its own body zones, it takes portions of the mother's body—the breast, the voice, and the gaze, for example—as its own, and these sources of plenitude and pleasure, when separated from the bodily territory of the infant, cause it to experience a sense of object loss. While this loss is necessary for its entry into the symbolic order, it also undermines permanently any sense of wholeness.

29. Ellie Ragland-Sullivan, *Jacques Lacan and the Philosophy of Psychoanalysis* (Urbana: University of Illinois Press, 1987), 296.

30. See, for example, Kaja Silverman, *The Acoustic Mirror: The Female Voice in Psychoanalysis and Cinema* (Bloomington: Indiana University Press, 1988), especially her chapter "Lost Objects and Mistaken Subjects," 15–27.

31. In arguing for castration as preceding knowledge of anatomical difference, Silverman goes on to suggest that "this refusal to identify castration with any of the divisions which occur prior to the registration of sexual difference reveals Freud's desire to place a maximum distance between the male subject and the notion of lack" (ibid., 15).

32. Ragland-Sullivan, *Jacques Lacan*, 296, suggests that "insofar as the primary unconscious Desire is the (m)Other's, the daughter is closer to the personal and narcissistic (the *moi*) while the son is urged by the oedipal structure and by language to 'transcend' the Other's influence, to find himself within the social (public) group."

2

Stopped Dead: Pathology as Development in *The Bell Jar*

> The woman is perfected
> Her dead
> Body wears the smile of accomplishment
> . . . Her bare
> Feet seem to be saying:
> We have come so far, it is over.
>
> —Sylvia Plath, "Edge"

Sylvia Plath's *The Bell Jar* (1963), although hardly "contemporary," does provide a useful point of departure for a study of textual escap(e)ades. For one thing, its mimetically rendered inscription of impaired mobility offers up an imaginary engagement with Sigmund Freud's theories of female psychosexual development; for another, its narrative structure betrays a lack of ease with the constraints of the *Bildungsroman* paradigm, while its imagery is marked not by stasis so much as by inversions of mobility—images of flattening, shrinking, and melting, to name a few. It is also a text in which the maternal presence becomes almost all-pervasive, operating in the form of spatial constructs as well as in the proliferation of surrogate maternal figures. Last, the novel has a compelling "unconscious" side to it, becoming, in Mary Jacobus's words, a text that "knows more than it knows (and more than the author intended),"[1] especially in Plath's treatment of lesbianism.

Unfortunately, because of the novel's autobiographical ingredients and the morbidly sensational nature of its content, it has attracted a diversity of readings. Those by male critics reflect an interest in probing Esther's behavior that is not unlike Freud's spirited excavations into the repressed secrets of his female hysterics.[2] Indeed, it is not difficult to make a case for Esther as a neurotic—or worse—but the horrified fascination that some male critics bring to their study of both Plath and her work is certainly troublesome for feminists more sensitive both to Plath's time and to the gender issues with which she appears to struggle.

Edward Butscher, whose admiration for Plath's poetry is never in doubt, displays a disturbing relish for the term "bitch goddess," which he applies ostensibly to the persona he sees in her later work. However, since he often has difficulty separating Plath from this persona, the epithet soon becomes suspect. He also has a tendency to construct a picture of Plath as driven by a lust for fame and possessed of an overweening narcissism.[3] Other psychoanalytic critics focus at length on Plath's father fixation and her puritanism. Their discussions have a reproachful air about them, and their pronouncements on the defects of both Plath and her fictional alter ego, Esther Greenwood, often become less attributable to illness than to their failings as women.[4]

Nevertheless, psychoanalytic readings seem unavoidable, and despite the rather transparent cultural bias that emerges in Freud's writing, his script for the girl's development has rather chilling echoes in *The Bell Jar*, especially in terms of his contention that the girl is "finished" by puberty. The denouement is the logical result of his relentless charting of the girl's developmental difficulties. The struggle begins with the girl's assignment to "two extra tasks,"[5] namely, the surrender of her "active" clitoral masturbatory activity for the passivity of her vaginal zone and the turning away from her mother. This change of object (which the boy does not undergo) seriously deprives the girl in terms of sexual activity; she experiences "a marked lowering of the active sexual impulses and a rise of the passive ones," says Freud ("Female Sexuality," *SE*, 21:239). But the turn from the mother to the father constitutes not the beginning of her development, but the end, since her entry into the "Oedipal situation" is described by Freud as "a haven or refuge" ("Femininity," *SE*, 22: 129). Freud also avers that because of her prolonged stay in the pre-oedipal phase, her superego will be insufficiently developed, with the result that her cultural contributions will be less significant as well.

Read against such constrictive pronouncements, Plath's novel of development can stand as a confirmation of the Freudian female journey. In any case, psychoanalytic readings are tempting, for Esther's descent into madness—if that is what it was[6]—seems to demand a reading, an analysis of cause and effects, both to explain the text and to offer clues to Plath's own behavior and its capping act of violence.

The Bell Jar also mirrors Freud's script of female development in another way. We might recall that Freud himself has difficulty keeping the line between the normal and the pathological distinct. This difficulty was attributed to the essence of female development itself, regarded by Freud as a constant battle against repression, a battle that is often expressed, as I have earlier indicated, in images of fixity and mobility. Like all literary texts, but perhaps to a greater degree, this novel has its uncanny side, where eruptive energies, which appear not only in images, but also in gaps that serve to contaminate the text and to produce slippage of meaning.

To begin, the disturbing ease with which the novel lends itself to both a description as a *Bildungsroman*[7] and a case history suggests the equally disturbing boundary confusion we find in Freud's scenarios for both "normal" and neurotic female development. We might suggest that both 'case history' and *Bildungsroman* fit this novel precisely because of the double-voiced discourse characteristic of women novelists such as Plath. However, the tensions resulting from this doubleness are also the source of a remarkable textual mobility. When we recall the ingredients of the typical *Bildungsroman*—the journey from country to city, the dilemma over career choice, the traumatic love relationships, the struggle to reconcile the hero to the community—we can readily see that when structured around a female protagonist, the asymmetry in development in terms of males and females is thrown into relief, also revealing the phallocentric bias of theoretical articulations of the developmental process itself. This bias is further highlighted when we examine the narrator's problems with mobility and fixity, problems that are revealed in images and narrative strategies, as well as in the presence of uncanny subject matter.

For example, keeping the *Bildungsroman* plot in mind, we can see that Esther Greenwood's story opens appropriately enough with a journey— her trip to New York for a month of editorial work in the offices of *Ladies' Day*. Here, however, the plot takes a wrong turn. For one thing, Esther has not been awarded a job; she has been given a prize, a pretend-job where she enters the world of the women's magazine where male-produced fantasies determine what the desired female image is to be. Hence, the job is one of the many labyrinthine dead ends of the story. In reality, the New York trip initiates a return to the country of the mothers, to Esther's hometown, whose "motherly breath enfold[s]" her.[8] This brief journey, which confuses egress and regress, exemplifies the Freudian view of the girl as finished before puberty. Indeed, Esther says as much when she declares that "after nineteen years of running after good marks and prizes and grants of one sort or another, I was letting up, slowing down, dropping clean out of the race" (*BJ*, 24).

Having correctly concluded that her race is over, the narrator is left to recount an increasingly episodic narrative that outlines attempts to move in some direction, but that ends in a maze of blind alleys. The second part of the novel, for example, can be characterized as possessed of a frenzied mobility, where Esther takes bus rides to Boston, returns to her childhood seaside town at Deer Island, and finally visits her father's grave. But each trip is regressive, moving outward from the hub of maternal space that structures and eventually determines a return, so that even Esther's imaginary journey by bus to Chicago, undertaken under the newly created identity of the orphan Elly Higginbottom, culminates in a stop "two blocks from my house" (*BJ*, 114). Like the closing/opening lines of *Finnegans Wake*, which she has been reading, Esther has also been brought "*by a commodious vicus of recirculation back*" to the site of the mothers (*BJ*, 101).

In fact, the only "getting out" Esther is able to accomplish is engineered by her mother and involves two agendas for normalizing her development and assuring her feminine destiny. One is a blind date at the beach, and the other involves appropriately ladylike work—volunteer work—at a hospital, where her job is to deliver flowers and candy to women in the maternity ward. In both instances she is forced to confirm "female" activities—both of which valorize those passive aims mapped by Freud: loving men and having babies. Esther is under no illusion about her hospital work: "If I had been getting paid," she says, "no matter how little, I could at least count this a proper job" (*BJ*, 32).

Her other journeys are undertaken in connection with her breakdown and further confirm her passivity. In these instances the maternal presence, represented by mother surrogates such as Dodo Conway and Philomela Guinea, is also imaged in vehicles: Her mother's car is described as a prison van (*BJ*, 151), and Dodo Conway's black station wagon—appropriately hearselike—is used to drive her to Walton to Dr. Gordon's private hospital for shock treatments. These vehicles convey Esther from her hometown hospital, then to a city hospital, and finally from the city hospital in another hearselike conveyance—Philomela Guinea's black Cadillac—to her ultimate destination.

This last hospital presents us with another disturbing configuration of the maternal presence. Its grouping of buildings not only maps the progression or the retrogression of its patients—Caplan (the middle ground), Belsize (for improving patients), and Waymark (for the backsliders)—but also provides the only kind of mobility available for the women it houses. Thus, moving through the buildings of the institution becomes finally the way in which space, always remaining linked to the maternal, continues to define Esther and her progress; worse, the agenda for recovery is scripted by patriarchal clinicians whose goal is to make women into better products. The buildings are also hierarchically structured and conceal beneath their ground floors a group of "mysterious basement corridors" that link, in "an elaborate network of tunnels and burrows, all the various buildings" (*BJ*, 174). Thus, even when pronounced improved and moved up to Belsize, Esther is never safe, for the tunnels can (and do) lead back to the underground room where shock treatment remains the ultimate "therapy." In its totality then, the institution is a topography that represents the control of female desire, a desire that, nonetheless, fails to remain repressed and often can be seen as erupting, contaminating from below.

Given the images of containment that dominate Esther's consciousness, it is not surprising to find the image of the bell jar coming to represent her mental disturbance. Also suggesting impasse, the place against which Esther moves, the bell jar signifies Esther's awareness that her condition is linked to that of the aborted fetuses she has seen floating in their jars. Thus, it is also no accident that Esther's experience of the bell jar is encountered in maternal space. Indeed, the first mention of it occurs in her mother's house, after her return from New York City, as she turns down the chance to share an apartment in Boston. Her surrender of the apartment is ambivalent, and Esther thinks of calling back to undo the damage: "My hand advanced a few inches, then retreated and fell limp. I forced it toward the receiver again, but again, it stopped short, as if it had collided with a pane of glass" (*BJ*, 97). In this instance Esther's hand seems as severed from her body as desire is from her consciousness. The second mention of the bell jar occurs during her ride in Philomela Guinea's car to the hospital, at a time when the seriousness of her illness has become evident.

Esther's loss of desire is connected most clearly to her deteriorating condition of the present, but we are also given glimpses of earlier behavior in which she is still capable of willed action. These earlier behaviors are, however, most often characterized by a mobility that is self-destructive.[9] Her skiing accident is perhaps the most memorable example of this kind of behavior, and Esther's explanation of it reflects the fact that she has transformed her anger at Buddy Willard into a punishment of herself.

Although she first accuses Buddy of making her break her leg (which in some convincing ways is the truth), she later admits, "I broke it myself," and appears to link her action to a need to punish herself for refusing to marry Buddy. The discussion of marriage takes place on her visit to the sanatorium where Buddy is recovering from TB, and it is clear to most women readers that he is coping with some problems of mobility himself. His own enforced immobility, the fattening process, which renders him less the competent athlete and more the feminized man, suggests that immobilizing Esther is a way of keeping his power over her. The power struggle that surfaces in their conversation is suggested by the way in which Buddy, as the dominant persuader, teacher, and diagnostician, proclaims Esther as neurotic because she is unable to choose between living in the country and living in the city. In one of her rare moments of overt defiance, Esther tells Buddy that "if neurotic is wanting two mutually exclusive things at one and the same time, then I'm neurotic as hell. I'll be flying back and forth between one mutually exclusive thing and another for the rest of my days" (*BJ*, 76).

"Flying" thus becomes linked in Esther's mind with her struggle against Buddy, a struggle that is acted out on the ski slopes, where Esther's "one careless superb gesture" (*BJ*, 77) results in a serious injury. That gesture is, in fact, a language of motion that articulates Esther's refusal to choose, to be channeled into one job, one life-style. Since Buddy is not only responsible for teaching Esther to ski, but also involved in Esther's choice of a more advanced slope on which to practice what he has taught her, he is also clearly implicated in the accident.

Esther, for her part, seems helpless to resist her dangerous descent, even though she has protested that she does not know "how to zig-zag" (a motion of escape that consists of moving in alternate directions). That she has not yet mastered this movement reinforces the impression we get that she is still trapped on a single path, and unlike the male who, as an arrow, can aim up, she can only aim "straight down." Also, while the male's trajectory is into the future, hers is into the past, and her flight thus becomes not only spatial, but also temporal. Momentarily happy because she moves "through year after year of doubleness and smiles and compromise," because she can believe she moves to a new beginning, her descent becomes a dark tunnel, a well, at the bottom of which lies "the white sweet baby" that is one aspect of her. But hers is a regressive fantasy, another dead end, another indication of her resemblance to the dead fetuses whom she views as dead before they are born. Buddy's "queer, satisfied expression" after the fall confirms his continued dominance and his ability to keep Esther immobilized, "stuck in a cast for months" (*BJ*, 79–80).

The skiing accident has, of course, occurred before Esther's New York trip and stands in contrast to present images of movement, which are mostly concerned with crawling. This verb dominates the middle portion of the text where Esther lies in the darkened bedroom she shares with her mother, questioning the point of "getting up." When she does get up, it is only to crawl to the window where she is rewarded with a tableau of maternity in the form of Dodo Conway, escorting five children, wheeling a sixth, pregnant with the seventh. Esther's response to the view beyond her window reveals her problem with subject/object boundaries, for this viewing is turned into a paranoid reaction where, instead of seeing Dodo, she imagines Dodo seeing her. Resistance of the maternal presence becomes, in the end, a submission to it as Esther not only crawls back into bed, but also settles herself between the mattress and the bedstead, thereby burying herself more deeply in the landscape of the mothers. Her final descent into the basement terminates in a crawlspace—a "dark gap," a "secret, earth-bottomed crevice," a "mouth" in which she can act out her ultimate dead end, mergence with the pre-oedipal mother (*BJ*, 138).

Esther's discourse is also marked by images of shrinking, melting, dissolving, and flattening. Watching the sexual play of the sexually sophisticated Doreen and Lenny, Esther wants to shrink "to a small black dot" (*BJ*, 14). In the bar with Doreen she feels like "melting into the shadows like the negative of a person I'd never known before" (*BJ*, 8). Mrs. Willard's kitchen mat—emblem of female creativity—is metaphorized as Woman herself, doomed in marriage to be flattened underneath the feet of men (*BJ*, 65).

Such negative images of mobility are extended into her aversion—sharpened doubtless by her internship at *Ladies' Day*—for the making of products. Esther's awareness of the ongoing transformation of process into product is the basis of her hatred of Technicolor movies, where the use of "lurid" colors defies natural colors, just as Technicolor plots turn women into objects of a patriarchally created landscape. To Esther the ends of such stories are predictable and fixed: "I could see the nice girl was going to end up with the nice football hero and the sexy girl was going to end up with nobody," she muses (*BJ*, 34).

Indeed, process increasingly loses out to product in Esther's imagination. This transformation occurs most vividly in the kitchens of *Ladies' Day*. In the beginning Esther, who loves food, especially exotic kinds, is seduced by the visual lushness of the food displayed at the *Ladies' Day* banquet; the "yellow green pear halves stuffed with crabmeat and mayonnaise and platters of rare roast beef and cold chicken" (*BJ*, 20) tantalize her. But after she has been poisoned, she reconstructs the image of the food in an altogether different way:

I had a vision of the celestially white kitchens of *Ladies' Day* stretching into infinity. I saw avocado pear after avocado pear being stuffed with crabmeat and mayonnaise and photographed under brilliant lights. I saw the delicate, pink mottled claw meat poking seductively through the blanket of mayonnaise and the bland yellow pear cup with its rim of alligator green cradling the whole mess. (*BJ*, 39)

Here the bland pears are linked with the seductive crabmeat; the pink mottling, the blanket, and the cup that cradles it all show a high incidence of maternal imagery, which, blended with images of seduction and poison, emphasize Esther's sensitive ambivalence, her tendency to distrust what is produced to represent the feminine. This later reconstruction of the banquet also reveals pre-oedipal material, feelings of being poisoned, which themselves point to anxiety over ego-body boundary problems and a fear of maternal devouring.

Arrayed against these pre-oedipal fears is her love of botany and language, two seemingly divergent topics, which she understands as crucially related to the making of art—and also to mobility. Not only does botany afford her a visualization of leaf shapes and "the holes the leaves breathe through," but also botanically related words evoke pleasurable sounds and seem "fascinating . . . like carotene and xanthophyl" (*BJ*, 29). On the other hand, the language of physics is hateful to her: "What I couldn't stand was this shrinking everything into letters and numbers"; these become "ugly abbreviations" and "hideous, scorpion-lettered formulas" (*BJ*, 29). In fact, physics, like other sciences, becomes for Esther a language associated with males and death, its abbreviated form suggesting to Esther an abstracting action that kills process.

These persistent feelings toward the male-related, disembodied, or abstracted forms of language evoke some tentative textual escap(e)ades.
Esther escapes the linguistic confines of her chemistry class by simply
refusing to hear the professor and by creating an alternative discourse: "I
shut his voice out of my ears," she tells us, "by pretending it was only a
mosquito in the distance and sat back enjoying the bright lights and the
colored fires and wrote page after page of villanelles and songs" (*BJ*, 30).
Her mother's insistence on shorthand lessons also evokes in Esther an
effort at escape, this time in terms of the visual. Rebelling against her
mother's blackboard shorthand samples, she "sees" in the place of the
sterile and abstracted shorthand signs "white curlicues," which "blur into
senselessness" as she imagines in their stead Joyce's 100-letter Wakean
word of origination and destruction.

Increasingly Esther, in her deteriorating condition, projects mobility
onto language, and "words dimly familiar but twisted all awry, like faces
in a fun house mirror," escape her and transform themselves into monster
shapes, while at the same time control over her hands and her writing
diminishes: "The letters grew barbs and rams' horns. I watched them
separate from each other, and jiggle up and down in a silly way. Then they
associated themselves in fantastic shapes, like Arabic or Chinese" (*BJ*, 102)

Finally, even plant images fail to connote creativity and instead become
linked with products and fixity. Beginning with the photo session at *Ladies'
Day*, where all the girls are posed with the symbols of their future occupa-
tions, and where Esther is posed with a paper rose, her identification with
plants grows more negative. During her brief attempt at volunteer work in
the maternity ward, for example, her anxiety about process is revealed
when she removes all the dying flowers from the arrangements to be given
to the mothers. Here it would appear that the dying and dead flowers
represent her association of the act of birthing and the child itself with
degenerative processes and lifeless products. Plant metaphors come more
clearly into focus as analogues for her own growth. After her first shock
treatment, she comes to view herself as a "split plant" whose sap has been
removed (*BJ*, 118). The thought of suicide forms in her mind like "a tree or
flower," and when she imagines slashing her wrists in a warm bath, the
blood from her imagined wounds also produces a flowering: "I thought it
would be easy, lying in the tub, seeing the redness flower" (*BJ*, 89).

Even the fig tree story—about the "beautiful dark nun" and the Jewish
man who meet to gather fruit from the fig tree, are separated after they share
a touch, and together witness the hatching of a bird from an egg—suggests
further ominous transformations involving process. Esther allegorizes the
story into a tale of herself, Buddy, and their witnessing of the troublesome
birth, but the story also seems to move her in ways that are not explained
by her fixing of thematic content. What she appears to find attractive ("I
thought it was a lovely story") is "the part about the fig tree in winter under

the snow and then the fig tree in spring with all the green fruit" (*BJ*, 45). Yet Esther's plot summary omits these seasonal ingredients, which appear instead as a kind of later interpretation. It may be that a healing process is a possibility to her, but her desire to "crawl in between those black lines of print . . . and go to sleep under that beautiful big green fig tree" again suggests the victory of her more regressive tendencies.

We might also wonder what has sent her into this regressive positioning. Could the answer lie in the two figures of the couple, who may, in this novel of mirror images and doubles, not be separate figures at all, but another split of Esther herself—the virginal, but potentially sexual, nun and the alien figure of the Jewish man, an intellectualized Other who might represent Esther's "masculine" nature, which, having touched the feminine nun, is censored by the Catholic kitchen maid? The answer to this question may require an examination of the role of Joan Gilling.

In any case, the fig tree story creates an organic analogy for Esther's dilemma. Representing choice for the desirous, yet starving, Esther is trapped in the crotch of the tree, and the figs, which remain beyond her reach, can only ripen and fall to the ground. Thus, while Esther's desires have been articulated in terms of mobility and simultaneity when she expressed to Buddy the wish to "shoot off in all directions like the colored arrows from a Fourth of July rocket" (*BJ*, 68), she becomes trapped instead in Buddy's discourse, the scripts of the male clinicians that diagnose desire as neurotic.[10]

Perhaps the most provocative commentary on the problems of mobility and fixity is articulated through the figure of Joan Gilling. In Esther's imaginary world, a world increasingly suffused with *imagos*, Joan Gilling would appear to be another of Esther's doubles, albeit a more prominent and problematic one. We may recall that Freud describes the double as originally an insurance against the destruction of the ego, a primitive infantile creation that has been repressed, but that can manifest itself in a later stage of experience. Freud and Otto Rank also theorize that what was once a friendly aspect of the psyche tends to take on a demonic aspect when it appears at a later time: Hence, what was repressed becomes the repressing force and can even take on the role of a pursuer.[11] Jeffrey Berman emphasizes this pursuing aspect of the double and calls our attention to the "ferocious competitiveness" with which Esther and Joan "torment" each other.[12] However, while Esther does at one point refer to Joan as tormenting her, that word really does not describe their relationship. Indeed, Esther has earlier described Joan as "the beaming double of my old best self" (*BJ*, 167).

If there is a pursuing aspect to Joan, it involves her lesbianism, a subject that seems to make critics either nervous or perfunctory. Vance Bourjaily, who rightly argues that Joan is the book's real double, envisions Joan and Esther as personifying the forces of homosexuality and heterosexuality, and evaluates the girls and their mental health in terms of their relationship to

men. Consequently, he can state that "Esther manages to get rid of her
virginity," while "Joan's new experience is homosexual"; therefore, "as
Esther improves, Joan declines." [13] Gordon Lameyer associates Joan's
lesbianism with puritanical sexual attitudes, seeing her as "representing all
the puritanical ethics present in the world."[14] I assume that he is referring
to Esther's attitudes projected on Joan. Nonetheless, this is still a rather
puzzling observation, since Joan would appear to be far less puritanical
than Esther. Joan is more relational, feels comfortable with the women at
Belsize, has an affair with Dee Dee, and later lives off campus with Nurse
Kennedy. Berman is closer to the mark in recognizing the "submerged
bisexuality" that is evident, a condition with which Plath, and hence Esther,
has difficulty.[15]

That difficulty is passed on to the critics. Usually, Joan is easily dispensed
with, and if we want to examine the dynamics of this relationship more
closely, we will be warned off by those who presume to know. For example,
Lameyer reassures us on the basis of his personal relationship with Sylvia:
"I knew her too well at the time of the incidents related to *The Bell Jar* to
conclude that she had lesbian tendencies"; his belief is reinforced by his
personal relationship with Jane Anderson, the student at Smith on whom
the Joan Gilling character was based: "I believe I am the only person who
has ever dated both Sylvia and the original Joan Gilling," Lameyer assures
us, not without pride, and concludes, "neither girl was inclined towards
lesbianism."[16] Butscher, on the other hand, discusses lesbianism not in
relation to *The Bell Jar*, but in relation to Plath's poem "Lesbos," claiming
that Plath's attention to the subject is either ironic or satiric. Referring to the
"bitchiness" of the poem, Butscher argues that it "does not accept or
support the fantasy of repressed homosexuality," that lesbianism as an
escape is the subject of "sardonic satire."[17]

In sum, either Joan is not discussed at all, or she is used to prop up
arguments for Esther's cure. Certainly this avoidance can, in part, be
blamed on Esther herself, who claims that "I'd never known Joan except at
a cool distance" (*BJ*, 60) and who also tells us that Joan gives her "a creepy
feeling" (*BJ*, 179), that "she always made me feel squirmy" (*BJ*, 48). Also,
Joan's appearance is "wrong"; she is "big as a horse" with "tombstone
teeth" (*BJ*, 48). When Joan expresses her love for Mrs. Willard, Esther thinks,
"Joan and Mrs. Willard, Joan . . . and Mrs. Willard . . ." (*BJ*, 178). The ellip-
ses, which speak in the place of words, point to the difficulty she has with
the subject, nor does troublesome content come to the surface until after
Esther's shock treatments. At that point the subject is discussed with Dr.
Nolan, and her answer to Esther's question about what women find in each
other is "tenderness," to which Esther replies, "That shut me up" (*BJ*, 179).
Also, it seems important to bear in mind that while Esther cannot imagine
a lesbian relationship ("But what were they *doing?*" she asks in regard to
an earlier college experience), her curiosity may belie unconscious desire.

In any case Joan is hardly a monster. She is the girl who is class president, a physics major, a gifted athlete and horsewoman, who likes "doing things outdoors," as Buddy puts it. In fact, we might assume from the preceding information that Joan has, in Freudian terminology, a masculinity complex, that she is indeed the classic lesbian, identifying with the father, desiring the mother. In contrast to Esther, Joan sees Mrs. Willard as a "wonderful woman who has been a real mother to me" *(BJ,* 128). Indeed, in all her interests and desires, Joan shows herself to be a kind of shadow figure, liking what Esther hates—especially physics and Mrs. Willard.

However, to dismiss her as only a shadowy double of Esther is to render the relationship static and frozen, whereas, in fact, the relationship between the two women is dynamic and challenges Woman as place and object. For example, Joan's sexual overtures to Esther occur during the time the two are at Belsize and after Esther's second series of shock treatments. The time and place of this confrontation are important because they point to a stage in the treatment of both girls where freedom, in terms of the expression of hitherto repressed feelings, is encouraged. Joan, also the more mobile of the pair at this point, has town and shopping privileges, and her appeal to Esther, "I like you," suggests her ease at actively expressing feelings. But she is met with Esther's insensitive, even vicious, response: "I don't like you. You make me puke if you want to know" *(BJ,* 180).

If we assume that Esther is "better" at this point, we can be tempted to accept her reaction as the "proper" one despite its brutality. Furthermore, clinical response to lesbianism and homosexuality in general was, at that time, negative, and treating homosexuality as a disease was the standard procedure. On the other hand, Dr. Nolan evinces no overt homophobia in her discussion of the subject, and Esther's own response seems overreactive. What this confrontation exposes is the gap between an active female libido and ideologically grounded assumptions about female mental health that repress alternative sexual possibilities and active experience for women. Plath's own stance, while on one level endorsing the status quo, is nonetheless not a simple or consistent one, and gaps in the text expose this inconsistency.

If we examine the relationship in terms of the images of mobility and fixity relative to it, we can see that on the most overt, linear level Joan seems initially activated by Esther's suicide attempt. But Joan pursues Esther only in the sense that she reads about her case in the newspaper; her own movement is to New York—to a city where anonymity is a possibility. But when we come to consider Joan as the pursuing double elsewhere, we have to note that she is moved to Belsize before Esther, is granted town privileges first, and is able to live off the grounds before Esther is. Only in the final days is this pattern reversed. Esther is to leave while Joan has returned. Indeed, the funeral and Esther's release coincide, certainly not by accident. What seems to emerge from this sketchy summary is a relationship that is neither one of leader and follower, nor one of pursuer and pursued, but one that intertwines, a relationship rendered complicated by internalizations about what is normal and what is deviant.

What is more important to me is the textual aspect of the two women's relationship, the fact that they provide each other with stories that, because of institutionalized repression, operate as a subtext. For example, Esther sees Joan's wrist scars as a story: they are like "a miniature mountain range, large reddish weals upheaved across the white flesh of her wrists" (*BJ*, 164), and it is Esther's reading of this story that makes her feel for the first time that she and Joan "might have something in common" (*BJ*, 164). More important, Joan carries Esther's story—the buried story of her attempted suicide—preserved in clippings. The positive nature of this text is reinforced by Esther's later reflection on what has happened to her. When her mother wants to regard the experience as a bad dream, Esther rebels: "I remembered everything . . . they were part of me. They were my landscape" (*BJ*, 194). Just as Joan's scars, emerging out of the whiteness of her skin, are her landscape, Esther's story is also a landscape, brought to the surface by Joan.

What these clippings mean to Esther is never directly told to us, but they do seem to articulate an experience that has been erased in her days of unconsciousness. Basically they consist of four separate stories, accompanied by four different pictures. The first two photographs of Esther recall her New York summer friendships with Doreen and Betsy—the "tarty" one suggesting the sexual self she identifies with the sophisticated Doreen and the smiling Esther suggesting the more innocent self linked to "Pollyanna Cowgirl" Betsy (*BJ*, 5). The third, taken at night, is not a picture of her at all, but of certain "moon faced people," some of whom "looked queer" and turn out to be bloodhounds (*BJ*, 163). This rather hellish image is succeeded by another night picture, showing a body with a "featureless cabbage head" being placed in an ambulance (*BJ*, 163). They serve to objectify Esther's experience, and perhaps promise change, even progression, since the first and second pictures represent the selves she has hated and attempted to reject, while the third shows her as an absence, and the last shows her as yet unformed, once again a fetal *tabula rasa* that may promise a new story. In any case, Esther does keep the pictures, and Joan has thereby served to fill the empty space in Esther's memory, giving her back her story.

But our understanding of Joan's function in the novel necessitates a close reading not only of the novel's ending, but also of its specific ingredients— Esther's sexual encounter with Irwin, Joan's suicide and burial, and Esther's emergence on the last page. Esther's sexual encounter certainly appears as problematic. Some critics may celebrate her sexual liberation, echoing Esther's "I was my own woman" (*BJ*, 182), but there are some subtextual elements here that would seem to undermine optimistic closure. Take, for example, the scene in the doctor's office where Esther is getting fitted for a diaphragm.[18] Ascending the table for her fitting, she thinks, "I am climbing to freedom, freedom from fear, freedom from marrying the wrong person" (*BJ*, 182), but there is something troubling about the juxtaposition of this utterance with the setting. Once again, she is offering herself to another examination table, rendering herself an immobilized object. In fact, her sexual initiation is framed in two such scenes where Esther lies passive and prostrate on an examination table, probed and penetrated by phallic instruments.

Irwin's space is not an improvement, for he is much like the other scientific, medical males whom Esther (or Plath) designates as Other. The room where Esther loses her virginity is a room filled with "incomprehensible books with huge formulas inset artistically on the page like poems" (*BJ*, 185). Does her sexual acceptance of Irwin connote a reconciliation between art and science, between poetry and physics formulas? It would hardly seem so.

But, of course, it is the hemorrhaging incident that perhaps offers the most telling evidence as to the ambivalence of both the author and her protagonist, especially since Plath's sensitivity to blood is well known.[19] Esther's response to the scene is also ambivalent at best, and it would appear that Esther registers the meaning of the experience in terms of the body. If this is so, then the bleeding operates as a kind of conversion symptom. While Esther may tell us that the blood makes her "part of a great tradition," she has, in other places, expressed too many doubts about that tradition for this statement to be positive, and as the bleeding intensifies, Esther recalls other details of that grand tradition, namely, the Victorian women who died giving birth "in torrents of blood" (*BJ*, 189).

The most theatricalized scene occurs at Joan's house, when Esther, attempting to make Joan aware of her problem, removes a blood-filled shoe and empties it on the floor before her: "I held the shoe up, before Joan's enlarged, pebbly eyes, tilted it, and watched her take in the stream of blood that cascaded onto the beige rug" (*BJ*, 188). Not only does Esther's gesture suggest the consequences of sexual mobility,[20] but also the hospital scene that follows her so-called liberation resonates in an even more sinister manner as Esther is laid out on a table amid all the appurtenances of the medical world that she had always linked to her own extinction.

Images linking sexuality and bloodletting have occurred once before in the text, namely, during Esther's encounter with Marco. In this earlier instance, Esther describes herself and Marco as "two bloody-minded adversaries" (*BJ*, 89). And in spite of her observation that "woman-haters were like gods: invulnerable and chock full of power" (*BJ*, 88), Esther marshals her own powers: "I fisted my fingers together and smashed them at his nose" (*BJ*, 89). Later, Marco marks her face with his own blood in a gesture that we might interpret as statement of power, a writing on the body of Esther. But this rather bizarre scene has even stranger consequences, for

Esther, clearly disturbed at this point, preserves these bloodied marks, likening them to "the relic of a dead lover" (*BJ*, 92). Here Esther seems to be inverting the essence of blood as taboo, as a living part of a person, which can, in the possession of an enemy, cause injury. Esther, having immobilized Marco, appropriates his power and wears his inscriptions as a mask.

In a typical Plathian inversion, however, the price is paid by the victim, as we see in Esther's commentary on the blood marks during the train ride home: "The blood would flake away in no time, so I kept my face immobile, and when I had to speak I spoke only through my teeth, without disturbing my lips" (*BJ*, 92). Here her badly traumatized consciousness articulates, by means of body language, her conviction that Marco is still the victor. By rendering her face mask-like she symbolizes her invulnerability, but also her increasing withdrawal from animate forms. Thus, her defense against injury becomes a hardening or covering that will prevent seepage, a word she uses in connection with her hemorrhaging, but also a word that characterizes her own leakages of self.

These problems, reflecting the crucial struggle written on the body regarding mobility and fixity, are expressed in the poem "In Plaster," composed by Plath during March 1961, after her miscarriage and during the time she was working on the novel. In it the speaker evokes two selves, the "new absolutely white person and the old yellow one." The plaster self is "one of the real saints," but also "like a dead body," unbreakable," and "with no complaints." While the speaker is at first in conflict with the plaster self, she also sees herself as existing through it, endowing it with life: "I bloomed out of her as a rose." The speaker also comes to see the plaster self as a necessity, but at the same time one that has a weakening effect on her: "I wasn't in any position to get rid of her/She'd supported me for so long I was quite limp." Although the speaker, yellow-bodied, "hairy and ugly," resolves to leave the plaster covering behind, the protagonist of *The Bell Jar* finds this severance more difficult. The opening lines, rather than the later ones, of "In Plaster" seem more descriptive of Esther's state ("I shall never get out of this! There are two of me now.")

I feel it is important that we connect these elements because they all converge in the final pages of the novel, whose ending has served to put critics in something of a bind. In part, readings have been ghosted over with the knowledge of Plath's suicide, which, combined with later biographical revelations, adds painful irony to discussions of it. Especially ironic is the fact that the "real" Joan Gilling did not die, but instead went on to become a successful psychologist. One question that critics have raised concerns the state of Esther as she is ready to leave the hospital. Critical ambivalence can be seen in, for example, Linda Wagner-Martin's work, where in one article she speaks of the ending as open-ended, while in her biography of Plath she describes Esther as a survivor.[21] I think Paula Bennett is closer to the mark when she describes the ending as "unbearably factitious" and argues that Plath wanted us to see Esther as cured, but that Plath's "emotional understanding" fails her. Bennett's frustration is reflected in the following commentary: "Plath ends *The Bell Jar* with Esther exiting triumphantly stage left bearing her diaphragm aloft while Joan, the defeated, is laid to rest beneath the pearly snow."[22]

What we seem to be dealing with here is a good deal of subtextual activity. Let us return, for a moment, to the sexual experiences of both Joan and Esther, which are interrelated, but not in the way that Bourjaily has argued. Each girl's sexual experience would appear to have an effect on the other, but to view these effects as vindicating heterosexuality is to read with an androcentric bias that moves male sexuality to the foreground. Esther's discovery of Joan's relationship with Dee Dee, as well as Joan's advances to Esther, certainly move Esther to discuss the subject of lesbianism and to acquire a diaphragm, but Esther's actions seem motivated not so much by a desire for freedom from pregnancy, or a desire for sex, as by a desire to escape from the implications of Joan's lesbian attachments which, in turn, suggest (an)other way. In this sense the shedding of her virginity and her immunization from pregnancy can be viewed as more defensive than affirmative.

We tend to overlook, or at least downplay, two facts about Esther's sexual initiation. First, it is Joan that she turns to for help when she is hemorrhaging, and, second, because Esther herself ignores it, we tend to pay little attention to the effects Esther's close call has on Joan. For Joan the hemorrhaging incident has doubtless been traumatic. Nevertheless, Joan calls for an ambulance, accompanies her to the hospital, and is described as standing beside Esther during her examination "rigid as a soldier . . . holding my hand" (*BJ*, 190). There is a kind of ceremonial quality about this last time the two have together: Joan, the upright "phallic" figure, standing beside her prone and bleeding counterpart, her fallen comrade, the girl who can now claim to be a woman because she is heterosexual. Yet the scene will be played again at the gravesite where Joan is the fallen one. The military metaphor Esther applies to Joan hints at, but again leaves unsaid, the possibility that another death has occurred.

Esther's response to Joan's death suggests not only her sense of complicity, but also her "covering over" of the possible chain of cause and effect. We have to assume that despite Esther's conviction that Joan has no idea what has caused her hemorrhaging, such is not the case, and Joan's return to Belsize "a few days later" would appear to confirm her upset. Nevertheless, Plath seems to go two ways here: She offers us a convenient suicide, but at the same time she surrounds Joan's death with elements of the uncanny. The connection between Esther's final dissociation from Joan (*BJ*, 191), a severance that takes place during the midnight visit of Dr. Quinn and would seem to coincide with Joan's actual suicide, suggests the neurotic's belief in the omnipotence of thoughts.[23] But the connection also validates the cause/effect sequence, for Esther has other thoughts about Joan as she tries to sleep: "Joan's face floated before me . . . I even thought I heard her voice, rustling and hushing through the dark" (*BJ*, 192).

Indeed, Esther has good reason to wonder what she is burying, and the answer is only indirectly articulated. Esther declares, for example, "I was perfectly free," but this statement is followed by a gap in the text, then the funeral scene. The answer is hinted at in the description of Joan's "pebbly eyes" (*BJ*, 48, 189), a description that causes us to recollect that other pebble at the bottom of Esther's metaphoric well. Joan, who plays the "bottom part" in the piano duets, is recognized by Esther in a more overt way during the funeral service as "the black shadow of something that isn't there" (*BJ*, 198).

To put it another way, Joan represents what is buried, unspeakable, unrepresentable, for Esther. In Luce Irigaray's terms, she represents the place of origins, the place that has no name in the phallic economy where it is covered over by absence and lack. By retaining her "masculine" identity, Joan displaces the phallic and retains not only her female origins, but also her active role. In Esther's plot, Joan becomes the wound that needs to be stanched and covered over. Like the "marble calm" (*BJ*, 198) that characterizes the landscape outside the institution grounds and the marble calm that covers Esther's own troubled topography, Joan's burial is also a covering over, a permanent fixing. The grave is a "gap . . . hacked in hard ground," an opening in the blanket of snow that will soon, however, be erased. Here Plath/Esther says more than she may know: That shadow would marry this shadow, and the peculiar yellowish soil of our locality seal the wound in the whiteness" (*BJ*, 198). What Esther has thus buried is her own bodily and psychological mobility. She has buried the active relational sexuality of Joan, her love of women, all the ingredients that Esther tries to repress, but cannot successfully cover over.

Esther's emergence from the institution, described in the very last lines, confirms the continuation of her problems. Despite her "brag of heart"—"I am, I am, I am," (*BJ*, 199), she never escapes her awareness of the fictional nature of the self—hence her interests in masks. Her exit through a door does not lead to the outside; instead, she moves into a space where she once again becomes the object contained in the gaze of others: "The eyes and the faces all turned themselves toward me, and *guiding myself by them*, as by a magical thread, I stepped into the room" (*BJ*, 200, italics mine).

NOTES

1. Mary Jacobus, *Reading Woman: Essays in Feminist Criticism* (New York: Columbia University Press, 1986), 233.

2. While I may sound like a disgruntled gynophile, it is also true that I find a number of discussions of the novel helpful despite their blind spots. See, for example, Murray M. Schwartz and Christopher Bollas, "The Absence at the Center: Sylvia Plath and Suicide," *Criticism* 18 (1976): 147–72; see also Jeffrey Berman,

"Sylvia Plath and the Art of Dying," *University of Hartford Studies in Literature* 10, nos. 1–3 (1978): 137–55.

3. Edward Butscher, *Sylvia Plath: Method and Madness* (New York: Seabury Press, 1976). Butscher explains his fondness for the term "bitch goddess" (the "persona who rages through the poetry of *Ariel* and *Winter Trees*") as follows: "As a combination, 'bitch goddess' has the additional advantage of a long metaphorical association—at least from the time of D.H. Lawrence—with fierce ambition and ruthless pursuit of success" (xi-xii). Butscher's tone is disturbing, projecting as it does not only a sexist stance, but also a profound ambivalence toward his subject matter. He tends to view Plath's use of biographical material in *The Bell Jar* as "distorted," and his argument that Plath is always masked is not very wrong, perhaps, but is itself distorted because of his tendency to see these masks as aggressive, rather than defensive. More revealing of his tone is his rather gratuitous attack on Robin Morgan, who had attacked Ted Hughes in one of her poems. Butscher refers to her as a "shrill feminist" and to her poem as "verbal afterbirth" (325).

4. Gordon Lameyer, "The Double in Sylvia Plath's *The Bell Jar*," in *Sylvia Plath: The Woman and the Work*, ed. Edward Butscher (New York: Dodd Mead, 1977), 145, indicts Esther Greenwood for her puritanism, views her excessive interest in virginity as the partial cause of her neurosis, and again seems to conflate both the author and her protagonist.

5. For the best analysis of Freud's views of women, see Sarah Kofman, *The Enigma of Woman: Woman in Freud's Writing*, trans. Catherine Porter (Ithaca, N.Y.: Cornell University Press, 1985); Luce Irigaray, "The Old Dream of Symmetry," in *Speculum of the Other Woman*, trans. Gillian C. Gill (Ithaca: Cornell University Press, 1985), 13–129; see also Madelon Sprengnether, *The Spectral Mother: Freud, Feminism and Psychoanalysis* (Ithaca, N.Y.: Cornell University Press, 1990).

6. Plath was never diagnosed as schizophrenic, although Edward Butscher, *Sylvia Plath: Method and Madness*, calls her illness "schizophrenic depression" and Jeffrey Berman, "Sylvia Plath and the Art of Dying," 145, judges this "an intelligent conjecture." The doctors found no trace of psychosis, and Olive Higgins Prouty's letters to Plath (*Letters Home*, ed. Aurelia Plath [New York: Harper and Row, 1975], 126) calls the illness a neurosis.

7. See Linda Wagner-Martin, "Plath's *The Bell Jar* as Female *Bildungsroman*," *Women's Studies* 12 (1986): 55–68. Martin is one of the first critics to argue for the novel as a *Bildungsroman*; she also observes that it has not been recognized as such because of its "tone of wrenching anger" (66).

8. Sylvia Plath, *The Bell Jar* (reprint; New York: Bantam, 1971), 93 (hereafter cited parenthetically in the text as *BJ*).

9. Schwartz and Bollas, "Absence at the Center," 157, argue that this incident shows Plath's phallic identification with the father. Her character "denies the arrowless, static definition of woman and instead imagines herself as the phallic man." They conclude that such actions show Plath to be appropriating the father's "masculine self-essence." Again, this interpretation assumes all female activity to be connected to lack.

10. This desire to "shoot off in all directions," the desire to have every fig on the tree, is also expressed in Esther's envy over Constantin's work as a simultane-

ous interpreter. Linguistic simultaneity is also imagined by Esther as a possible "way out."

11. See Freud's "The Uncanny," in *The Standard Edition of the Complete Psychological Works of Sigmund Freud*, ed. James Strachey (London: Hogarth Press, 1953–74), 17:234–36.

12. Berman's description, "Sylvia Plath and the Art of Dying," 151, of a competition "so intense as to threaten their individual identities" seems exaggerated and reflects a persistent tendency to use emotionally toned language. Berman also speaks of the "theatricality of their suicide attempts," of their love of "notoriety" and "sensationalism," and he sees "a sadistic element" in Joan's desire to become a psychiatrist (150). In a recent biography by Anne Stevenson, *Bitter Fame: A Life of Sylvia Plath* (Boston: Houghton Mifflin, 1989), 164, the author observes that Plath's "preoccupation" with doubles is accompanied by both a need to have them and, "when such doubles showed their autonomy" and became "hated rivals," a need to kill them off.

13. Vance Bourjaily, "Victoria Lucas and Elly Higginbottom," in *Ariel Ascending: Writings About Sylvia Plath*, ed. Paul Alexander (New York: Harper and Row, 1985), 138–39.

14. Lameyer, "The Double," 165.

15. Berman, "The Art of Dying," 151. Bourjaily, "Victoria Lucas," and Butscher, *Sylvia Plath: Method and Madness*, both associate lesbianism with sterility.

16. Lameyer, "The Double," 165. Stevenson, *Bitter Fame*, as the "authoritative" biographer of Plath, makes no mention of lesbianism and refers only once to Jane Anderson as a brief rival (26).

17. Butscher, *Sylvia Plath: Method and Madness*, 323.

18. Butscher, ibid., 125, discussing Sylvia's sexual liberation and her need to escape from her mother's puritanical attitudes, says, "Sylvia acquired a douche and decided with typical energy and efficiency, that the common-sense approach to sex was best." *Douche?* Has Plath fictionalized a diaphragm fitting? Or is this Butscher's blind spot?

19. Plath's image clusters are complex, but she often associates infants and birthing with poems and poetry-making (see "Stillborn," for example). Blood is also associated with writing.

20. Joan also has trouble with her feet, a trouble that inhibited her work and may have precipitated her illness: "I had these bunions," she tells Esther, "I could hardly walk" (*BJ*, 160).

21. Wagner-Martin, "Plath's *The Bell Jar*," 62, characterizes the ending as "somewhat ambivalent." In discussing Esther's final scene, she concludes, "in contrast to the doorless blankness of tunnels, sacks, and bell jars, this open door and Esther's ability to breathe are surely positive images" (64). In her biography *Sylvia Plath: A Biography* (New York: Simon and Schuster, 1987), 186, she sees Esther as having undergone a "healthy rebirth." Schwartz and Bollas also see the ending as positive, as does Lameyer, who, in "The Double," 144, sees Esther as "psychically reborn."

22. Paula Bennett, *My Life a Loaded Gun: Female Creativity and Feminist Poetics* (Boston: Beacon Press, 1986), 131.

23. Her biographers affirm Plath's own psychokinetic sensibility.

3

Writing to the Other Side: Metafictional Mobility in Atwood's *Lady Oracle*

> Woman is neither open nor closed. She is indefinite, in-finite, *form is never complete in her.*
>
> —Luce Irigaray
> *Speculum of the Other Woman*

Moving from the mimetic world of *The Bell Jar* to the metafictional world of Margaret Atwood's 1976 novel *Lady Oracle*, we encounter an altogether different strategic approach to sometimes similar content. Like Plath's novel, *Lady Oracle* has been regarded as a novel of development, even a *Künstlerroman*. Both novels are in some sense "road" novels, and the two writers make use of labyrinthine imagery both to evoke the maternal body and to show the problematics of movement. Both works use first-person narratives, even though neither protagonist can be said to project herself as a stable or centered subject. Although Esther seems able to believe in the possibility of an integrated self beneath her "marble calm," Atwood's protagonist, Joan Foster, has many selves. Unlike Plath, Atwood is interested in using intertextual ingredients—especially those relating to gothic conventions—as well as uncanny, or non-realistic, material to both evoke and subvert female entrapment. Gayle Greene has observed that *Lady Oracle* is "a brilliant exposé of escape fiction,"[1] but its comedic and metafictional nature suggests Atwood has constructed a textual escap(e)ade that goes much further, making something altogether different of "escape" fiction.

Like its predecessor *Surfacing* (1972), *Lady Oracle* can be seen as a road novel, although Atwood has suggested that this later work was intended to be "a kind of antithesis to *Surfacing*" and a work that instead would be "all tangents."[2] While Plath has her protagonist evoke firecracker imagery to project an invigorating dispersal, a going off in all directions, Atwood builds this disruption into the very structure of her novel. Perhaps because of the novel's puzzling stance and confusing structure—not to mention its obese protagonist—early critics seemed compelled to seek a convenient generic category for the work, although none agreed on exactly what its label should be. Robert Lecker called it a "failed romance," while Jerome H. Rosenberg regarded it as a parody of a gothic romance. Judith McCombs saw it as a portrait of the artist, but dismissed the gothic elements as "genre, fantasy, commercial art"; both Sherrill E. Grace and Ann McMillan rightfully noted the importance of its gothic elements, but differed on just what those elements mean; Lucy M. Freibert saw the novel as picaresque.[3] Later critics seem to agree on the crucial function of gothic components in the novel; Molly Hite argues for the novel as a satire that results from "the clash of conventions belonging to different discursive practices."[4]

When it came to dealing with Atwood's protagonist and narrator, critics tended to be especially judgmental, perhaps because, like the structure of the novel, Joan was difficult to classify, in part because she seems to have difficulty classifying herself or rather because she classifies herself in so many ways. By the time of her affair with the Royal Porcupine she is aware of her dilemma: "I was more than double, I was triple, multiple, and now I could see that there was more than one life to come, there were many."[5]

Many recent critics have used such observations as the basis of psychologically based readings of the novel. In some of these analyses Joan is again criticized for a lack of integration, for an inability to establish distinctions "between reality and fantasy,"[6] and her multiple selfhood is read as symptomatic of serious disturbance. Roberta Rubenstein describes Joan's multiplicity of selves as an "extreme defense against engulfment by the monstrous mother."[7] Greene, also viewing Joan's multiple selfhood as in reality a split between two basic identities, one "passive-acquiescent" and the other "active-aggressive," argues that it is these oppositions that enable Joan to imagine that her life is "more than double"; thus, while she has thereby managed to elude entrapment by the mother, in reality she only exchanges one kind of confinement for another.[8] Hite, however, takes such readings to task, first, because *Lady Oracle* would appear, as a text, to resist "the unequivocal privileging of a 'real self'" and, second, because the reading of women's fictional representations in negative terms suggests that readers have allowed themselves to become aligned with "gender-coded assumptions" that the text itself questions in the guise of the protagonist, namely, Woman as represented in western culture.[9] Furthermore, given postmodernist views of the fiction of subjectivity and Jacques Lacan's descriptions of the subject as constituted by way of complex identificatory (and alienating) processes, Joan's proclamation of multiple selfhood is comic, but it is also closer to the truth and, for her, finally empowering.[10]

It would appear that Joan's own description of herself as an escape artist suggests the importance of fluidity and mobility for Atwood, especially in relation to the troublesome question of containment in male-inscripted cultural myths, a question that is most pointedly addressed by the gothic novel. Furthermore, the manner in which Atwood's critical study *Survival* (the title itself is suggestive) resonates with questions relative to escape— Canada from its entrapment in its role as a colony of the United States, the Canadian writer from entrapment in American narrative strategies and conventions, and women from containment in stereotypical role expectations and other cultural myths—suggests her interest in this topic. At the same time, viewing escape as merely "escapist" denies the comic, even trickster, elements that are so prominent in this work. Indeed, Joan Foster's ability to change selves, which is later replicated in her ability to change genres, enables her to escape both the males who would immobilize her and the plots that would constrain her. Her writing from the Other Side— from the small Italian town in which she hides after staging her most spectacular escape—her own death—provides us with the narrative that is *Lady Oracle*, a text that has appropriated gothic material, but that has, in transforming it, engineered its own escape from the fixing constraints of gothic conventions. *Lady Oracle* thus becomes a text that, lacking a neat gothic resolution, remains true to its tendency to go off in all directions and to blur boundaries between realism and fantasy, self and other.

The narrator's response to problems centered on mobility and fixity in life and art is suggestively rendered in a passage early in the novel, where, outside the wall of her Italian flat, she is beset with voracious ants who feast on the sugar water she provides. Tracing this mixture on her windowsill in her own initials, because she desires to "see my name spelled out for me in ants: a living legend" (*LO*, 19), she expresses her ongoing need to blur the boundaries that would divide life and art, mobility and fixity. Yet while she attempts to re-present herself in a form of art that would stabilize both it and her own identity, she is also cursed with another desire, namely, that art should be living, rather than merely *life-like*. However, toward the end of her narrative, we learn that the saucer has gone dry; the sugar water has hardened into a glue, and the ants have become as trapped in their gluey script as Joan has in her plots. Always uncomfortable with such "hardenings," Joan is left to worry about the converse tendency of her life to "spread, to get flabby, to scroll and festoon like the frame of a baroque mirror" (*LO*, 3).

Joan's problems with fixity and mobility clearly derive from her early life and, more specifically, from a mother who is containment and entrapment incarnate. Mrs. Delacourt is herself the victim of entrapment (her marriage is a result of an unwanted pregnancy), and perhaps as a consequence of this rather compelling boundary violation, her domestic spaces are representations of the imagined settings of others—"museum displays"— which suggest her compulsive need for boundary maintenance and fixity. In any case Mrs. Delacourt struggles to create what Joan describes as a world that is "static and dustless and final" (LO, 74), where furniture is covered in plastic and carpets cannot be walked upon with shoes.

Not surprisingly, the mother attempts to project this containment and fixity upon her daughter by turning her into a product.[11] "Our relationship was professionalized early," says Joan; "she was to be the manager, the creator, the agent; I was to be the product" (LO, 70). But Joan resists her mother's fixing tendencies by using her own body—which she describes to us as "a huge cloud of inchoate matter"—to resist such shaping and containment. Becoming the "disputed territory" (LO, 71) over which she and her mother do battle, Joan's body is empowered by overeating. In language that conflates imagery that is both martial and culinary, Joan tells us, "I swelled visibly, relentlessly before her very eyes, I rose like dough, my body advanced inch by inch toward her" (LO, 73). Thus, childhood mobility involves primarily a control over process, a struggle that is expressed in outlandish growth against a mother whose methods of "fixing" her are numerous and complex.

Joan is able at first to foil her mother by means of failure. Besides "failing" to moderate her eating habits, Joan also fails at being a Brownie. Among those drab replicas of one another who speak only in meaningless chants that reinforce prevalent culture myths about girls, Joan's overlarge shape makes her an inevitable misfit. But a more serious clash between Joan and her mother involves Joan's role in the school ballet. While dancing is a kind of mobility deemed appropriate for girls ("something girls could do" [LO, 44]), only girls with the proper bodies are allowed to engage in it. Joan's obesity clearly stands in her way. Indeed, her mother, who describes her dancing as "thumping" and relegates her to the basement where her damage can be controlled, plots with the dance teacher to deny Joan a role in the school's "Butterfly Frolic," thereby colluding to construct one of the many alien and confining plots to which Joan falls victim.

The result of this early maternal manipulation is that Joan, awaiting the wings that her butterfly role has promised, finds herself instead in a plot that grounds her as MOTHBALL. The demotion from a transformational flying creature to a product intended for its destruction is cruel and traumatic for Joan. Nevertheless, she is not to be denied her dance, and her comic and contingency-governed response to attempts to fix her as a mothball says much about the way she will escape constrictive art forms as well as social roles in her adult life: "I danced. There were no steps to my dance, as I hadn't been taught any, so I made it up as I went along. I swung my arms, I bumped into the butterflies, I spun in circles and stamped my feet as hard as I could." (LO, 51). The fact that she is the hit of the play is only a momentary source of gratification, for she has already linked the image of the butterfly to gendering processes, to prescribed standards of beauty, which create attractive objects for male desire. Thus, although at this time Joan understands only that no one "would think of marrying a mothball" (*LO*, 52), she will learn to construct alternative scripts.

This incident both foreshadows Joan's lifelong love of dancing and movement, and underscores the role of improvisation and contingency in her life. It also serves to explain her ability to escape the textual impositions of others and her aptitude for moving between boundaries. Indeed, Joan's childhood is early rendered problematic by words (again her mother's discourse is the culprit) that set such boundaries. For example, her mother's warnings regarding "bad men" is taken at face value and understood in its abstract form, but Joan often finds that her mother's distinctions cannot be relied upon. When accompanied by her Brownie friends across a dangerous ravine where "bad men" are supposed to lurk, Joan encounters "bad" girls who tie her to a tree and abandon her. When a man rescues her, she cannot be sure if he is "bad" or not. When she encounters an actual flasher who exposes himself behind an offering of daffodils, Joan is not disturbed, much less terrified. And she does accept the man's offering. Not only is differentiating between good and bad a complicated task for her, but also the men from the ravine, both rescuer and flasher, become blended in her mind so that she muses, "I still wasn't sure, though. . . . Was the man who untied me a rescuer or a villain? Or, an even more baffling thought: was it possible for a man to be both at once?" (*LO*, 67). Yet her awareness of such transformational potentials becomes a crucial key to the construction of her own selves, which are both multiple and simultaneous.

Joan's instinct for escape is further nourished by a mother surrogate, her Aunt Lou, and increasingly takes place in her imagination. Not surprisingly, Aunt Lou is the antithesis of her mother. While Mrs. Delacourt is neat and dresses in navy blue suits and white gloves, Aunt Lou is sloppy—"soft, billowy, woolly, befurred" (*LO*, 95). Joan's mother is small, Aunt Lou is large; her mother is plain, Aunt Lou is ornamented: "things dangled from her," Joan observes (*LO*, 113). The mother is all containment; Aunt Lou personifies escape: "wisps escaped from her head, threads from her hems, sweetish odors from the spaces between her collar and her neck" (*LO*, 95); she expands, filling space, dissolving boundaries. The mother's description of Lou as "beyond the pale" is appropriate because the pale, originally a stake driven into the ground to designate a boundary, here marks Lou and Joan as positioned on (an)Other side. Indeed, Aunt Lou opens up spaces for Joan, creating the possibility of self and motion. As a public relations writer, Aunt Lou has authored a text entitled "You Are Growing Up," which not only acknowledges process, but also articulates female functions that Joan's more puritanical mother has failed to articulate.

Another means of escape that Lou offers her niece is by way of the movie theater, which demarcates a kind of maternal space Joan describes as "furry, soothing darkness" (*LO*, 87). Here she is introduced to conventional romantic images and narratives, which, nonetheless, suggest the possibilities of escape and transformation. *The Red Shoes* is a particular favorite of Joan's because it concerns dancing and also because it contains a red-haired protagonist heroine and is, therefore, an attractive projection. This figure, caught between her lover and her career, is entrapped and ultimately commits suicide, but the film's scenario still offers Joan some kind of catharsis, a chance to objectify problems, a lesson on escape from which Joan will be able to benefit.[12]

Even Aunt Lou's censorship of certain circus acts—the harem of dancing girls and the Fat Lady—fails to wilt Joan's imagination and, instead, feeds it. Indeed, it is through the presence of the Fat Lady—Hite describes her as Joan's "embodiment . . . of the female potential for excess"[13]—that Joan performs another imaginarily liberating escape. Conflating the dancing girls and the Fat Lady, Joan dresses the static Fat Lady in the costume of the harem dancer— "gauze pants, and a maroon brassiere and red slippers"— and fantasizes her future rebellion (*LO*, 97). Slowly liberated by Aunt Lou, Joan, in turn, liberates the Fat Lady by giving her mobility, the chance to be both dancer and performer. Placing her on a high wire with only a small pink umbrella to balance with, Joan takes her "across, past the lumbering enterprises of the West Coast, over the wheatlands of the prairies, walking high above the mines" (*LO*, 111). The Fat Lady would also appear to replicate Joan's early perilous crossing of the ravine; yet she also must return to her static existence—to sit in her tent, just as Joan at this point in her life is forced to subside behind her mask of "dogged" friendliness and her "calm," set smile (*LO*, 100).

Aunt Lou's beneficial effects on Joan ultimately include freeing her from both her economic dependency on her mother and ultimately from the burden of her form, since her legacy to Joan cannot be claimed without the shedding of 100 pounds. Nevertheless, early childhood influences cannot be so easily escaped, and these have set the pattern for Joan. While she has been allowed (she thinks) an escape from an older self, she remains in need of determining who she is. Having struggled to transform herself into the butterfly—the image that conforms to the cultural myth about women's shape—she experiences a different kind of alienation: "It was like being born fully grown at the age of nineteen: I was the right shape, but I had the wrong past. I'd have to get rid of it entirely and construct a different one for myself, a more agreeable one" (*LO*, 157). Thus, her narrative becomes a recounting of her constructions of self, and while she continuously becomes mired in plots that have inscripted the suppression of female desire, she nonetheless manages to escape, turning her lovers into fictional constructs and plotting their narratives according to her own submerged desire.

Doubtless because of her early confusion over men as rescuers or villains, her three major relationships with men become projections of this dichotomy. Her first lover, Paul, rescuing her as she falls off a bus near Trafalgar Square, has the right story for her as well: He is aristocratic in background, a Polish exile who has escaped the Russians. Her second lover, Arthur, rescues her from Paul. As his name suggests, Arthur is a crusader. For Joan he becomes "a melancholy fighter for almost lost causes, idealistic and doomed, sort of like Lord Byron whose biography I'd just been skimming" (*LO*, 184). Her third lover, the Royal Porcupine, also fits her image of Byron ("there was something Byronic about him," Joan comments [*LO*, 283]), but he is even more Romantic for her than Arthur, perhaps because he has more deliberately constructed himself. Having the proper costumes—a cloak, spats, a goldheaded cane, white gloves and top hat—he is also red-haired, is elegant in his mustache and beard, and has successfully escaped his own name and vocation and entered into an earlier time period.

But all Joan's lovers become villains who entrap her in their own scripts. Paul is obsessively neat like her mother—"a systematic man. . . . His idea of the good life was that it should be tidy" (*LO*, 169). The nurse novels he writes under a pseudonym, replete with pursuing men and pursued women, serve to reinforce Joan's own assumptions about male behavior. Furthermore, Paul forces her to live according to his rigid sex stereotyping, and Joan, finding herself increasingly trapped in a reality that includes a jealous possession of her, almost comes to believe his "story." Accused of infidelity, she finds herself once again oppressed by another's script and not only concludes that "maybe he was right, maybe I did have a secret lover" (*LO*, 180), but also acquires one. But a new lover leaves her still contained in Paul's plot: "How," she asks, "did I get into this thoroughly sealed place and how could I get out?" (*LO*, 177). Only when boundaries once again blur, when Paul becomes less the romantic rescuer and more a villainous jailer, can she escape.

Arthur's crusader image also undergoes some transformation with marriage, and Joan finds herself trapped in another's patriarchal plot and even more immobilized than she had been with Paul, since her role as wife is even more oppressive. Paradoxically, she acknowledges that "for years I wanted to turn into what Arthur thought I was" (*LO*, 235). And while she does attempt to conform to the roles he constructs for her, she remains unshaped, "a nourishing blob" (*LO*, 236). In reality, it is Arthur who is truly immobilized, whose "crusading" is an illusion. A manic depressive, he moves only in terms of emotional ups and downs, which correlate with the success or failure of his most recent crusade. In fact, he never moves; he only changes causes, a behavioral pattern that is described in terms of movement as "going through"—"Vietnam sheltering draft dodgers, student revolt, and an infatuation with Mao" (*LO*, 235), Joan tells us—but his activism is a parody of mobility. The journal he edits, with the rather ironic title of *Resurgence*, is commentary on his own futile resurrections—his attempts to remain in control of all discourses while Joan is rendered voiceless.

Joan's need to escape Arthur is clinched during a trip to Italy, where she encounters, in the gardens of Tivoli, a disturbing image of stasis and passivity—the statue of Diana of Ephesus: "She had a serene face perched on top of a body shaped like a mound of grapes. She was draped in breasts from neck to ankle, as though afflicted with a case of yaws" (*LO*, 282). Recognizing herself in the goddess, in terms of body shape (she never escapes the ghostly fat Joan) and also as nurturer, Joan observes that, unlike the statue, she is not "inexhaustible," not "serene," not, in other words, a frozen reflection of male need. She consciously accepts the desire articulated heretofore only within the fictional confines of the gothic: "I wanted things, for myself," she says (*LO*, 282).

While the Royal Porcupine is her most liberating lover, he, too, ends by entrapping and immobilizing her. In the beginning of their relationship, his appeal is, in part, due to his rejection of language. Having once "done words" (*LO*, 288), he has opted for an "unwritten biography" (*LO*, 298)—an impossible achievement and instantly suspect. Indeed, one manifestation of his tendencies toward fixity can be seen in his art, the art of the "con-cre-ate"—what he describes as the poetry of things. Claiming to be the man who put "creativity back into concrete" (*LO*, 268), he practices his aesthetics by collecting the corpses of road kills and freezing them for an art showing titled SQUAWSHT. Despite his protestation that "I don't squash them, I just recycle them," (*LO*, 269), his tendency is also to fix, and Joan becomes almost as much a collectable as his road kills. In fact, he is first attracted to Joan as an image—telling her, "I've always wanted to know what it was like to fuck a cult figure" (*LO*, 272). Eventually, he almost succeeds in making her not only into an art object, but also into a past event. As Joan observes, "he started seeing the present as though it was already the past, bandaged in gauzy nostalgia" (*LO*, 298), a mummification that becomes alarmingly displayed for Joan as "each of my gestures was petrified as I performed it, each kiss embalmed. . . . I felt like a collectable" (*LO*, 298).

Given her childhood, Joan's aptitude for writing gothic novels comes as no surprise. Yet Atwood's use of gothic material led some critics to question Joan's susceptibility to this very conservative genre. Some have pointed to its weaknesses—its elements of fantasy and titillation, its failure to confront the maternal presence,[14] its validation of a heroine who is also victim and who, although sometimes intrepid, ultimately reverts to being a passive figure in need of rescue. In sum, they would argue that the gothic story valorizes "a conservative relationship to social norms."[15] Worse, Joan, in her fondness for the genre, "models her role as innocent victim" on that of the gothic heroine.[16] Grace, aware that Atwood herself has described the novel as "anti-Gothic," concludes that the novel exposes the perils of gothic thinking, and that because Joan allows the genre to invade her life, the gap between reality and gothic fantasy all but disappears.[17] However, Grace's argument needs some qualification.

Certainly Atwood is intent on disrupting the easy dichotomy of "reality" and "fantasy" (a subject to which I shall return), but Joan's problems with boundary dissolution are not made to reflect her preoccupation with fantasy as much as they are to represent her awareness—albeit not always conceptualized—of the gap between what is "real" and what is perceived to be real. While there is no denying that the content of Joan's gothic novels reflects her life, it seems incorrect to see her as trapped in them, especially in view of Joan's almost always developing need to undermine their plots. In the beginning the gothics serve to provide her not only with a conventionalized representation of genuine female entrapment, but also with a space where desire may be articulated. While her plots correlate with the difficulties she has with her lovers, she uses those plots to effect escape.

Taking Paul's idea that writing should be an escape for the writer as well as the reader (*LO*, 173), Joan's choice of gothic is a natural one, having to do with her predilection for costumes (and the shedding of them) as well as with her fascination with, and confusion about, rescuers and villains. Gothics also provide her with a way of countering the slippages of her own life and her sense of multiple selfhood, offering up stereotypic characters whose transformations from villain to rescuer can be controlled. More important, the gothics she writes violate their own fictional boundaries, becoming scripts of her escape from men. For example, *Escape from Love*, written during her escape from Paul and her early days with Arthur, depicts its heroine Samantha as on the road, fleeing a seducer. Replete with other gothic ingredients—the fleeing governess, the seducer-employer, the cold dark streets of a fallen world—the text is never completed because Joan moves in with Arthur. During her marriage to Arthur, on the other hand, she writes another book entitled *Love My Ransom*, where the plot is centered on entrapment. Guilt-ridden over her affair with the Royal Porcupine, she creates *Terror at Casa Loma*, where male jealousy is the central focus.

Always it is the unconscious source of this material that Atwood's narrator needs to deal with, a need revealed most clearly, perhaps, at the point where the writing of the gothic becomes itself something of a dead end in the work called *Love My Ransom*. Confronted with a character named Penelope, for whom she cannot supply a plot, Joan needs "something new, some new twist" (*LO*, 242) and finds her Aunt Lou's spiritualistic beliefs in the Other Side coming to her rescue. These beliefs enable her to think in new ways about space and boundaries. While Joan professes to be uncomfortable with the idea of an astral body that "could float around by itself, attached to you by something like a long rubber band" (*LO*, 121)—especially when she imagines her now-deceased mother as one—"some kind of spiritual jello" from whom she has never really been disconnected, she is, nonetheless, attracted to the ways in which spiritualism blurs boundaries between the world of the dead and that of the living, a blurring that also allows for the intrusion of non-realistic material, ghostly ingredients that seriously affect Joan's consciousness and that Atwood's metafictional narrative strategies allow to exist unexplained alongside the novel's more realistic material. The uncanniness associated with these beliefs offers Joan a means of dealing with deeper problems of self and (m)Other, whereas Atwood uses the uncanny to unsettle patriarchal assumptions about the female body.[18]

Beginning with her most immediate need to devise a plot with which to liberate her captured heroine Penelope, whom she has placed before a candlelit mirror (this itself is both a new plot ingredient for Joan and an unconscious attempt to deal with the specular aspect of subjectivity), Joan enters the story herself. Setting herself before her mirror, she is first aware of seeing something there and then of the need to "find someone" (LO, 245). As she stares into the mirror, she experiences an awakening of her own desire to "go down that dark, shining corridor . . . to see what was at the other end" (LO, 246). It is at this point that Joan's escape from the writing of gothics seems to originate and to suggest that gothics are yet another kind of entrapping mirror. In her experimentation with mirrors, she is enabled to escape gothic plots and discover a new kind of writing, namely, the mystifying poetic pieces that make her the cult heroine Lady Oracle. While her desire to enter mirror space may appear regressive, it also suggests an attempt to create a new story of origins, to escape the identificatory and culturally grounded formations of infancy that Lacan describes in his mirror-stage theory. That this period of infancy was an especially troublesome period for Joan seems a strong possibility, given the narcissism and coldness of the mother and the subsequent absence of positive mirroring for her.

Yet Joan's escape from the constraints of gothic plots does not signify her escape from gothic ingredients, which, like the uncanny material they point to, suggest the deeper source of gothic images in that mystifying and unrepresentable space of the mother—evidenced by her desire to see "what was at the other end." Thus, despite Joan's preoccupation with the men in her life, it is the ever-recurring image of her mother that is the energizing force behind both her attraction to gothic material and its ultimate failure as an escape route for her. In an important (and psychoanalytic) reading of this genre, Claire Kahane critiques the earlier view of the gothic as the female protagonist's struggle against a seductive father figure; she argues instead for the presence of the dead or absent mother. Older readings, Kahane argues, exclude female desire, whereas the true center of the gothic novel is "the spectral presence of a dead-undead mother, archaic and all-encompassing, a ghost signifying the problematics of femininity which the heroine must confront."[19] Kahane goes on to defend this confrontation as one involving "the mysteries of identity and the temptation to lose it by merging with a mother *imago* who threatens all boundaries between self and other."[20] Space then, for the gothic novel, is usually represented by a castle, or some other ultimately labyrinthine structure, which serves as a projection of the maternal body with its accompanying abundance of claustrophobic dead-end passages, places where "boundaries between inner and outer, me and not-me, are still not sharply drawn, and self cannot distinguish itself from the mother," as Norman N. Holland puts it.[21]

Indeed, Joan's problems with the mother, which have only been superficially discussed so far, are complex and intimately bound up with Joan's multiplicity of selves. We get some inkling of the mother's importance by way of two recurring childhood dreams that Joan relates to us, "bad" dreams, both of which center on the mother. In the first one Joan is crossing the bridge over her infamous ravine while the mother stands on the other side. The bridge begins to collapse, and Joan, terrified of plunging into the ravine, calls out to her mother "who could still have saved me . . . she could have pulled me back with her to firm ground" (*LO*, 68). Instead, the mother, her face toward a male figure, ignores the struggling daughter. This dream evokes pre-mirror and mirror-stage experiences, the sense of body dissolution and the disruption of the mother-child dyad by the third term, the law of the Father, here represented in the male who turns the mother's attention away from the falling Joan. But it also suggests, once again, the inadequate mirroring, the mother's failure to grant to the child its image. Thus, while the withdrawal of the gaze is a part of the process whereby the infant becomes a subject, the withdrawn gaze also represents a part of the subject's self and hence serves as a traumatic experience of castration that opens up the void, the repressed material from infancy, for the child.

While all mothers undermine that image, even as they grant it,[22] the young Joan's deprivation seems beyond the normative, especially given the fact that Joan's constitution as subject has taken place in an atmosphere where the mother's hostility and resentment have been ill-concealed, where Joan has been provided with only an "inconstant source of self."[23] This fact accounts for Joan's increased alienation and her less well developed sense of boundaries. Therefore, the mother's turning to the male figure in Joan's dream seems less a representation of the oedipal drama than an evocation of pre-specular fantasies. The diminution of the influence of the paternal signifier suggested here appears to intensify the problem of separation for Joan. Indeed, Atwood has even constructed for Joan a childhood marked by the absence of the father. Away in France for the war, the father never does constitute a noteworthy presence in the household, a fact that Joan understands on some level because she tells us that "he wasn't there, which is probably why I remember him as nicer than my mother" (*LO*, 80).

Joan's second dream appears as almost a continuation of the first, or perhaps it would be more accurate to describe its contents as an elaboration of the problem with the mother. In this recurring dream Joan's mother sits at her makeup table before a triple mirror. In her waking existence Joan's interest in the mirror activities of her mother has constituted one of the rare positive experiences Joan shares with her, even though it is always the mother, and never Joan, who dominates mirror space. Ironically, although Joan is denied mirror space, she is allowed to watch her mother make up as a "reward" for good behavior. In her dream, however, the mother is viewed in her triple mirror not as she appears to the social world, but as Joan knows her, with "three actual heads," which rise "from her toweled shoulders from three separate necks" (*LO*, 70).[24] The image of her mother as hydra-headed, as a kind of monster, does not terrify Joan, however; what seems more disturbing in this strange drama of the specular is the presence of a man who appears to have knowledge—perhaps the knowledge that Joan herself possesses— and who is, therefore, threatening. It is possible to speculate that in this world of condensation and displacement, the observing figure represents the part of Joan who both knows of the mother and knows of her own bond to the mother (and hence her own monstrous nature), but who, at the same time, can stand apart. Empowered by the gaze, the dreaming Joan seems to fear that power and its accompanying knowledge. Hence, Joan fears that the knowledge will result in something terrible happening—not just to her mother, but also to Joan herself, who, after all, is her mother.

Yet Joan has very early learned a truth about the mirror that she does not know she knows. She acquires this knowledge watching her mother make up, and as I mentioned above, it is her mother's image, and hence her mother's narcissism, of which we are made aware. This condition suggests the mother's own regression, her own inadequate formation of object relations, her own unstable sense of self. She is the one trapped in the mirror, trapped in (an)Other's reflection of male desire. The most important manifestation of this condition is the fact that Joan's mother tries to be someone else—Bette Davis— and her makeup becomes a bizarre ritual of substitution: "Her lips were thin, but she made a larger mouth with lipstick over and around them, like Bette Davis" (*LO*, 71). But what Joan observes is the slippage between her mother's specular self *and* the tracings of the ghostly movie star self behind it; Joan is also aware of another truth about her mother—that "instead of making her happier, these sessions appeared to make her sadder, *as if she saw behind or within the mirror some fleeting image she was unable to capture*" (*LO*, 69–70, italics mine). With her most memorable childhood images involving mirrors and ghostly escaping presences associated with them, it is not surprising that Joan spends much of her energy in adulthood acting out a pursuit of such fleeting images.

While Joan's own mirror experiments can be viewed as comic depictions of self-hypnosis that satirize the creative process, her desire to get to the Other Side is not a frivolous one. It has been brought to the surface by Aunt

Lou, whose interest in spiritualism legitimizes not only (an)Other side, but also a blurring of boundaries between the two. The Other Side is a dominant image, worked in complicated ways by Atwood. It connotes the space to which "Woman" has always been relegated as a sign of difference for patriarchal consciousness. It is also, more important, the space to which the young Joan—as a violator of the normal boundaries of self—has been banished. But the Other Side is also an imaginary construct—a place where, in Lacanian terms, the world of intersubjectivity is veiled by mirrors. It is also a space that the text consistently undermines, for, as Hite has argued, in the fictional world of *Lady Oracle*, things do not stay in their places despite the socially mandated will to impose containment and to maintain "sides."[25]

Thus, Joan's desire for the Other Side is not a simple initiation experience, although at times it seems to endanger her. At one point during her acting out of Penelope's dilemma, for example, Joan does find herself immobilized beyond the mirror: "I was stuck there, in the midst of the darkness, unable to move. I'd lost all sense of direction" (*LO*, 249). Nevertheless, there is more movement to be found in Joan's rather unusual attempt to write Penelope out of her bind by getting to the other side of the mirror—here the gothic mirror—herself. What Joan brings back from her re-enactments of Penelope's journey are words that center around a female image, a woman "like a goddess," but a goddess with "an unhappy power," a woman who puzzles Joan because "she wasn't like anyone I'd ever imagined and certainly she had nothing to do with me" (*LO*, 248). Joan's denial of this introjected image, an elaboration of ego ideals, or *moi* fixations, does not, however, hold. Certainly Joan's recognition of herself as the goddess with the unhappy power is a self-alienating admission. But this kind of activity appears to have enabled her to confront the loss that the mother symbolizes, but that is ultimately unconscious.[26]

Thus, the writing produced from Joan's mirror experiments is a new kind of writing—automatic writing, or writing that is "automatic" because it is (symbolically) less mediated by consciousness. This writing from the Other Side seems to resemble, at least in its most fragmented state, an utterance best described by Julia Kristeva as the *semiotique*—"a whirl of words, a complete absence of meaning and seeing; it is feeling, displacement, sound, flashes. . . ."[27] In any case, this writing seems to be Joan's way out of the gothic.

In their finished state, these writings become her Lady Oracle poems, especially notable for their echoings from "The Lady of Shalott" (*Her glass wings are gone/She floats down the river/singing her last song"* [*LO*, 252]), echoes that are comical, but hardly accidental. As a child Joan has been drawn to the image of the Lady, although over time, the Lady has, like Joan, undergone a number of transformations. In Joan's childhood the Lady is a romantic figure, associated with castles, princes, rivers, and happy endings.²⁸ What Joan does not readily see is that the poem is an inscripting of the masculine fantasy of the ideal maiden, virginal, passive, and, finally,—dead. In the poem the mirror represents the external world out of which the Lady weaves her art, but the image also operates as an appropriate metaphorization for the operations of the imaginary. Locked in her tower, where the world can enter only through a mirror, the Lady believes that by breaking the mirror and exiting the tower she will escape the world of shadows, not realizing that she is part of the mirroring process, too, that there is no leaving that world, that the real world is, for women, a world of shadows, where they exist as the reflector of male desires. Drifting on the river in a barge that bears her name—that fixes her identity as an object—the Lady glides on to her passive destiny—to present her face for Lancelot to gaze upon for confirmation of his own subject status.

Joan's understanding of the poem and the Lady does not really occur, however, until she has constructed her own "Other Side," where her problems with her mother and her gothic writing converge in a representation of the labyrinthine center that is the subject (and object) of her latest writing effort. It is during this time that Joan dreams once again of her mother, who appears "crying soundlessly," her face pressed against a glass that separates her from her daughter. Joan perceives the barrier, but is aware now that it is her mother who is the trapped one, that, in fact, that glass that separates them is the same mirror that served as their imprisoning "tower." Joan also recognizes her own complicity: "She'd never really let go of me because I had never let her go." She then can see that her mother "needed her freedom also: she had been my reflection too long" (LO, 363).

In reversing the perception of the daughter trapped in the reflection of the mother, Joan has come to understand her own world of shadows as a world where her otherness to herself is revealed, where primary identifications involving the mother are seen as replaying themselves in later echoes of mirror-stage dynamics. With the realization of the mother as an introjected image, Joan appears to have established an important boundary for herself—a separation from the (m)Other in the sense that she no longer exists as an outside force invading her. Rather than escaping the mother, Joan recognizes the need to understand exactly where she resides and to withdraw the projection. "What was the charm that would set her free?" Joan asks. Instead of seeing her mother as a personalized image, Joan now recognizes her for what she has really been all along: a "vortex," a "dark vacuum," the void that is loss, original separation, the fate of the speaking subject (LO, 363).

This partial liberation of mother and daughter is reflected in the way in which Joan resolves her difficulties in writing Stalked by Love, the gothic that has been her project since her "death" and her residency on the Other Side. Her problem—and perhaps its solution—is demonstrated in the fact that her feelings of entrapment and her need of rescue from her "death" become represented in the actions of her fictional characters as they are invaded by elements from her "real" life. One indication that this invasion is perhaps a good, if not inevitable, thing is the fact that, as I have noted earlier, it forces her to abandon gothic plots and aids in one kind of successful "escape." For example, although gothic convention has already determined that Charlotte—her plain, submissive, and conventional heroine and alter ego—will marry the unscrupulous, but sexually attractive, Redmond, and that the beautiful, erotic, and amoral Felicia must be killed off first. However, Joan finds it difficult to kill off Felicia because the character has escaped its stereotype, has refused to stay in its proper place: "She was losing more and more of her radiant beauty," Joan says, and continues: "Circles were appearing beneath her eyes, lines between her brows, she had a pimple on her neck, and her complexion was becoming sallow. Charlotte, on the other hand, had roses in her cheeks and a spring in her step" (*LO*, 349). In fact, Joan has begun to dislike the proper Charlotte with "her intact virtue and her tidy ways" (*LO*, 352). Yet Joan knows that gothic conventions preclude any escape from assigned roles: "Sympathy for Felicia was out of the question, it was against the rules, it would foul up the plot. . . . In my books all wives were eventually either mad or dead" (*LO*, 352).

Nevertheless, Joan finds herself writing a different Felicia, a women more like herself, sexually active, but vulnerable, one who wants to keep Redmond and give up her affairs. And yet as she and her character blend, so do Redmond and Arthur, who begin to share a concern about female mobility. About this new Felicia, Redmond has some reservations: "*He'd become tired of the extravagance of Felicia: of her figure that spread like crabgrass, her hair that spread like fire, her mind that spread like cancer or pubic lice. 'Contain yourself,' he'd said to her more than once*" (*LO*, 351)

As the crisis produced at home by her "death" grows increasingly complicated, Joan's paranoia about discovery increases,[29] as does her need for a closure that can only be constructed by means of the maze and its problematic center. Her first attempt to force Charlotte to enter the maze only results in Charlotte's loss of consciousness and Joan's loss of plot line. "I must have taken a wrong turn somewhere," she muses (*LO*, 366). However, a reconsideration of this wrong turn leads her to exchange a more passive representative of herself for the more active one—Felicia—who can, and in fact does, get to the center. Not surprisingly perhaps, the center is full of Joan's discarded or repressed selves: two who "*looked a lot like her*," a third that is middle-aged and "*dressed in a strange garment that ended halfway up her calves, with a ratty piece of fur around her neck*," and a fourth who is "*enormously fat*," with "*a pair of pink tights and a short pink skirt*" (*LO*, 375), complete with butterfly antennae. These older selves may inhabit the center of the maze, but they are not the answer, although they in part objectify the problem of specular selfhood.

There is one final gothic ingredient left for Joan to integrate into her plot, namely, the secret door, which can be opened only by Felicia. Behind this door lies not the secret of the feminine self, the Woman who must be known, not even the Mother. Instead, Felicia encounters a protean male figure: *"his face grew a white gauze mask, then a pair of mauve-tinted spectacles, then a red beard and moustache" (LO,* 377). What is protean about this figure, however, is his attributes—the mask of the father, the glasses of Arthur, the beard of the Royal Porcupine, all of which mask male desire to fix. The words of Arthur/Redmond articulate the conflict that lies at the maze's center—the struggle between female mobility and the male desire to fix—and the monster at the center is the romance plot itself: *"Let me rescue you. We will dance together forever, always" (LO,* 377), the male voice urges. But words like *forever* and *always* deny any dancing for women.

Rescue and dancing are, Joan realizes, incompatible. Dancing, on the other hand, is part of Joan's conceptualization of escape. Having realized that "the real romance of my life was like that between Houdini and his ropes and locked trunk; entering the embrace of bondage, slithering out again" *(LO,* 367), Joan celebrates this moment of illumination—her liminal nature—with a "light-hearted" dance. But the dance ends disastrously as, once again oblivious of boundaries, she dances out of her apartment and onto the broken glass of her porch. She can only conclude, "You could dance, or you could have the love of a good man. But you were afraid to dance, because you had this unnatural fear that if you danced they'd cut your feet off so you wouldn't be able to dance. Finally you overcame your fear and danced, and they cut your feet off" *(LO,* 368).

It is, after all, "the feet punished for dancing" that are the "real" Red Shoes *(LO,* 368), and out of this realization Joan can write Felicia's escape: *"I know who you are",* Felicia tells Redmond, who, metamorphosing into a figure of death (*"the flesh fell away from his face, revealing the skull behind it"* [*LO,* 377]), also reveals the deadly fixing strategies of the patriarchal romance plot.

Joan's own narrative is even more difficult to resolve. We understand that she will return to Canada, that she will perhaps get involved with the hapless reporter whom she believes to be stalking her. However, in the final scenario, it is worth noting that it is Joan who becomes the villain-rescuer—when, after braining the reporter with the Cinzano bottle, she oversees his recovery in the hospital. It would seem that with her abandonment of the gothic world of mirrors, she will move to another kind of imaginary expression, and her admission that she will never be a "tidy person" (*LO,* 380) suggests that she will continue to be a boundary violator, having many selves, and that she will continue to refine her ability to slither out of the tight places of patriarchal discourse. Surely Joan, like her heroine Felicia, has discovered that escape also serves as a way to "refuse to be doomed" (*LO,* 377).

Atwood's metafictional text has constructed a less domesticated protagonist—a woman whose multiple selves articulate the impossibility of patriarchal containment, of the fixing of Woman-as-Image—while her configuration of the immobilized and domesticated mother renders domestic space the true habitat of monstrousness. But Atwood's narrative strategies ensure an escape, first, from the realistic mode in which the Foster women's lives are rendered by introducing a gothic intertextuality that critiques that "real" world and, second, from the imaginarily constructed gothic mirror world. At the same time, Atwood allows supernatural elements—with their suggestions of ontological instability—their "side" of the story as well.

NOTES

1. Gayle Greene, *Changing the Story: Feminist Fiction and the Tradition* (Bloomington: Indiana University Press, 1991), 170, Green differentiates between Atwood's writing of the novel *Lady Oracle* and Joan's own negotiations of escape; Joan is, she says, "expert at fabricating escape for others" through her creation of gothic romances, but is also thereby enabled to "avoid knowing herself or the past" and therefore prone to repetitive pattern-making (167). I would argue, however, that Joan's very comic nature does suggest that she can be read as more successful at making her way past the constraints of her existence if the comedic ingredients of the novel are not lost sight of.

2. Quoted by Jerome H. Rosenberg, *Margaret Atwood* (Boston: Twayne, 1984), 112.

3. Robert Lecker, "Janus Through the Looking Glass: Atwood's First Three Novels," in *The Art of Margaret Atwood: Essays in Criticism*, ed. Arnold E. Davidson and Cathy N. Davidson (Toronto: Anansi, 1981), 201; Rosenberg, *Margaret Atwood*, 112; Judith McCombs, "Atwood's Fictive Portraits of the Artist: From Victim to Surfacer, from Oracle to Birth," *Women's Studies* 12 (1986): 78; Sherrill E. Grace, *Violent Duality: A Study of Margaret Atwood*, ed. Ken Norris (Montreal: Véhicule Press, 1980), 122; Ann McMillan, "The Transforming Eye: *Lady Oracle* and the Gothic Tradition," in *Margaret Atwood: Visions and Forms*, ed. Kathryn Van Spanckeren and Jan Garden Castro (Carbondale: Southern Illinois University Press, 1988), 48–64; Lucy M. Friebert, "The Artist as Picaro: The Revelation of Margaret Atwood's *Lady Oracle*," *Canadian Literature* 92 (Spring 1982): 24. See also Clara Thomas, "*Lady Oracle*: The Narrative of a Fool-Heroine," in Davidson and Davidson, *The Art of Margaret Atwood*, 159–75.

4. Molly Hite, *The Other Side of the Story: Structures and Strategies of Contemporary Women's Narratives* (Ithaca: N.Y.: Cornell University Press, 1989), 134.

5. Margaret Atwood, *Lady Oracle* (New York: Fawcett Crest, 1976), 274 (hereafter cited parenthetically in the text as *LO*).

6. Grace, *Violent Duality*, 125.

7. Roberta Rubenstein, *Boundaries of the Self: Gender, Culture, Fiction* (Urbana: University of Illinois Press, 1987), 86.

8. Greene, *Changing the Story*, 178.

9. Hite, *The Other Side of the Story*, 131.

10. Ellie Ragland-Sullivan, echoing Lacan, notes the impossibility of any centered or stabilized self and concludes, "the early traumas of prematuration, separation and repression mark humans for life as the creatures of contingency they are, as opposed to the creatures of knowledge they imagine themselves to be" (*Jacques Lacan and the Philosophy of Psychoanalysis* [Urbana: University of Illinois Press, 1987], 85).

11. See Linda Hutcheon, "From Poetic to Narrative Structures: The Novels of Margaret Atwood," in *Margaret Atwood: Language, Text, and System*, ed. Sherrill E. Grace and Lorraine Weir (Vancouver: University of British Columbia Press, l983), 17–31, for an insightful discussion on the important conflict between process and product in Atwood's work, as well as the importance of ice images in *Lady Oracle*.

12. See Emily Jensen, "Margaret Atwood"s *Lady Oracle*: A Modern Parable," *Essays on Canadian Writing* 33 (Fall 1986): 29–49, for an interesting discussion on *The Red Shoes*.

13. Hite, *The Other Side of the Story*, 139, goes on to describe the Fat Lady as a threatening configuration that suggests "that unmutilated, unchecked femininity will overflow boundaries, obliterating distinctions and violating proprieties." Finally, the conflation of the two forbidden circus acts, the Fat Lady and the dancers, comes to signify Joan and the self that desires too much.

14. Greene, *Changing the Story*, 173, observes that while the gothic allows the woman to achieve separation from the mother, it is only so that she can become the submissive wife. By elevating the father-husband to the role of rescuer and projecting menace onto the mother, the daughter is "bamboozled into denying the mother even as she is in the process of *becoming* her."

15. McMillan, "The Transforming Eye," 52.

16. Ibid., 58.

17. Grace, *Violent Duality*, 125.

18. Hite, *The Other Side of the Story*, 137–41, notes that the appearances of the mother, for example, are not hallucinatory, that the first one is observed by the spiritualist Leda Sprout, while the second, a visitation by the dead mother, is seen by Joan before she knows that her mother is, in fact, dead. Such autonomously functioning intrusions are Atwood's way of foregrounding what lives beyond patriarchal consciousness and what, according to its lights, is invisible and, therefore, non-existent. Says Hite, "such bodies are also surplus that the realist narrative cannot accommodate, representations of 'woman' that exceed the patriarchal gesture whereby the real is defined and contained" (141).

19. Claire Kahane, "The Gothic Mirror," in *The (M)other Tongue: Essays in Feminist Psychoanalytic Interpretation*, ed. Shirley Nelson Garner, Claire Kahane and Madelon Sprengnether, (Ithaca, N.Y.: Cornell University Press, 1985), 336.

20. Ibid., 340.

21. Norman N. Holland and Leona F. Sherman, "Gothic Possibilities," in *Gender and Reading: Essays on Readers, Texts and Contexts*, ed. Elizabeth A. Flynn and Patricinio Schweikart (Baltimore: Johns Hopkins University Press, 1986), 215–33. McMillan, "The Transforming Eye," 51, associates the labyrinth with chastity and views it as a structure that becomes a projection of fear of violation.

22. Jacqueline Rose, "Introduction II," in *Feminine Sexuality: Jacques Lacan and the École Freudiènne*, ed. Juliet Mitchell and Jacqueline Rose (New York: W. W. Norton, 1981) 30.

23. Ragland-Sullivan, *Jacques Lacan*, 73.

24. Pamela S. Bromberg, "The Two Faces of the Mirror in *The Edible Woman* and *Lady Oracle*," in Van Spanckeren and Castro, *Margaret Atwood: Visions and Forms*, 22, sees the episode as evidence of the "failed rituals of specular transformation."

25. Hite, *The Other Side of the Story*, 132, says, "this is a book in which the activity of marking limits and designating 'sides' is at once a social imperative and an ontological impossibility."

26. Ragland-Sullivan, *Jacques Lacan*, 288.

27. Julia Kristeva, *Desire in Language: A Semiotic Approach to Literature and Art*, ed. Louis S. Roudiez (New York: Columbia University Press, 1980), 239–40.

28. It is also a poem that is mistranslated by the young Joan, who reads *shalott* as a green onion and takes the line "the curse has come upon me" to refer to menstruation, though both the Lady's curse and menstruation share a relationship to immobility forced upon the female body.

29. Joan's paranoia has important ramifications for our understanding of subjectivity. Mary Ann Doane, in discussing paranoia and film, notes that the paranoiac has difficulty separating self from other, inside and outside, because internal representation has been transformed into exterior perception (*The Desire to Desire: The Woman's Film of the 1940s* [Bloomington: Indiana University Press, 1987], 130). Paranoia also points to an absence of the paternal signifier, necessary for separation and entry into the symbolic order. The weakness of the paternal signifier results in a displacement of the problem of knowing, which is now rendered in spatial terms (in gothic material as images of staircases, closed doors, winding corridors). Whereas in most genres Woman is the object of knowledge—the space to be penetrated and demystified— in gothic fiction Woman becomes the subject of the desire to know, "the instigator of the gaze, . . . investigator in charge of the epistemological trajectory of the text, . . . the one for whom the 'secret beyond the door' is really at stake" (134).

Textualizing the Journey: *Her Mothers* and the Spaces of Re-Search

Like *Lady Oracle*, E. M. Broner's *Her Mothers* articulates an escape from the limitations of genre. Like Atwood, Broner is intent on subverting narrative modes associated with patriarchal discourse, and, like other women experimentalists, she employs non-linear, non-hierarchical, and decentered structures to that end. What she produces is what Ellen G. Friedman and Miriam Fuchs have described as "an alternate fictional space, a space in which the feminine, marginalized in traditional fiction and patriarchal culture, can be expressed."[1] Aware of the tendency of Western culture in general, and Jewish culture in particular, to "fix" women, Broner, using the diaspora (Gr. "a scattering") as both trope and structural device, constructs a text that is all mobility. Not only is Bea "a wanderer among wanderers," to use Nancy Gray's description,[2] but also the text itself "wanders," moving into pasts that are alternately historical, mythical and personal, into futures that resist closure, even as it brings together a number of voices that are biographical, scholarly, realistic, and imaginary, in order that a multiplicity of stories can be gathered that will together constitute the recovery of the mother and, through her, the daughter as well.

Clearly Broner has located the problem of female immobility in the Jewish tradition, but her art is also a response in more specifically literary terms to the post–World War II Jewish novel. The typical work of this sub-genre, with its themes of tradition and assimilation, usually has as its protagonist a solipsistic, albeit sensitive, young male, as well as a mother who, as Marilyn French notes in her introduction to the 1985 edition of the novel, is usually "a monstrous devouring caricature."[3] But while the Jewish mother is hardly apotheosized in Broner's novel (since she is, after all, the conservator and perpetuator of the patriarchy), she is credited with heroism, and, more important, she is allowed utterance. Furthermore, Broner's artistic vision involves a complex recovery of the maternal voice, accompanied by a recognition of the inevitable boundary problems that will characterize the mother-daughter relationship. The Mother is never, for Broner, the "vortex" that she is for Atwood's protagonist. Instead, she is particularized—in lists of names that are "real" as well as fictional, in photographs, in words from letters and diaries of famous women writers. Thus, Broner constructs a textual escape from the Mother that nevertheless demands a textual embrace of Her, an embrace that requires recognition of Her multiple manifestations and is engineered by means of Broner's major structural and thematic motif: research.

Broner has said of her approach, "I speak out of a history, but I re-search it."[4] What the crucial hyphenation of the term *research* seems to suggest is that research involves a return, a re-examination. It further suggests that re-search is not only historical, but also archaeological—historical because it re-examines people and events of the past, but archaeological because it involves excavation, which is defined as the process of making holes or hollows, a process of exposing or uncovering.

But exposure and recovery are, for Broner, to be accomplished by textualizing the feminine, which must be accomplished on the level of structure. Beyond rejecting linear plot development and closure, Broner's reflexive text emphasizes not only relationality, but also fragmentation, the single story meshed with the collective, third-person narration slipping into first. Divisions of the text call attention to structure in textual terms through the use of headings and sub-headings; blocks of text are introduced with letters of the alphabet; upper-cased lines foreground certain passages.

One of Broner's most unusual textual creations is the short, refrain-like question-answer exchange between mother and daughter. These appear extensively throughout the text and are constructed much like the following two, which open the novel:

A.
"I'm pregnant, Mother."
"Have a girl."
"Why?"
"A girl should have a girl."
B.
"Mother, I'm pregnant with a girl."
"How old is she?"
"Seventeen years old."
"Then you're pregnant with me."[5]

What Broner articulates here is the inextricable interrelationship of mother and daughter, who share spaces and reproduce each other. However, the extensive use of such interpositions (I count 125 of them) suggests their functional importance. Gray has rightly observed that "it is the daughter's questions of the mother about bearing girl children that set the text in motion and punctuate it."[6] Such interpolations also appear to serve as bridges between narrative segments, offering sometimes playful comment on what has transpired, but at times also providing what are best characterized as angry and satiric revelations of culturally-produced gender bias. For example:

"Mother, I am pregnant with a baby girl and you will be proud of her."
"Why?"
"She is pleasant to the customers, respectful to her parents, distant from her friends."
"An ideal daughter." (*HM*, 47)
and
"Mama, I'm pregnant with a baby girl."
"What does she want to know?"
"Will she be happy in marriage?"
"Let her stay in the womb, for once she is out of it, she could marry a baby boy who would crouch in *her* womb and refuse ever to leave." (*HM*, 49)

What is also important about these passages is the fact that they dominate the first two parts of the novel, with sixty-three of them appearing in the section called "Looking for Friends" and fifty-six appearing in the section called "Historical Mothers."[7] They seem related to Bea's movement through texts that first contain personal biography and focus on the doings of family and friends, but that next treat her re-searching of "historical" mothers, a quest that widens and deepens her sphere of action and embraces the personal and historical, the present and past. In these sections the utterances of the transpersonal mother-voice, speaking as a subtext from regions buried by patriarchal discourse, serve to energize the rest of text.

To this end the refrains appearing in the "Historical Mothers" section are more political and generalized, and comment particularly on the problematics of mobility that Bea uncovers, for example, in the double-voiced discourse in Emily Dickinson's letters to Reverend Higginson. In one instance the daughter-voice repeats Bea's perception of Dickinson's strategic pose of containment before Higginson, "begging for advice," "being modest, maidenly and retreating," to which the maternal voice responds, "Then she is manipulating her correspondent" (*HM*, 75). When Bea notes the numerous references to Margaret Fuller's plainness, the maternal voice urges, "Then let her be the eldest and the support of her family" (*HM*, 84), which is, of course, what Fuller was. When Bea discovers in one of Fuller's love letters to James Nathan a desire that is not desire—namely, "to be as that good soil, a shelter, and to bear fruit"—the mother-voice observes that obviously "she wants nothing from life" (*HM*, 87). Louisa May Alcott's devotion to an "active" father is also seen as producing for the daughter only containment and immobility. About Alcott's irresponsible and exploitive father, Bronson, the daughter-voice comments, "my baby girl's father is a wanderer," to which the mother responds, "Then she will stay close to home" (*HM*, 104).

In the "Foremothers" section, however, only two refrains appear, and they seem to oppose one another. The first evokes the false, and immobilizing, definition of matriarchy: "May she be the mother of heroes" (*HM*, 149), while the concluding one focuses instead on the daughter and a recovery of mobility. Since this section of the novel also includes a present-day narrative of Israeli women encountered by Bea in her search for her daughter, Lena, the final maternal exhortation seems appropriate. The daughter's mobility is exchanged with, rather than canceled by, the mother:

"Mother, I am pregnant with a baby girl and she has left me."
"Then you must spend the rest of your life looking for her." (*HM*, 172)

This transformation from the vegetative state of mothering heroes to the active search for the daughter thus promises, in Broner's text, the recovery of the mother herself—and her mobility. This other narrative recalls an altogether different kind of ritual and myth, one popular with contemporary women writers—namely, the Eleusinian mysteries, whose rituals are repeated in the later Greek myth of the sorrowing Demeter, searching for the abducted Kore. These interpositions thus serve to excavate the maternal voice in order that it may effect the mother-daughter awakening. While this maternal voice remains present in the later sections of the novel, it has apparently done its work, and in the later sections it appears only occasionally to direct the search for the lost daughter. At this later point, Bea's journey has become spatial; that is, the journey takes place less in terms of history and more in terms of personal events that occur in physical places—the Northeast, the Midwest, and the West.

It soon becomes apparent to the reader of *Her Mothers* that Broner's extensive textualizing evokes the archetypal quest as both a retelling of the dominant patriarchal myths and a means of escaping entrapment in these narratives. Broner's interest in the journey can be seen most obviously in the section titles, "Looking for Friends," "Looking for Fathers," and "Looking for Daughters," and subtitles involving "Looking for Mothers." Yet these titles are tentative, inconclusive, and open-ended, and even point to difficulties in the search. While Broner's protagonist, Beatrix Palmer, is always recognized as the quester, it is also clear that a portion of her quest is focused on the difficulty of the initial undertaking itself, especially since Bea moves not only through linear space and time, but also through the texts of other women who have lived historically, prehistorically, and mythically. However, her initial immobility is clearly represented as the result of being Jewish and female in the America of the 1940s and 1950s.

Broner has also described *Her Mothers* as "a search, a holy pilgrimage."[8] French has noted that the character's last name *Palmer* resonates with connections to a Christian journey and describes a pilgrim who "completed a spiritual journey to Jerusalem" and also that the name *Beatrice* (Beatrix) evokes the name of the inspirational force behind Dante's journey.[9] If it is indeed Broner's intention to bring Christian resonances to bear on the journey motif, then it would appear that she also intends for her protagonist to escape from all biblical and classical narrative, as well as from the conventions of the Jewish novel itself.

Indeed, Broner's larger target seems to be all the immobilizing cultural forces that characterize Western discourse. Calling her novel "a very conscious counter Telemachus,"[10] she is intent on undercutting the narrative of the son's search for the father and opts instead for the older and perhaps even more influential myth of Demeter and Kore—the descent of the goddess and the *heurisis* of the daughter. Of the transformational power of this myth, as it was once acted out in the Eleusinian mysteries, Erich Neumann has this to say: "The one essential motif in the Eleusinian mysteries and hence in all matriarchal mysteries is the *heuresis* of the daughter by the mother, the "finding again" of Kore by Demeter, the reunion of mother and daughter."[11] Furthermore, this "finding again" signifies, in psychological symbolism, the annulment of the male rape with its accompanying intrusion into the female mysteries, even as it recovers the lost significance of the mother-daughter bond.

In contrast, biblical mythology used by Broner serves to delineate for Bea the source of women's immobility, since women move only as objects of exchange. In "Foremothers," the section of the text that treats this older material, the Four Matriarchs—Sarai, Rivka, Leah, and Rahel—bequeath to their daughters a legacy of bondage and betrayal where the exchange of women is a given, and where the reproductive organs link women to vegetation and earth. Sarai, although of royal blood, is transformed upon her marriage to Abraham into an object first offered to Abraham, then to the Pharaoh to ensure Abraham's safety. She is later spurned by Abraham for Hagar, who betters her reproductively. In the second generation, Rivka's favoritism for Jacob sets up the oedipal configuration, while her lack of fertility repeats Sarai's history and assures the control of Jehovah and his male worshippers over the processes of fertility. In the third generation, the rivalry to produce children is carried on by Rahel and Leah. Yet these stories—which tell of women who are ultimately entrapped by wombs that are their literal and metaphorical prisons, who betray other women, and who regard their children as prizes—are the result of Bea's literary excavation. It is in the way of her own telling that *matriarchy* is exposed as a masculine construction. "Who named you my mothers" cries Bea, "who named *this* a matriarchy?" (*HM*, 168).

As mentioned earlier, Broner seems to suggest that Jewish tradition is the formidable immobilizer of girls,[12] and embedded in the stories of her four childhood friends are patterns of entrapment and immobility that reverberate throughout the material that constitutes the present day and are shown to have both shaped and confirmed Bea's own experiences. The family of "Romanian Lois" offers an example of the mother who favors the male child and the father who offers the daughter only false comfort, with their double-voiced discourse encouraging mobility, but ultimately denying it. A tragic figure in the end, Lois's aptitude for chemistry does not allow her entry into the all-male high school chemistry club, and this loss of opportunity is represented in a later gesture reminiscent of Esther Greenwood, a jump out of the window of the medical building in which her doctor-husband has an office.

Other friends' lives repeat patterns of containment and immobility. Shirley, who in her adult life exists in an attic room and "cannot walk without help" (*HM*, 63), is the daughter of a artistically gifted mother who is killed by the Nazis. Later, her own artistic sensibility is killed by an abusive father. A third friend, known as Black Janice, has problems with containment, stemming mainly from her mother's tendency to buy clothes that are too small for her in an attempt to deny a body that is too athletic, too muscular. While ignoring Janice's athletic prowess, the family instead follows the achievements of the brother. Her way out is accomplished by her internalization of blackness and her marriage to a black man, after which her family abandons her. Bea's fourth and last friend, Pauline, also exists in a closet-like apartment and gradually ceases to speak. Only after the death of an indifferent working mother do her ambitions to be an architect become fulfilled and her ability to speak return.

Bea's own development is problematized in ways similar to those of her friends, but her ways of coping with the immobilizing constraints of patriarchal socialization are different. She does not flee into marriage like Janice who, abandoned by husband and family, becomes a total projection of otherness; nor is she reduced to hobbling on crutches like Lois. Instead, Bea consciously opts for heroism. Like Joan Foster, Bea's limitations are body-related and are exacerbated by her early awareness that she is never going to fit the culturally determined image of female beauty. Indeed, Bea seems able to describe herself only in terms of lack: "Her hair is not as neat as Inez Miller's. She does not have lifted eyebrows and an amused smile like Marcia S. Liebowitz. She is not blonde, blue-eyed, frilly, like Razel Schiller" (*HM*, 5). At one point her excesses are "mapped out" in a section with an upper-cased heading of CARTOGRAPHY OF BEA. Here Bea enumerates all her despised body parts—breasts ("too small, nipples too large"); thighs ("Hate thighs.

Loose."); legs ("too full); shoulders ("too wide"); hair ("all that hair") (*HM*, 81–82).

Strangely, despite the presence of the mother-daughter refrains discussed above, there is a disturbing absence of mothers in the texts of both Bea's historical mothers and her own, perhaps because Broner is more intent on exposing the role of the fathers in the suppression and seduction of the daughters. While the stories of Bea's friends reveal unsympathetic father figures, which can be courtly seducers or vengeful logos figures, Bea's own father is exposed as a more subtle kind of seducer. He is responsible for her early political attitudes, as well as her adolescent literary productions (the mother, we are told, never reads books). Bea's father goads her into action with a question that, in spite of variants, remains essentially the same: "Bea, what will *we* do to free Sacco and Vanzetti?" and "they're killing our people. What will *we* do?" and, finally, "what will *you* do about the British?" (*HM*, 57–58, italics mine).

What Bea does is to write a report on the Nazi death camps, which appears in the high school paper, and a report on the British prevention of the Jews' entry into Palestine, which is to appear in the college paper. In each case her father has been the source of her social awareness and a spur to her writing efforts, yet each of her texts is suppressed. The principal censors her exposé of the Nazi death camps; the Army Information Service and the journalism department of the college urge the suppression of her "anti-British propaganda" (*HM*, 58). In each instance the parents collude in the silencing of Bea and continue to favor her less ambitious and far less talented brothers.

Despite her early and frequent silencings, Bea, whose writing is always recognized on some level as a writing of her self, is successful in finding a way out at last through her research of nineteenth-century American women. Writing becomes, in fact, a descent not only into history, but also into myth, which itself represents the daughter's re-entry into the body of the Mother, the subsequent need to escape from that body, and the important transformation that is the goal of that re-entry. Bea's mothers—Emily Dickinson, Margaret Fuller, Louisa May Alcott, and Charlotte Forten—will serve to "birth" her as they, in turn, become re-presented in her re-searched texts, thereby becoming her daughters.

Relying on biographies and letters, but also feeling like Adrienne Rich's androgynous diver who seeks not the story but the wreck itself.[13] Bea wants to expose the ways in which these women's stories have been constructed. What she unearths is a spectrum of containment narratives. In Dickinson's letters to Higginson, Bea discovers a duplicitous voice, one that is obsequious before males (a voice that addresses Reverend Higginson as "Master" and "Preceptor") while—in an intriguing inversion of the process of self-naming—designating herself as "Gnome."[14] However, it is through this false and masking voice that Bea comes to recognize the modification of her own "rich" and "low" voice to a "high nervous Mother Emily voice" (*HM*, 79) that she, like Dickinson, feels forced to use around males. Bea also associates Dickinson's well-known lifelong confinement in the house in which she was born with the repressed mobility that manifests itself in the poet's "fluttering" and "retreating" movements (*HM*, 75), and even in her "scrawly handwriting" (*HM*, 74). Nor is Bea unaware of the irony in the fact that Dickinson's pretentious mentor also has a housebound wife who is confined to a wheelchair "in order not to have to move anywhere" (*HM*, 75).

Thus, Broner's (Bea's) collection of excerpts and her very careful documentation of her biographical sources give the reader a view of accomplished women trapped in the narratives of male scholars, who present their writings as scholarly and objective, and who are, therefore, blind to their gender biases. Bea's research acts to expose the ideologies of those scholars through whom we read only the story of the fathers. In Bea's research on the life of Fuller, for example, we are given excerpts from personal reminiscences put together after Fuller's death and edited by Ralph Waldo Emerson, William Henry Chain, and James Freeman Clark. What these commentaries reveal, however, is the kind of usurpation male writers practice to gain control of the words of women, even as they draw attention away from those words to the female body. In the case of Fuller, her plainness becomes a popular topic. Emerson's description: "Her appearance had nothing prepossessing. Her extreme plainness—a trick of incessantly opening and shutting her eyelids, the nasal tone of her voice— all repelled" (*HM*, 83). Responding to the unconscious fear and revulsion of femaleness expressed in such pronouncements, Broner's narrator replies in kind: "Ugly Emerson, hypochondriac, effeminate Higginson, short, egocentric Mr. James Nathan . . . undersized, long-nosed Thoreau!" (*HM*, 83). Yet by stripping away the masking language of the seemingly dispassionate observer, the narrator reveals the emotionally toned underside of such commentary. The reader who is disturbed by the inappropriateness of such remarks has only fallen into Broner's trap.

Yet Fuller's own accomplishments, like those of Emerson, Higginson, and Thoreau, are formidable and suggest a high degree of mobility. Fuller has served as an editor of *The Dial* and as a literary editor of Horace Greeley's *Tribune*; she has traveled to Oregon in a covered wagon; she has fought for the rights of American Indians and prisoners. She has also authored a feminist tract, from which Broner has extracted some of her more telling comments and uppercased them. Some examples:

FRAILTY, THY NAME IS MAN. (*HM* 87)
. . . THERE EXISTS IN THE MINDS OF MEN A TONE OF FEELING TOWARD WOMAN AS TOWARD SLAVES. (*HM*,88)

Such captioned declarations, by means of which Broner/Bea foregrounds women's words, are of only minimal comfort to Bea, since her research on Fuller also presents her with another side of this woman who, like Dickinson, is a victim of another variant of patriarchal containment. Her letters to men—in this instance, James Nathan, a man with whom she was in love—reveal another self, which, in spite of the accomplishments of their author, is a diminished self enclosed in culturally dictated responses to a male love object. Fuller's letters to Nathan make a plea for domination and crave a self-diminution. Like Dickinson, Fuller has also internalized the culture myths about women's beauty and describes herself to Nathan as an "ugly dwarf changeling" (*HM*, 87). In another letter she becomes passive, receptive, the reflecting object, a moon to Nathan's sun, and she continues, "I open my thoughts to the loved soul who has brought me so much sunlight" (*HM*, 98).

A discouraged Bea observes that, like her Matriarchs, these women are victims of exchange, except that these women actively participate in their own passivity and "bring themselves to their gentlemen" (*HM*, 84). They also remake themselves in a language prison, in which they censor their own discourse. Says Bea, "We must learn to read the love letters women write . . . we must learn they are lies" (*HM*, 92).

Re-searching Louisa May Alcott reveals to Bea an even more sinister situation of entrapment in which the father plays a major part. Born on her father's thirty-third birthday, Alcott outlives her father by one day and dies as a result of her efforts to nurse him. Bea reads the symbolism of this happpenstance as especially appropriate because Alcott has been, in fact, trapped in her father's life span. And although Alcott was a creator of texts, Bea's examination of Alcott's life reveals the insidious subordination of the daughter's desire to the needs of the father, which at the same time points up not the strength of such fathers, but their overriding weaknesses. For example, despite his notoriety, Bronson Alcott, Bea decides, has been the product of women. His mother is responsible for publishing his texts on teaching. His wife and daughters endure inconvenience and poverty during his Fruitlands experiment, and while at its failure Bronson Alcott indulges in thoughts of suicide, the women are the ones who must manage to carry on, as well as to distract him from his rather histrionic depression. Always it is Bronson Alcott who travels (Emerson pays for his England trip) and the women—especially Louisa and her mother—who remain at home to run the household and support the family. Mobility for Louisa means learning to "shovel snow, carry water . . . split kindling, make fires . . . do sewing, teach children, take in washing, or write a book" (*HM*, 111).

Not surprisingly, such constraints engender in Louisa a lifelong battle with depression. Always self-hating because she is not a male ("I have a fellow feeling for lads and always owed Fate a grudge because I wasn't a lord of creation" [*HM* 106]), she nonetheless writes nineteen books whose titles (for example, *Under the Lilacs* and *Flower Fables*) belie their seriousness and their author's despair. Alcott is also betrayed by her body. She is ungainly—over six feet tall—and her only asset is her long chestnut-colored hair which she loses in an illness.

Perhaps because for the African-American woman mobility is both an important correlative of a free identity and a literary tradition devolving from the early slave narrative, Charlotte Forten, Bea's last literary foremother, is more successful at being mobile. Her trip to Sea island, undertaken when she was twenty-two, marks a crucial event in her life and an important area of research for Bea, for whom re-search now becomes a truly mobilizing act. For Bea moves imaginatively not only into a textual life, but also into the very space that Forten herself has occupied. Accompanied by Forten's journal, Bea travels to the Sea Islands in an attempt to recover both the words of the woman and the context of her life there, and perhaps to resurrect the actual process of journal writing. (Ironically, as Bea discovers, Forten, who makes for herself a career teaching runaway slaves, is never able to escape either her color or her sex.)

As Bea enters the world of Charlotte Forten, she enters the past in a more meaningful way than she has heretofore done. There is a suggestion of entry into an underworld—she is ferried across to the island by a silent, mysterious boatman—and her own past seems to recede. The world she enters even has a touch of the uncanny about it, and her joke to her ferryman that she is looking for ghosts is accepted as a possibility: "You'll find those aplenty! . . . more ghosts than egrets" (*HM*, 122), he tells her.

This ghostly presence is in part evoked through Forten's journal, which Bea carries with her on her long walks along the beaches and through the woods. However, in doing everything that she has never done in "real life," Bea invokes an *unreal* life, an animated environment that seems to enter "her bedroom through the walk-in closet, the rose-decorated bedsteads and dressers, the orange-tiled bathroom floor, the double windows looking out on the river" (*HM*, 124). Even the spider crab shell on her dresser begins to move.[15]

Like other literary underworlds, this one comes replete with "shades," the source of which is, Bea thinks, Forten's journal itself, which becomes almost animated and which Bea imagines as "breathing out loud" (*HM*, 138). Bea's discomfiture, doubtless evoked through the recitation of bits of song, "a mother song"—about Jerusalem, mother death, salvation—is also stirred in the presence of a special kind of text: slave bills of sale that read "Old Rose, age seventy-five . . . $20; Peg, thirty-eight, . . . $500" (*HM*, 130). Yet her confrontation with the uncanny seems appropriate, and while it might be argued that the ghosts are caused by a kind of psychic paralysis or by Bea's projection of energy onto this alien world, they seem a necessary part of her underworld experience and suggest an encounter with the unconscious aspects of both body and text. Bea's cry of "Enter me, ghosts of my Mothers!" articulates a desire for the lost pre-oedipal unity, which is answered only with the silence of absence, and Bea understands that the ghosts must eventually be laid to rest. Going past them, first to her to prehistorical mothers—the foremothers—she must eventually come to "the opening of caves of herself" (*HM*, 140).

There are thus a number of disturbing similarities about the lives of Bea's historical mothers, ones she is quick to recognize. Each is trapped in a body that does not conform to culture's prescribed standards of beauty. Beyond the imprisoning effects of their bodies, these historical mothers also suffer hysterical symptoms: Alcott aches in her joints; Forten suffers some kind of recurrent illness; Fuller has migraines. Bea concludes: "My mothers were not trained to run the race, and, when a few of them did, their chests ached, their legs stiffened, they panted long before the finish line" (*HM*, 126).

Bea's historical mothers also make escapes, albeit futile ones, usually when they are in their thirties. Fuller journeys to the West Coast and later to Rome, but is drowned on her return to the United States, and her text on the 1848 Roman revolution is lost at sea, drowned with her. Alcott spends six weeks in Washington, D.C., as a hospital nurse during the Civil War, but returns home with typhoid pneumonia. Forten goes to Sea Island; Dickinson never really escapes at all, except metaphorically ("inside of an envelope, inside of another envelope" [*HM*, 104]). Like Bea, they can only effect escape through their writing, which, however, becomes more a record of entrapment than an account of mobility. The journals of Fuller and Alcott, for example, document their lack of importance to the outside world and chronicle, with fascination and self-contempt, the minutiae of their lives.

What Bea's re-searches reveal is that the daughters belong to the fathers, and by becoming what she calls "Bearers of the Dream," they remain chained to reproductive processes. By being trapped in the metaphor of motherhood in this manner, they assume the same domestic containment of their own mothers. The tragedy of the daughters' metaphoric pregnancies is illustrated through the narratives of the young Israeli women. The father of Naomi, the biologist at Tel Aviv University, whose Zionism has "impregnated" her with a dream to return to the Land, ultimately disinherits his daughter because she has not remained home. The father of Bea's second friend, Rina, is a singer whose relationship with his daughter was created at the expense of her mother who is "always dead" (*HM*, 163). "We were a team, my father and I," Rina tells Bea. Yet when Rina succeeds in becoming a singer in Haifa, she, too, is rejected because she escapes domestic confinement and violates the axiom that girl singers do not go on the road. Ilana, a potter whom Bea meets, has a rejecting mother ("she gave birth and saw it was a girl and never spoke again" [*HM*, 169]). Instead, Ilana is close to her father, a "man of culture" and a collector who, unfortunately, desires that Ilana remain home as one of the collected. Rut'y, a social worker in the ministry, is the daughter of a labor organizer and, as a child, had been given a privileged mobility. Allowed to attend strike meetings, to visit women's prisons and Arab communities, Rut'y is also "disinherited." Broner's repeated use of this term suggests that she intends for the patrilineal interference to be heard, that the word must serve to underscore the linguistic fictionality of relationships based on patrilineage, thereby exposing the real loss to both mother and daughter.

In the light of the father-bonding as a formative factor in later heterosexual relationships, Bea's lesbian relationship with Naomi serves as a subversion, the introduction of a new script where fatherless daughters reaffirm, at least indirectly, the mother-bond. The sexual relationship between Bea and Naomi also serves to represent a reclamation of the female body, and it is noteworthy that Broner structures the description of what these women share as a counter text to the script of the fathers: Here the women do *not* ask, "Do you love me?" "Did you have other lovers?" "How did you lose your virginity?" since "virginity is neither valuable nor valueless between women" (*HM*, 156). Appropriating the Golden Rule (doing unto another "as you would have her do unto you" [*HM*, 156]) to a very different end, patriarchal law is transformed into a text in which the body is joined to law and speaks to women.

But *Her Mother*s is also a specific search for a lost daughter, and it is in the character of the resentful, yet enigmatic, daughter Lena that we "read" the consequences of Bea's mothering, the problems with mergence and separation that have not been overcome in Bea's re-search. It is an intended irony that Bea, in spite of herself, lives within the confines of the patriarchal myth and becomes in her own time the prescribing, engulfing mother. The difference is that Bea is aware of her and Lena's fates and her awareness becomes part of the textual fabric of Broner's work. Bea's surrender to patriarchal tradition is summarized by a listing of items that the newborn infant Lena will not need in the world. She will not need boxing gloves: "no fighting . . . rather taming. . . . No coming fighting from a corner. The idea is to corner"; she will not need "*trains, schooners, buses*": "Lena would not be a railroad woman. She will not aspire to Lionel trains, to skipper a schooner, unleash a Greyhound. By land, sea, or air, she will have to be taken there"; there will be no Superman pajamas for Lena: "No quick changing . . . no walking through walls"; nor will there be maps: "why should she find her way? Let her stay close to home" (*HM*, 99–100). Given her name by her grandfather, Lena also becomes for him a "living doll," that is, until her nose is broken and her face acquires a "fault."

Whatever Lena's genuine wounds, her childhood behavior indicates in ways both comic and horrific her fear of mergence with the mother, especially as evidenced in her drawings of monster figures and in her particular accusation—"You have stolen my name!"—when she learns of Bea's interest in writing a children's book from Lena's own stories. Her enactment of female immobility at the age of twelve—when she appears at a costume party clad in a white dress and carrying a plastic flower as the dead Ann Rutledge, only to spend the entire party "on the floor . . . not speaking, eyes closed, holding that stiff flower" (*HM*, 105)—suggests that she has learned much from her mother. Wearing the trappings of her mother's failed marriage, Lena seems quite aware of every woman's fate in a patriarchal system, as she becomes a bride of death (Hades), a parodic Sleeping Beauty.

It also becomes evident that Lena is in many ways her mother's daughter, and that her anger and rebellion are a maternal legacy, for Lena, like her mother, resists constraints. Given the nature of Bea's interference, this resistance is understandable. In a short, primer-like section entitled "Ten Ways to Lose Daughters," Broner offers up a comical, yet meaningful, listing of maternal strategies, all of which involve appropriation, silencing, and immobilizing injunctions, which seem to encompass a good number of the mothers' fixing tendencies. Under the heading "Talk Too Much," Bea is shown speaking "without pagination, inserting marginalia, notation"; under the heading "Compare," the daughter is specularized; under the heading "Be Helpful," the daughter's tasks are appropriated; and under the heading "Have Historical Perspective," difference is reduced to sameness (*HM*, 175–78). Not surprisingly, Lena's response to all the mother's efforts is the repeated refrain, "Shut up."

Lena is also shown to be as socially and politically conscious as her mother. The difference is that her world is not at war with Naziism; Lena is of the generation that watched the assassinations of King and the Kennedys. But she deals with her anger and pain in the same way the young Bea did: She transforms them into a text, thereby acquiring a voice of her own. In spite of her self-dramatizing pronouncement that "I can't write, I can't speak," Lena, at age sixteen, offers strong countering evidence that she does both.

Broner's novel is full of references to Sweet Sixteen parties, and as a degenerate form of older daughter rites, they are placed in the text to parody the Eleusinian mysteries and Sleeping Beauty stories. In fact, the Sweet Sixteen party is anything but a rite of passage and, instead, encapsulates the cultural fixing of daughters. Instead of marking the girl's passage into meaningful activity, it involves the trivialization of activity, the consignment of girls to parties and beauty parlors, all of which partake of a process of arresting development and turning girls into products. It is significant then that Lena fails to show up at her Sweet Sixteen party. Escaping to Canada, she leaves her birthday cake to "harden" in the refrigerator. Broner's suggestion here seems to be that it is better that the cake should be consigned to the refrigeration processes than the daughter. Furthermore, what the reader knows of Lena's absence, gleaned through the little information that Bea herself possesses, suggests that it is spent in wandering, and although Bea considers her daughter "nowhere bound," the truth may be that this separation, and the activity it engenders, is energizing and

preferable to the house-bound daughter that has dominated Bea's re-
searched texts.

Nevertheless, Bea does stay connected to her child, even if only through
texts that would appear to deny that connection, as, for example, Lena's
suggestive pronouncement on the back of one envelope that "NO THING
UNITES US" (*HM*, 232). This enigmatic message seems true in at least two
ways. Mother and daughter are doomed to separation as they fulfill the
Freudian script, the romance plot. Also, the fact that "no thing" unites
mother with daughter does not deny their permanent connection, since the
ties are based on imaginary connections and, therefore, doomed to be
haunting ones. Interestingly, these words are scrawled on the *outside* of the
envelope, the words appearing to stand where Lena herself wishes to
stand—outside the enveloping presence of the maternal. Unfortunately,
this and other bits of texts where Lena speaks to her mother are misunder-
stood by Bea who, unable to "read" her daughter's texts, seems to regard
them as points of argument and catalysts for still more discord. Thus, while
Bea is able to read the doubleness of her historical mothers, she fails to hear
the double-voiced pronouncements of the daughter, fails to ask herself why
Lena bothers to write at all.

Part of the resolution to the paradoxical nature of the mother-daughter
relationship is to be found once again in the structure of this work, especially in the two final sections of the novel, which present Bea at the end of
her life (even though the thread of chronology that weaves its way through
the narrative suggests that Lena has only been gone about three years and
that two years have passed since Bea's trip to Sea Island.) The two final
sections, entitled "Bea at Home" and "Looking for Shells," suggest the fixity
and mobility that, in fact, characterize each. "Bea at Home" is told in the
present tense, suggesting immediacy, but not action, since Bea within
domestic space spends her time trying to arrest her body's aging processes.
Attention is, therefore, paid to her weight, her exercises—for both face and
body—her hair dying, her menstruation. Her only other activities are
cooking and television watching.

On the other hand, in the "Looking for Shells" section Bea is seen walking
alone on a beach on a small key off Florida's west coast. The chapter announces itself as a story and is narrated in the future tense, thereby
undercutting the reader's inclination to regard these events as a realistic
representation of Bea's encounter with her daughter. In it Bea has become
a seeker after shells, accumulating large numbers of them and memorizing
their names. The shells serve as a rich, if rather puzzling, symbol here. They
are remnants, cast upon the beach by the sea. But, more important, each is
"a carnivore that engulfed and smothered other shellfish" (*HM*, 231).
Despite the fact that they are dead things, inanimate fragments that have
lost their living substance as well as their ability to grow, the shells have
beautiful, vividly colored insides. Bea, who has always associated her

journeys with "the caves of herself," is naturally responsive to the beauty of these cavities with their vaginal associations. Furthermore, as Bea herself knows, the shells can revive their external color only by being submerged in sea water. All these properties symbolize aspects of the mother-daughter relationship. Thus, the corroded shells are associated with Lena's corrosive letters, while other shells are cemented together, suggesting an ongoing bond (*HM*, 232).

The sea also leads away from fixity and recalls, for example, the moisture of the female body, which, earlier in the work, Broner has textualized under the heading of "From Embryo to Out You Go." Here the embryo, described as soaking in "that female brine . . . all of life . . . pickled and floating" (*HM*, 217), is linked to the sea. In terms of signification then, the sea and the beach suggest space along the margins, an appropriate place for the confrontation of mother and daughter, a place of beginnings.

It is along this strand that Bea records a futuristic encounter with her daughter. No banal or cloying reunion takes place, however. Instead, there is a night-long battle—appropriately mythic—that culminates in an interesting sea immersion where the paradox of mothering is expressed in Bea's thought: "was she strangling that baby . . . when she nurtured her? . . . Was she pressing that face into her chest to keep the nose from breathing?" (*HM*, 240). The immersion in the sea seems to provide the answer to Bea's question: "At the pressing down of Lena's head through the water, Bea's obsession with the past, with fixed objects such as photographs, is dissolved: "albums were spilled and snapshots cracked. Ink ran from letters, stamps loosened, envelopes opened" (*HM*, 240).

But destruction is really only disruption. Broner returns her characters to the place where subjectivity can be shared, where fluidity can be recaptured and re-experienced, a place where Luce Irigaray's "playful crossings" can take place. Like the shells that have their colors restored to them by immersion in the sea, the mother-daughter text has been allowed to recover its *jouissance*.

NOTES

1. Ellen G. Friedman and Miriam Fuchs, "Contexts and Continuities," in *Breaking the Sequence: Women's Experimental Fiction*, ed. Friedman and Fuchs (Princeton, N.J.: Princeton University Press, 1989), 4.

2. Nancy Gray, *Language Unbound: On Experimental Writing by Women* (Urbana: University of Illinois Press, 1992), 161.

3. Marilyn French, Introduction to *Her Mothers*, by E. M. Broner (1972; reprint, Bloomington: Indiana University Press, l985), xi.

4. Judy Hoy, "Of Holy Writing and Priestly Voices: A Talk with Esther Broner," *Massachusetts Review* 24, no. 2 (Summer l983): 264.

5. E. M. Broner, *Her Mothers* (1972; reprint, Bloomington: Indiana University Press, 1985), 3 (hereafter cited parenthetically in the text as *HM*).

6. Gray, *Language Unbound*, 152.

7. For readers less familiar with this novel I offer the following breakdown:

Section	Number of Interpositions
I. "Looking for Friends"	63
II. "Historical Mothers"	56
III. "Foremothers"	2
IV. "Looking for Daughters"	1
V. "Looking for Fathers"	1
VI. "Bea at Home"	1
VII. "Looking for Shells"	1

8. Hoy, "Of Holy Writing," 255.

9. French, Introduction to *Her Mothers*, xiii.

10. Hoy, "Of Holy Writing," 259. Broner explains this need as due to the fact that "the men were not active enough in that search [for the past]."

11. Erich Neumann, *The Great Mother*, trans. Ralph Manheim (Princeton, N.J.: Princeton University Press, 1963), 309–10. Neumann's androcentric reading of the Demeter-Kore myth focuses more fully on what he designates as the "second mystery," namely, the birth of the son, which symbolizes the beginning of the concept of the luminous male principle. On the other hand, Adrienne Rich, *Of Woman Born: Motherhood as Experience and Institution* (New York: W. W. Norton, 1976), 238–39, emphasizes the mother's role as a catalyst in the rescue of birth and death processes from "paternal splitting." In other words, the ritual affirms process and movement between two supposedly alien states.

12. Broner, in her interview with Hoy, "Of Holy Writing," 264, admits that Judaism is a force from which she cannot escape: "I can't separate my Judaism from myself," she says, "because the world defines me always as a Jew." She goes on to conclude, "The world will still destroy me in the name of Jew."

13. Adrienne Rich, "Diving into the Wreck," *Diving into the Wreck: Poems 1971–1972* (New York: W. W. Norton, 1973), 23.

14. Dickinson may herself be engaging in some textual playfulness here, since "gnome" not only means "a small misshapen dwarf," but also refers to an earth-dwelling guardian of treasure and to a wise or pithy saying.

15. As in the case of Atwood's novel, supernatural ingredients present in Broner's text resist "naturalization" or explanation.

5

Walking the Red Road: Mobility, Maternity, and Native American Myth in *Meridian*

Live by the Word and keep walking.

—Alice Walker
"Advice of the Two Headed Woman"
Living by the Word: Selected Wrtings

In her essay entitled "Choice: A Tribute to Dr. Martin Luther King, Jr.," Alice Walker writes this interesting bit of family history:

My great-great-great-grandmother walked as a slave from Virginia to Eatonton, Georgia—which passes for the Walker ancestral home—with two babies on her hips. She lived to be a hundred and twenty-five years old and my own father knew her as a boy. (It is in memory of this walk that I choose to keep and to embrace my "maiden" name, Walker.)[1]

This anecdote, suggestive of a slave narrative, appears as yet another example of Walker's well-known veneration for her foremothers, but the story also suggests a less discussed concern of Walker: the problematic conjunction of mobility and maternity. Yet the importance that Walker places on mobility is evidenced in her textual appropriation of the legacy of her slave foremother's walk.

Walker demonstrates in many places in her writings a need for such confirmation, for although she has celebrated The Mothers, both literary and ancestral, telling us that "so many of the stories I write, that we all write, are my mother's stories" (*MG*, 240), she also describes those same mothers as artists "driven to a numb and bleeding madness by the springs of creativity in them for which there was no release" (*MG*, 233). It would appear that Walker has a problem with this maternal legacy, a problem that manifests itself thematically in numerous images of entrapment and paralysis, as well as in images of surrogate motherhood.[2] Furthermore, paralysis and a lack of mobility seem clearly linked in her novels to the problem of black woman as artist. This problem forces Walker to look beyond the merely thematic representations of mobility and leads her ultimately into the question of textual mobility as well.

Walker's interest in the relationship of mobility to maternity doubtless explains, at least in part, her interest in that looming figure of the Harlem Renaissance Zora Neale Hurston. While Walker finds Hurston's autobiography *Dust Tracks on a Road* disappointing, she also admits, "I loved the part where [Zora] ran off from home after falling out with her brother's wife" (*MG*, 110). In fact, both Hurston and her protagonist Janie Starks of *Their Eyes Were Watching God* demonstrate a remarkable mobility, and the road is, for them, an ever-recurring symbol of freedom and self-creation.

Hurston's influence on Walker cannot be overestimated. In a recent and important study on the relationship between the two, Dianne F. Sadoff offers some insightful commentary, which has at least an indirect bearing on mobility and textuality. Sadoff argues that both Walker and Hurston tend to idealize the mothers, Hurston because her mother died when she was nine, Walker because of her need for literary vindication.[3] Using Nancy Chodorow's model of family configurations and Harold Bloom's anxiety-of-influence theories, Sadoff suggests that Walker suffers from a kind of matrilineal anxiety, and that before she can define and validate her own texts, she must "invent" Hurston as a viable author and source. Nevertheless, Sadoff says, Walker is caught by her need to idealize black matrilineage, while at the same time she feels anger "at her black slave mother's disinheritance."[4] That anger, I would argue, is not leveled so much at the disinheritance of those slave mothers as at the immobility that is symptomatic of that legacy. Therefore, while Walker honors the mothers, she clearly chooses not to become one of them.[5]

Sadoff's argument has a special relevance for Walker's 1976 novel *Meridian*. Because ambivalence toward her maternal slave history is particularly in evidence in this novel, it serves as an important textual locus for the struggle between mobility and maternity. It is also the novel in which Walker crystallizes her own role as a creative artist. Walker's dilemma would seem to involve her need to use that maternal slave history, while at the same time she escapes the constraints of its discourse. I will argue here that Walker accomplishes this escape by drawing on another part of her heritage, namely, that of Native American myth. What she is able to achieve through her use of this special mythology is a different kind of mobility—one that allows her to escape the bonds of realism and to engage in a more dynamic structuring of her novel. At the same time she is able to discover for herself a resolution to the problem of the black woman artist and her maternal slave history. For Native American mythology offers her a special kind of creatrix, a maker not of humans, but of human activity, known variously as Thought Woman, or Spider Woman, who is not She Who Bears, but She Who Thinks.

First, a brief discussion of the novel's realistic subject matter seems called for. Certainly a young black girl's coming of age in the South of the turbulent sixties and her involvement with the Civil Rights Movement are the stuff of realism. But while politics and race are central concerns, there is another, almost subtextual, ingredient that determines Meridian's involvement in these perhaps larger, but more removed, issues, namely, the immobilizing effects of pregnancy and gender. Much of the conflict in the novel involves not only a hostile white patriarchal society, but also the paralyzing effects of Meridian's black maternal slave heritage.

Meridian's mother is an almost stereotypical Black Matriarch—the "Black Mother personified" as Meridian denotes her, a woman conceived of as "huge, a giant, a woman who *could* trust in God."[6] Indeed, Mrs. Hill's voice, identified with the god-voice derived from patriarchal discourse, speaks of long-suffering, self-sacrificing motherhood. Yet while black maternal self-sacrifice is almost legendary to Meridian, she also understands another, suppressed script, one that expresses her mother's real attitude about childbearing and rearing. She knows of her mother's surrender of a teaching career to marriage, a fate that Meridian likens to being "buried alive," to being "walled away from her own life brick by brick" (*M*, 51). As marriage and childbirth took away her mother's mobility and made her dependent, they also divided her from her newly emergent self and, worse, from the right to express any anger about her entrapment. While the mother's mobility might have been limited to choosing to teach in a nearby town, the mother has nonetheless surrendered even this much opportunity, and her mobility has been reduced to "blind, enduring stumbling" (*M*, 77).

Not too surprisingly perhaps, Meridian feels guilty, regarding her own birth as a theft of her mother's life. She sees herself as responsible for "shattering her mother's emerging self" (*M*, 51). This guilt has the same effect that the daughter's bonding to the mother would, and Meridian, awakened to her guilt by the mother's constant question, "Have you stolen anything?" is also immobilized: "the question literally stopped her in her tracks" (*M*, 51). Thus, Meridian's journey to Atlanta to college is conceived of as an escape, and her involvement with the Movement vies in her thoughts with her guilt over her mother. This guilt is further exacerbated by Meridian's rejection of her own child, a rejection that represents the refusal to reproduce her mother's story.

Meridian's immobility, derived from her status as both mother and daughter, is, in part, expressed by means of the numerous examples of pregnant women in the novel, all of whom become victims of entrapment. There is Nelda, Meridian's childhood friend, who, pregnant at fourteen, surrenders both education and mobility, but achieves in return the status of the good daughter. There is the Wild Child, an abandoned girl whose lifelong survival alone on the streets is terminated by pregnancy. Escaping Meridian's care, and "running heavily across a street, her stomach the largest part of her," she is finally killed by a car (*M*, 37). There is Fast Mary of the Tower, the Saxon college student guilty of infant murder, whose fate is celebrated by all the women on the campus in a yearly commemorative rite. There is the thirteen-year-old child-murderer Meridian visits in prison, whose awful act engenders in Meridian more sympathy for the mother than for the murdered child.

Most of all, however, it is Meridian's guilt over the surrender of her own child and her mother's accusing voice that bring on the central conflict of the novel, along with Meridian's paralyzing illness. Viewing her life as a young mother as "slavery," and harboring thoughts about murdering the child—or herself—Meridian's existence at age seventeen is characterized by a numbing lethargy. She becomes activated only when the house of some civil rights workers is demolished by a fire bomb, and clearly—since Meridian has never evinced any interest in political activism before this incident—we might theorize that it is the visual destruction of an imprisoning domestic space that helps to activate her: "something about the bombing had attracted her, the obliteration of the house, the knowledge that had foreseen this destruction" (*M*, 80). This objectification of her own containment—and its destruction—frees her to join the Movement, to attend college—but also to surrender her child.

Her guilt over this last act, even though she rationalizes that she has "saved a small person's life" (*M*, 91), is kept alive by the voice of her mother, which repeats patriarchal scripts about mothering: "You should *want* Eddie Jr. . . . unless you're some kind of monster. And no daughter of mine is a monster, surely" (*M*, 89). But, rather than resisting, Meridian internalizes this "voice that curses": "It said, over and over, until she would literally reel in the streets, her head between her hands: Why don't you die? Why not kill yourself? Jump into traffic! Lie down under the wheels of that big truck! . . . Always, the voice urging her on" (*M*, 91). This reeling motion ("to reel" is defined as "to give way; fall back, sway, swing, or stagger in shock") alternates with her marching, and to some extent the two neutralize one another. Nevertheless, the result of Meridian's responsiveness to the voice of the mother is immobilizing illness—nightmares, headaches, anorexia, temporary blindness, but especially paralysis and a kind of catatonia.[7]

Thus, the opening of the novel, where Meridian marches on behalf of some children barred from seeing the traveling display of the Mummy Woman—albeit a rather bizarre and puzzling incident—can be seen as artistically appropriate because it encapsulates Meridian's problems with mobility and transforms the conflict into textual terms as well. The mummified woman, advertised as "Dead for Twenty-Five Years" and "Preserved in Life-Like Condition," is accompanied by another grouping of static captions—noun phrases that freeze women's stories in clichés. These are "Obedient Daughter," "Devoted Wife," "Adoring Mother," but they are followed by a fourth caption: "Gone Wrong" (*M*, 19). This last caption contains a verb, but also a delimiting adverb suggesting in textual terms the fate (and vector) of the woman who moves.[8] The Mummy Woman's story, told by the husband, describes a woman who, as a "goddess," had nothing to do but "lay back and be pleasured," but who had instead "gone *outside the home* to seek her 'pleasuring'" (*M*, 20, italics mine). Strangled, thrown into a salt lake, reclaimed, and now displayed as the perfect female object, the woman also objectifies Meridian's own immobilizing text and the resultant pronouncement of deviancy. Truman, puzzled by Meridian's curious political target, asks, "What good did it do for those kids to see that freak's freaky wife?" But Meridian replies that "She was a fake. They discovered that" (*M*, 26).

Nevertheless, the woman and her accompanying texts are not so easily debunked by Meridian herself, for her confrontation is followed by a collapse and she is carried home by four men, "hoisted across their shoulders, *exactly as they would carry a coffin*, her eyes closed, barely breathing, arms folded across her chest, legs straight" (*M*, 24, italics mine). Meridian's thinness and her skin tone, which Truman describes as "wasted and rough" and as "a sallow, unhealthy brown" (*M*, 24), also suggest the correlation that Walker is making between her protagonist and the mummified woman.

Thus, Walker provides us with a realistic representation of the struggle between the imperatives of Meridian's heroic revolutionary activity and the wasting paralysis that accompanies that activity. But mimetic representation seems as binding as Meridian's own conflict, and Walker seeks an escape into a less mimetic mode of fiction-making, one whose essence seems to be mobility. She suggests as much when she discusses *Meridian* as a "crazy quilt story," going on to define this kind of story as "one that can jump back and forth in time, work on many different levels, and one that can include myth."[9] This less realistic mode is seen in Meridian's strange out-of-body experience, related in the "Indians and Ecstasy" chapter, and in her later physical crisis with its accompanying visions. Such experiences are thematically and structurally coherent only when we move into the realm of Indian mythology.[10] There is also the epigraph of Black Elk, which introduces the novel. But in less obvious ways as well, the novel is permeated with American Indian myth, and it is this myth that offers mobility to Meridian, and structural cohesion to Walker, even as it provides the latter with an escape from binding narrative conventions and white textual inscriptions.

Indian myth is attractive to Walker for personal reasons, as she tells us: "There was my mother's mostly Cherokee grandmother to contend with in myself. . . . There was my gravitation toward Indian art and artifacts . . . and Indian pottery, jewelry. . . . And there was my study of Cherokee folklore and folkways.[11] And while acknowledging aspects of sexism in some Indian attitudes, Walker also allows that "it is their light step upon the Earth that I admire and would have us emulate" (LW, 43).[12]

Black Elk is perhaps most frequently mentioned in her writings. His story, recorded in 1932 by John G. Neihardt, remains not only a moving indictment of white genocidal policies, but also an extraordinary expression of sacred consciousness. It is the influence of his story on the making of *Meridian* that I especially wish to explore.

The epigraph Walker uses to introduce the novel is taken from a later portion of Neihardt's text and refers to the destruction of the Indian nations at Wounded Knee in 1890. In this passage Black Elk describes the scene of "butchered women and children lying heaped and scattered all along the crooked gulch" and concludes with these crucial words: "*A people's dream died there. It was a beautiful dream. . . . the nation's hoop is broken and scattered. There is no center any longer, and the sacred tree is dead.*"[13]

Certainly Black Elk's words articulate the fate that Walker perceives to be in store for the Civil Rights Movement of the early sixties, a fate that by the time of the present action of the novel—1968—has already become something of a reality. For Indians, Wounded Knee was the end because the people's dream had died. Walker, as an artist as well as an activist, knows that if the dream is to be kept alive, it must be maintained through a special weaving of the political with the personal, the artistic with the sacred. To put it another way, Walker creates a protagonist who must encounter the sacred, who must experience a vision that will both liberate her from her immobilizing illness and prepare her for her role as a revolutionary, but one who is an artist and a seer.

Meridian's unusual illness, which serves as a threshold to a special kind of healing, is related to a number of so-called conversion experiences. That tradition helps us, I think, to explain her psychological and physiological crisis, recounted in the chapter entitled "The Recurring Dream." The title would appear to refer to Meridian's disturbing dream, which has sprung from her reading of traditional realistic narratives and their conventional punishments for ambitious—that is, mobile heroines.[14] This thrice-repeated bit of narration reads as follows: "She dreamed she was a character in a novel and that her existence presented an insoluble problem, one that would be solved only by her death at the end" (M, 117). Nevertheless, Walker rejects this kind of closure, this "recurring dream," for an altogether different kind of dreaming. What she takes for her model of the dream is Black Elk's "great vision." While Black Elk's vision was experienced when he was a boy of nine and Meridian's occurs during her college years when the activity of the Movement and her guilt over her child have become particularly trying, there are similarities between the two experiences.

Black Elk's vision, which transpires while he lies in a coma for twelve days, is preceded by an immobilizing illness. His illness is nonetheless succeeded by a feeling of freedom, which culminates in what is best described as an out-of-body experience during which Black Elk encounters the Six Grandfathers. These figures he recognizes as "not old men, but the Powers of the World" (*BES*, 25).[15] Four of the six figures represent the four directions—West, North, East, and South; the other two represent Sky and Earth. Each gives Black Elk empowering objects. From the First Grandfather (of the West) he receives the cup to make things live and the bow to destroy. The Second Grandfather (of the North) gives him the healing herb and the power of the cleansing wind; the Third Grandfather (of the East) offers the peace pipe and promises the power of "roots and legs and wings" (*BES*, 27). The Fourth (of the South) offers him the red stick, which becomes the sacred tree. The Powers of the Sky and Earth give him mobility in terms of wings, stars, and winds and in terms of walking the black and red roads on earth. Furthermore, Black Elk is given a view of his own history through "four ascents"—that is, four generations—a history that embraces both the living and the dead.

Similarly, Meridian's vision occurs in conjunction with the crisis engendered by her illness. Blinded, anorexic, and paralyzed, Meridian appears to frightened roommate Anne-Marion to be "slipping away" (*M*, 119). While Black Elk's vision evokes a confrontation with the Grandfathers, Meridian's "vision" involves—appropriately—the Grandmothers, figures who also represent power, who will evoke maternal history as a source of healing and creativity.[16]

There are also six personages involved in Meridian's crisis. Four are her maternal ancestors, and the other two are her roommate, Anne-Marion, the revolutionary, and Miss Winters, the college teacher from Meridian's home town. As a revolutionary who endorses violence, Anne-Marion seems to suggest a possible future, while Miss Winters appears to represent the past. Yet the appearance of Miss Winters is important because, as one of the college's three black faculty members, she had risen "against Saxon tradition" (*M*, 120)—that is, against a tradition that is white and patriarchal—by teaching jazz and blues.

Just as Black Elk's illness and recovery involve a confrontation with the ancestors, Meridian, too, must confront her ancestors in order that she may remember maternal history, a history that has, until now, only served to paralyze her. With the entry of Miss Winters (whose name associates her with the Indians' northern cleansing wind) we are presented with another point of view and one that is crucial to that remembering. What Miss Winters recalls is Meridian's high school speech on the U.S. Constitution, an oration that Meridian, recognizing its falsity, is incapable of concluding. While this rather spontaneous rebellion is the cause of a rift between Meridian and her mother, Miss Winters remembers it as a stance to be respected and—more important—to be remembered. It is this knowledge that allows Miss Winters to take on the role of mediator, even the role of surrogate mother, so that when Meridian in her delirium utters, "Mama, I *love* you. Let me go," Miss Winters can reply, "I forgive you" (*M*, 125).

What Meridian herself remembers—literally dreams— in her illness is her mother's achievement and its marked characteristic—mobility: "Mrs. Hill had persisted in bringing them all . . . to a point beyond where she, in her mother's place, her grandmother's place, her great-grandmother's place, would have stopped" (*M*, 122). Yet this is not the final word on those "places," for the repetition of the word *place* points to movement along a line, and from there to the genuine mobilizing ability of maternal history. Indeed, Meridian is forced to go beyond her mother, but in order to do so, she must recognize her maternal history and its empowering dynamism.

Meridian's remembering of maternal history begins with the story of the great-great-great-grandmother slave who steals her children back at great personal cost. The next story is not about a mother, however, so much as it is about an artist—the great-great-grandmother who painted barn decorations, buying her own freedom with the money she earned from her art. The third story again emphasizes maternity and tells of the grandmother who endured brutal beatings from her husband and the bearing of twelve children. The final story is one about her mother, who paid for her own education and that of her four siblings as well. Meridian, as Walker's alter ego, may have difficulty with the mother, but Walker, the artist, sees the need to include both the maternal and the artistic in a text that weaves into its design the work of both the mothers and the artists.

Beyond these similar illnesses and their resulting conversion experiences, Walker uses a number of empowering symbols derived from Black Elk's vision, symbols that are important to tribal consciousness. Two of these, referred to in the epigraph quoted above, are the concept of the nation's hoop and the sacred flowering tree. Also frequently mentioned in *Black Elk Speaks* is the metaphor of the red road. Connected to both the hoop and the tree, the red road must be walked "in a sacred manner." But this injunction can be obeyed only when the hoop is unbroken and surrounds the people, and when the tree, planted in the center of the hoop, is able to bear leaves and thereby to flourish. These ingredients, crucial for community survival, also embrace mobility.

The American Indian concept of the circle is used by Walker to give structure to the novel. Black Elk describes the importance of the circle to Neihardt as follows: "You have noticed that everything an Indian does is in a circle, and that is because the Power of the World always works in circles, and everything tries to be round. . . . Everything the Power of the World does is done in a circle. . . . The life of a man is a circle from childhood to childhood, and so it is in everything where power moves" (*BES*, 198).

Nevertheless, the circle is not to be taken as a static configuration. In a sense, because the figure of the circle tends to take on a static aspect, it is often better represented in a dynamic way—as a spiral. Cherokee author Dhyani Ywahoo best illustrates the connection when she says, "The circle teachings represent the cycle of all things that spiral in the ever-moving universe, a process of constant movement and subtle change in harmony together."[17]

Thus, life and death go on within a circle, but this configuration is less appropriate than that of the spiral if, using the circle, we envision a fixed point of return. Furthermore, the spiral seems to better describe the structure of *Meridian*. We can note, for example, that the novel begins in the present, moves part way into the past, and then moves forward into the present again. Then it spins out into the points of view of Truman and Lynne. The opening chapter is entitled "The Last Return" and describes Meridian's present political activities, while the last portions of the book (entitled "Travels," "Pilgrimage," "Settling Accounts," and "Release") all have to do with a different kind of movement—Meridian's movement among the impoverished and brutalized blacks she tries to help. The center portions of the novel take us back to Meridian's college days, and then to her childhood, her pregnancy and marriage, and conclude with her entry into the Civil Rights Movement. However, there is never a return to a particular point of departure or point of origin. Finally, while the opening pages have shown Truman moving into town, the final pages show Meridian moving out.

In the only portion of the novel that deals explicitly with Indian consciousness— the "Indians and Ecstasy" chapter— the spiral plays a critical role. This chapter tells us of Meridian's father—a man who chronicles the history of the now-absent Indians and who is himself "a wanderer and a mourner," and owner of land upon which there is an ancient burial mound. This sacred land has imprinted on it the signature of a five-hundred-yard-long serpent, which forms a "curling twisting hill" (*M*, 56), and is itself a locus of mobility. As part of a field of energy, it has been known to Meridian's great-grandmother Feather Mae. Feather Mae's story is an important part of Meridian's legacy because she represents another grandmother figure, but especially because of her extraordinary experience in the burial mound and her conversion to an ecstatic religion, which stands in contrast to the "white" religion that Meridian's mother has internalized as her own discourse. Furthermore, the serpent in the burial mound is another link to the Grandmothers—the creative Dreamers of Indian myth.[18]

The story told of Feather Mae is that she discovers the energy contained in the burial mound when she ventures into the deep pit formed from the coiled tail of the Serpent. Caught up in the energies of the place, the Grandmother feels that she has "stepped into another world" where "the next thing she knew she was getting up off the ground" (*M*, 57). Renewed by her encounter with the sacred, Feather Mae practices ecstatic religion—a religion of mobility, an Indian religion.

But the story passed on to Meridian does not lose its mobility; its power is retained in the telling, and both Meridian and her father also experience the energy buried in the coil of the serpent's tail. Meridian's encounter, which also describes a spiral, is as follows:

> It was in her head that the lightness started. It was as if the walls of earth that enclosed her rushed outward, leveling themselves at a dizzying rate, and then spinning wildly, lifting her out of her body and giving her the feeling of flying. And in this movement she saw the faces of her family, the branches of trees, the wings of birds, the corners of houses, blades of grass and petals of flowers rush toward a central point high above her and she was drawn with them, as whirling, as bright, as free as they. (*M*, 58)

This rather unusual experience, clearly a departure from the realistic mode of the novel, establishes another kind of consciousness, another kind of knowing, which foreshadows the liberation of Meridian, while it also reinforces the importance of the spiral as a symbol of the dynamic nature of the cosmos.

There is even more persuasive evidence of Walker's use of the spiral in Meridian's very name. It is evident from Walker's positioning of rather lengthy definitional material just prior to the start of the novel that she means us to regard the name as important. And, indeed, the name does suggest the same dynamic configuration. It seems to promise her movement, even to mandate her destiny. However, it is also apparent from the length and multiplicity of Walker's definitions that she is not desirous of fixing the term. "Meridian" can mean an apex or point, but also a vector or track, something that is both fixed and moving. "Meridian" is also "an imaginary great circle," and it is, most important, a longitudinal and intersecting line that, running from North to South, represents, according to Indian myth, the road of life and death. Such tracking lines between North and South designate the cleansing powers of the wind (abstracted as will) and the regenerative powers of the South (abstracted as renewal).[19]

Thus, Walker's elaborate, yet ambiguous, textualizing of Meridian's name leads us to some interesting speculations regarding Meridian's function. For example, as *prime meridian*, which is defined as "a carefully located meridian from which secondary or guide meridians may be constructed," Meridian serves to hold other characters in place, to keep them on track. She herself serves as a vector (but always in Indian terms dynamic and unfixed). Thus, Truman Held is the *true man* who is *held* in line by Meridian, so that he continues in the movement, living the dream. Furthermore, by placing this material before the novel, Walker has established the importance of the term as a word in a text, not as sign, but as signifier.

Returning to Black Elk and his reference to the nation's hoop, we find that the idea of the hoop offers us another way of thinking about the circle as dynamic, for to conceive of the circle as a hoop restores its dynamism; the hoop can move. Furthermore, it can have a center around which it moves. For Indians the Sacred Hoop, or Medicine Wheel, designates the space in which the nation lives and the means by which it thrives. But it is not a space that is static; it moves with its people. And, most important, within the Sacred Hoop is the sacred tree.

We may recall that from the Fourth Grandfather, representing the power of the South (the power related to growth), Black Elk receives a red stick, which the voice describes as "the living center of a nation" (*BES*, 28). As Black Elk watches, the red stick sprouts branches and leaves. In Black Elk's vision, the villages of the people circle the tree and thrive. But when, in another part of the vision, Black Elk enters the village and sees that the people are sick and dying, the voice of his vision tells him that he must give them "the flowering stick that they may flourish" (*BES*, 34). When Black Elk plants the red stick "at the center of the nation's hoop," both the animals and the people are restored (*BES*, 34).

Walker's version of the sacred tree is, of course, The Sojourner, the ancient magnolia that stands in the center of the campus and that possesses magical powers of song. As an archetypal symbol for maternity, a locus of black history and magical transformations, it is one of her richest symbols. The name of the tree is evocative of the great Sojourner Truth, and Walker clearly intends for us to make this connection. Indeed, the connection does not stop with Sojourner and a tree. In *Living by the Word*, Walker weaves her own name into Sojourner Truth, explaining that both *Alice* and *Truth* combine, as do *Sojourner* and *Walker*.[20] And she goes on to say, "I get a power from this name that Sojourner Truth and I share. And when I walk into a room of strangers who are hostile to the words of women, I do so with her/our cloak of authority—as black women and beloved expressions of the universe" (*LW*, 98).

Thus, the Sojourner tree serves many functions. The tree is large enough to protect the girls who climb its branches and hide there to make love. It is also the locus of the Commemoration of Fast Mary of the Tower and in other times concealed runaway slaves. It stands in opposition to that other connective symbol—the chapel—which refuses to accept the body of the Wild Child. When the college president refuses to admit Wild Child's coffin, the students, without needing to say anything, carry it to The Sojourner, "whose heavy, flower-lit leaves hovered over [the coffin] like the inverted peaks of a mother's half-straightened kinky hair" (*M*, 48). Here Walker has animated the Pieta image, given it a vegetative form, and moved it out of the church.

The Sojourner is also connected with the fate of a West African slave named Louvinie, who came from a family of storytellers and was herself able to terrify white children with her stories. This African power to conjure is terrifyingly realized when a child actually dies of fright, causing Louvinie to be punished by having her tongue torn out. But Louvinie is not totally silenced. Understanding the need to find a special place for her tongue in order to save her soul, she buries it under The Sojourner. This act, reaffirming the interpenetration of all forms of life, seems to mitigate the curse on her, and the tree comes to possess magic—it can talk and make music.

Nevertheless, despite the tree's history and significance, it is the object that the girls destroy in their anger and frustration over the treatment of the Wild Child by the school authorities. Besides her intent to show that the anger of women is so often turned upon themselves, Walker appears to use The Sojourner as a different kind of maternal symbol.

The Sojourner's textual significance is not fully apparent, however, until the final pages of the novel. Then it appears transformed into a photograph, one Meridian has placed on her wall. To Truman it looks at first like "an enormous bull's eye," but he soon correctly perceives it to be a stump of a tree, one with "a tiny branch, no larger than his finger . . . growing out of one side" (*M*, 217). Truman's readings may be persistently phallic,[21] but the bull's-eye image is also evocative of a circle and a center—hoop and tree. The photograph, sent by Anne-Marion with the accompanying comment, "who would be happier than you that The Sojourner did not die?" (*M*, 217), seems an assurance for both Meridian and the reader that African Americans need not suffer the fate of Native Americans. Furthermore, with her fondness for merging plant, animal, and human life, Walker has Truman perceive Meridian as a kind of tree. While he understands by the end of the novel that he has lost the "old Meridian," there is a "new part" of her that has "grown out of the old," like the new life out of the old stump.[22]

It would be a mistake to assume that the foregoing symbols—the hoop and the flowering tree— suggest one place. The Plains Indians were, of course, a highly mobile people, and they took their hoop with them. Therefore, Black Elk's vision does not provide a picture of stasis, even when the hoop is in place and the holy tree flourishes. Accordingly, even when the voice in Black Elk's vision declares the power and eternity of the nation's hoop, it also concludes with another injunction: "Now they shall break camp and go forth upon the red road, and your Grandfathers shall walk with you" (*BES*, 35).

But the good nation "walking in a sacred manner" does not comprise only the living, for in his vision Black Elk sees behind him, accompanying the people, the "ghosts of people like a trailing fog . . . grandfathers of grandfathers and grandmothers of grandmothers without number" (*BES*, 36). The ancestors are the nation as well.

Meridian also desires to walk in a sacred manner, but in order to do so she must acquire a new sense of community, that tribal consciousness that embraces both living and dead. This she accomplishes in a surprising place—in a Christian church. We know that Meridian has always resisted church because she has identified it with her mother. But this church experience proves to have a different effect on her. When Meridian enters, she expects to find everything the way she experienced it as a child. Yet she notices immediately that the music is different. It has been revitalized, reappropriated, and it has become a music that possesses "triumphant forcefulness," an "oddly death-defying music" (*M*, 195). The minister is also different. He speaks in the voice of Martin Luther King, and Meridian comes to see this "imitation" not as a mockery but as a means of "keeping that voice alive. It was like a *play*. . . . and the preacher's voice—not his own voice at all, but rather the voice of millions who could no longer speak" (*M*, 196). The "ahmens" have also been transformed and are now uttered not with resignation and despair, but with anger and determination.

Most important of all, perhaps, is the commemorative nature of the service, a memorial service for a murdered civil rights worker, whose grieving and maddened father adds another moving element to the ceremony. What the commemoration of the young man's death does for Meridian is to make her more aware of true ceremony as a "righteous convergence"—one of the features of a meridian— and as yet another reference to an interchange between the grieving parent and the community that expresses itself as a communal voice. Such a voice now appears to say to Meridian: "If you let us weave your story and your son's life and death into what we already know—into the songs and sermons, the 'brother and sister' we will be so angry we cannot help but move" (*M*, 199).

However, the anger does not make Meridian violent. While she recognizes the obligation "to kill before she allowed anyone to murder" the man's son again, she also sees more clearly that her own role is to walk the road, but "to walk behind the real revolutionaries" (*M*, 201). At this point she knowingly assumes the role of the healer, the visionary, the dreamer, and concludes, "I will come forward and sing from memory songs they will need once more to hear. For it is the song of the people, transformed by the experiences of each generation, *that holds them together*, and if any part of it is lost the people suffer and are without soul. (*M*, 201 italics mine)

Here we have another convergence—a meeting of author and protagonist to share a vision of a creative destiny. Black Elk says of his own destiny that he was to "bring the hoop together with the power that was given . . . and make the holy tree to flower in the center and find the red road again" (*BES*, 151). Walker's destiny as an artist involves a similar vision, but she must become empowered through images that validate the feminine. Indian myth offers her that validation in the figure of a special Creatrix: the woman variously called Thought Woman or Spider Woman. This figure, described by Susan J. Scarberry as "keeper of sacred traditional knowledge,"[23] differs from the archetype of the Great Mother because she is concerned not with maternity, but with essential *processes* of creation, including the making of pictures, songs, and stories. She is, in other words, the maker of culture, and it is her original act that the people emulate in the creation of language and art.

As Grandmother Spider, her creativity becomes imaged in the web spun out of her body. Here, as Scarberry observes, the spider and the web, long devalued in Western mythology, are recovered as positive images. Most important, the orb replicates the image of the sacred hoop: "The orb web is an orderly arrangement of threads radiating out from a central hub and linked to one another in a spiral."[24]

So Meridian walks the red road, singing the songs of each generation in order that they will remain a people. Walker also weaves together the voices of the people—reflected in the multiple-voiced narration of the text—and thereby emulates not the reproductive Earth Mother—She Who Bears—but Thought Woman or Spider Woman—She Who Thinks. Empowered by the Grandmother who is the maker not of humans, but of human activity, Walker can emulate this essential creativity—a creativity that makes not a solipsistic art, but a truly tribal art, an art by which the people live and thrive as a people.

NOTES

1. Alice Walker, *In Search of Our Mothers' Gardens* (New York: Harcourt, Brace Jovanovich, 1983), 142 (hereafter cited parenthetically in the text as *MG*).

2. In *The Color Purple* (New York: Washington Square Press, 1982), mothers are absent or dead. Celie's mother has died from overwork and excessive child-bearing, as has Sofia's mother. While Sofia is the mother of six children, they are mostly raised by her sisters and Squeak. On the other hand, when Sofia is released from prison and Squeak goes off with Celie and Shug, Sofia undertakes the rearing of Squeak's child. Nettie helps to raise Corinne's children (who are really Celie's anyway), and Celie raises Albert's children. The message seems to be that mothering is better done by surrogates, and the children raised in this more extended familial structure seem to survive without noticeable damage.

3. Dianne F. Sadoff, "Black Matrilineage: The Case of Alice Walker and Zora Neale Hurston," *Signs* 11, no. 1 (Autumn 1985): 4–26.

4. Ibid., 11.

5. For studies on Walker and maternity, see especially Barbara Christian's works, "Alice Walker: The Black Woman Artist as Wayward," in *Black Women Writers (1950–1980): A Critical Evaluation*, ed. Mari Evans (Garden City, N.Y.: Doubleday, 1984), 456–77; and *Black Women Novelists: The Development of a Tradition 1892–1976* (1980; reprint, Westport, Conn.: Greenwood Press, 1985), 204–34. When asked about having children herself, Walker (who has a daughter) replies that a single child is best: "With one you can move. . . . With more than one you're a sitting duck" (*MG*, 363).

6. Alice Walker, *Meridian* (New York: Washington Square Press, 1976), 121 (hereafter cited parenthetically in the text as *M*).

7. In an interview with Claudia Tate, *Black Women Writers at Work* (New York: Continuum, 1983), 179–80, Walker comments on Meridian's illness, arguing that it is stress- and guilt-related.

8. Rachel Blau DuPlessis, *Writing Beyond the Ending: Narrative Strategies of Twentieth-Century Women Writers* (Bloomington: Indiana University Press, 1987), 159, observes that these captions describe "pickled roles . . . a series of conventional endings, which Meridian as multiple individual will painfully displace from narrative hegemony."

9. Tate, *Black Women Writers at Work*, 176.

10. Myth has by now numberless definitions. Alan W. Watts, *Myth and Ritual in Christianity* (Boston: Beacon Press, 1968), 28, defines it as "any narrative, factual or fanciful, which is taken to signify the inner meaning of life." Jungians see myth as projections of psychic images; Roland Barthes sees myth as a system of signs. Paula Gunn Allen, *The Sacred Hoop: Recovering the Feminine in American Indian Traditions* (Boston: Beacon Press, 1986), 104, sees myth as embodying "a sense of reality that includes all human capacities, ideal or actual," and "an expression of the tendency to make stories of power out of the life we live in imagination" (105).

11. Alice Walker, *Living by the Word: Selected Writings 1973–1987* (New York: Harcourt, Brace, Jovanovich, 1988), 43 (hereafter cited parenthetically in the text as *LW*).

12. Walker makes reference to James Mooney's *Myths of the Cherokee and Sacred Formulas of the Cherokees*, as well as to Anne Cameron's *Daughters of Copper Woman*, and especially to *Black Elk Speaks*. Her fullest discussion of Indian consciousness occurs in the essay entitled "Everything Is a Human Being" (*LW*, 139–52).

13. The above is a partial quote from Walker's abridgement. The full quote from *Black Elk Speaks*, transcribed and edited by John G. Neihardt (New York: William Morrow, 1932), 276, is as follows:

I did not know then how much was ended. When I look back now from this high hill of my old age, I can still see the butchered women and children lying heaped and scattered all along the crooked gulch as plain as when I saw them with eyes still young. And I can see that something else died there in the bloody mud, and was buried in the blizzard. A people's dream died there. It was a beautiful dream.

And I, to whom so great a vision was given in my youth,—you see me now a pitiful old man who has done nothing, for the nation's hoop is broken and scattered. There is no center any longer, and the sacred tree is dead.

Subsequent references to this work will be cited parenthetically in the text as *BES*.

14. DuPlessis, *Writing Beyond the Ending*, 158, argues that Meridian escapes from romance plots that would make her either a martyr or the wife of Truman and says, "Walker takes Meridian beyond all the endings of romance and death" so that she becomes a "multiple individual in a new plot."

15. Black Elk's vision (*BES*, 20–47) is most notable not only for its recurrent images of the hoop and the sacred tree, but also for the vectors and quadrants used to describe the Sioux cosmos. To summarize briefly, after the Grandfathers give him the symbols of power, he finds himself on a bay horse before the black horses of the West, the sorrels of the East, and the buckskins of the South. A voice next repeats the gifts and their powers and also prophesies struggle, the walking on the

black road. In the next segment of his vision Black Elk rides the storm clouds to his village and defeats a blue man who represents drought, after which he plants the red stick in the center of the village. Another segment of his vision involves four ascents, which he interprets as "the generations I should know." In each ascent the people's fortunes are shown as declining. First, the road becomes steeper; then it turns into the black road. By the end of the third ascent, the nation's hoop has been broken, and by the fourth, the holy tree has disappeared.

The vision does not end there, however, for even as a storm approaches, Black Elk is enabled to sing a song of power that evokes his ability to cure. As the horses once again gather from the four quadrants and make a hoop to perform a dance, the voice tells Black Elk that "the day is yours to make" (*BES*, 42). Then Black Elk is taken to a high mountain and is given the herb of understanding. When he returns to the Grandfathers, one of them proclaims of Black Elk, "in a sacred manner I have made him to walk" (*BES*, 45).

16. Allen, *The Sacred Hoop*, 11, describes the importance of the Grandmother figure to Native American consciousness as follows: "She is the Old Woman who tends the fires of life. . . . She is the Eldest God, the one who Remembers and Re-members."

17. Dhyani Ywahoo, *Voices of Our Ancestors* (Boston: Shambala, 1987), 37.

18. Allen, *The Sacred Hoop*, 204–5, explains the Dreamer in Native American myth as the one "responsible for the continued existence of the people as a psychic (that is, tribal) entity." And she goes on, "It is by virtue of her gift, her ability, that the people live and are a people."

19. Ywahoo, *Voices of Our Ancestors*, 77, speaks of meridians as carriers of elemental energy.

20. Walker, *Living by the Word*, 97, explains about Sojourner: "we share a certain 'mystical' bent, Sojourner ('Walker'— in the sense of traveler, journeyer, wanderer) Truth (which 'Alice' means in Old Greek) is also my name."

21. Margaret Homans, "'Her Very Own Howl': The Ambiguities of Representation in Women's Fiction," *Signs* 9, no. 2 (Winter 1983): 186–205, does a close reading of The Sojourner portion and the wall-hung texts. Homans emphasizes the phallic misreading of Truman who, she says, sees "a target where there is a living tree" (195).

22. In his painful last lament to the Great Spirit, Black Elk mourns the withered tree, but as he recalls his great vision, he declares, "it may be that some little root of the sacred tree still lives. Nourish it then, that it may leaf and bloom and fill with singing birds" (*BES*, 280).

23. Susan J. Scarberry, "Grandmother Spider's Lifeline," in *Studies in American Indian Literature: Critical Essays and Course Designs*, ed. Paula Gunn Allen (New York: Modern Language Association of America, 1983), 101.

24. Ibid., 105.

6

Morrison's Desolated Centers: Mobility, Desire, and Subjectivity in *Sula* and *Beloved*

I put frames into windows and discover they are holes in the void.
Dacia Maraini
Letters to Marina

As mentioned earlier, African American writing is perhaps most consistently marked by the trope of the journey, which, echoing the experience of the African diaspora, appears in impressionist renderings of the Middle Passage, in the autobiographical accounts of the slave's escape to freedom, and in the myth of the flying Africans who manage to return to their homeland. Toni Morrison seems especially attracted to narratives of mobility, and her work abounds with journeys that are literal, symbolic, historical, mythical, and personal. In her earlier works journeys appear in the main as simple initiation experiences, as in the case of Nel's visit to New Orleans (*Sula*, 1973) and Milkman's return to his people's homeland (*Song of Solomon*, 1977). Sometimes they are likely to represent a psychic/social crippling, usually the result of encounters with white society. Some of the most noteworthy of these occur in *Sula*, where Eva Peace returns to The Bottom after an eighteen-month absence with "two crutches, a new black pocketbook and one leg,"[1] Shadrack returns home from the war a schizophrenic, and Eva's son Plum returns a heroin addict.

Often Morrison represents movement in terms of startling descents, as in Robert Smith's plunge from the cupola of Mercy Hospital and Milkman's final ecstatic flight over Solomon's Leap (*Song of Solomon*), in Eva's desperate flight from her third-floor bedroom to save her burning daughter and Chicken Little's last flight out of the grasp of Sula and into the lake. Some characters, like Jadine and Son (*Tar Baby*, 1981), appear to incarnate mobility, again of a more destructive kind, since, in the case of Jadine, it is based on her escape from her African-ness, while for Son it signifies perpetual homelessness and weakened selfhood.

Perhaps because of the problematics of African American subjectivity, Morrison configures the trope of the journey as a centrifugal force, often imaged as a vortex or spiral, in which people move out and away, ultimately even vanishing. The prevalence of this dispersal and dissipation is in part responsible for what may be the most notable feature of Morrison's work, namely, presence of absence, which has been noted by more than one critic as central to her writing. Robert Grant argues, for example, that *Sula* is "'about' gaps, lacks, 'missing' subjects, and ambiguous psychic space, all of which must be 'filled' and interpreted by the reader."[2] Morrison has herself expressed her desire to draw the reader's attention to empty spaces for the reasons that Grant suggests, but her discussion of the meaning of such spaces suggests that more is involved: " We can agree, I think, that invisible things are not necessarily "not there" that a void may be empty, but is not a vacuum. In addition, certain absences are so stressed, so ornate, so planned, they call attention to themselves; arrest us with intentionality and purpose. . . ."[3]

I would argue that such "intentionality and purpose" convey the idea that absences function as affects that escape the bounds of discourse. To present such escaped material in her texts, Morrison attempts to use language not only to evoke what is there, but also to expose what is not there, echoing Jacques Lacan's idea that what is said cannot be measured against what *is*, namely, the real, which is lost to consciousness and unrecoverable within the symbolic order, but which nonetheless makes its presence known by way of certain disruptions in language and text, especially those that point to linguistic inadequacy.

Thus, I would argue that absence goes beyond the reader's involvement with the text, that it plays such a crucial role in Morrison's work because it "speaks" to the question of the subject, especially the African American female subject who comes into the symbolic world in a manner that is complicated by the presence of the white world. This white Other ensnares the black world in its signifying practices and, as a consequence, also serves to problematize the so-called normative splitting of the mother-child dyad. Because Morrison's "desolated centers" articulate the African American experience of this primordial separation trauma, as well as the experience of object loss and the unstable nature of the subject as constructed in language, I will draw on both Lacan's pre-mirror and mirror stages theories and Julia Kristeva's *semiotique*[4] to discuss the striking ways in which Morrison explores the mother-daughter relationship against a background of castration and loss, and the reconstitution of subjectivity by means of textual mobility that uses language and its discontinuities, especially as they operate in *Beloved*, her richest, most multivalent novel to date.[5]

While the mergence/separation problems of the daughters are rendered in the extreme in Morrison's work, they are played out against a textualized uncanniness that has as much to do with the white community as it does with the mothers. Thus, while the prominence of images of dismemberment and fragmentation points not only to the conditions of subjectivity under slavery, the representation of lack obviously leads back to infancy. In Morrison's work then, uncanniness involves the white community as an experience of boundary invasion. In this respect, it is similar to the uncanniness that Sigmund Freud attributes to the double that stands over "against the rest of the ego" and is capable of treating that portion of itself "like an object" (*SE*, 17:235). Although the white community is not the space in which Morrison's narratives take place, it is always present—an absence characterized by inscrutable and unpredictable powers. It possesses the powers of the gaze, always surrounds the black subject, and, enfolding her/him in its symbolic system thereby constitutes the African American subject "discursively, ontologically and politically" as Other.[6]

Indeed, the problematic nature of *all* boundaries in Morrison's work originates in this condition (mediated through the mother, of course). As all the characters in *Beloved* know, "anybody white could take your whole self."[7] In *Sula*, for example, Morrison represents the dissolution of an entire community in the slow slide of The Bottom from its hillside location to its diminished and fragmented reconstitution on the valley floor. Similarly, in *Beloved*, Sweet Home is both the site of "enlightened" slavery and the place of rape, torture, and mutilation. Nor do the boundaries between slave state (Kentucky) and free state (Ohio) succeed in keeping the slave world from intruding on the free, and even the Suggs household—a center of mothering and nurturance—also becomes, because of the failure of black boundaries to withstand white invasion, the place where the mother can murder her child.

It is against this background that Morrison, in the configurations of mothers and daughters, literalizes castration. Her women do not simply stand for lack; they bear the marks of castration on their bodies. We have only to think of Eva's amputated leg and of Sethe's two mothers, the surrogate one missing an arm, the biological one branded and ultimately eradicated through violent death. For Morrison, fragmentation and dismemberment are not simply infantile fantasies, but also intrusions of the real. I shall first explore the relationship of mobility to desire (and hence absence) in *Sula*.

"SULA": THE LONG FALL OF SPACE

In Morrison's 1973 novel we find that journeys are used to signify initiation experiences, at least initially. Helene's painful return to her disturbing childhood origins in New Orleans becomes for Nel a journey that marks a symbolic separation from her mother. Eva's triumphal return from her long absence marks her emergent power. However, Sula's journey, undertaken on the day when Nel surrenders her life to the constraints of marriage, and lasting for the next ten years, undermines any easy quest patterning.

Other kinds of mobility are problematic as well. Often mobility within domestic parameters—especially with respect to the Peace household—is associated with death. We are given the horrific dance of the burning Hannah and the menacing moves of her mother Eva, who trundles back and forth in her wagon in the upper reaches of the house. If one journey initiates her emergence into power, Eva's two later descents from her upper room involve her in the deaths of her children. In the first instance she takes to her crutches and, "swinging and swooping like a giant heron," enters Plum's room to end his life (S, 46). In the second instance she throws herself from her third-floor window in an attempt to save her burning daughter. "Trying to aim her body toward the flaming, dancing figure" (S, 76), Eva misses, much to her regret survives, and spends her remaining years with the window of her room sealed.

This destabalizing and decentering kind of mobility also characterizes the tenuous subjectivity of a number of other characters. Shadrack learns the fragility of selfhood during World War I when he witnesses the headless running soldier whose movement is counterpointed by the "drip and slide of brain tissue" down his back (S, 8). Confronted by this image of liquified dismemberment, Shadrack drops into a psychotic state where he possesses "no past, no language, no tribe" (S, 12), and where his own being threatens to slip and slide away (his fingers, for instance, begin to "grow in higgledy-piggledy fashion" [S, 9]).[8] He only recovers his tenuous selfhood and escapes the slip and slide of his always-growing extremities when he sees his image reflected in the water of a toilet bowl, an image that is only somewhat stabalized, but still remains watery, changeable, and therefore, impossible to hold.

The remainder of his life is spent in the attempt to contain death (most specifically rendered for him as dismemberment). In his establishment of National Suicide Day, where he makes "a place for fear as a way of controlling it" (S, 14), he does, in fact, effect a temporary containment for himself as well as the community, who thereby also come to know "the boundaries and nature of his madness" and can, therefore, fit him "into the scheme of things" (S, 15). Nonetheless, Shadrack's yearly march becomes, in the end, a dancing parade that ends up, in a sense, where it always was: at a hole, the tunnel excavation, that represents the white world and its negation of the black subject. Perceived by the community as a 'non-prom-ise' of work 'not given' to black men, of "teeth unrepaired, the coal credit cut off, the chest pains unattended, the school shoes unbought" (S, 161), it becomes a real void, which, when the residents attempt to "kill" it, instead swallows them.

Lack of another kind is represented in the characters of Nel and Sula, both of whom seem to represent extremes of fixity and mobility. Nel, who is never to leave the town after her childhood trip to New Orleans, is the product of a mother intent on driving "her daughter's imagination underground" (*S*, 18). In her futile attempts to straighten Nel's hair and to lengthen her nose, Helene molds her into a product that will reflect white middle-class cultural myths. In this sense Helene is much like Joan Foster's mother, intent on containing female excessiveness, in this instance identified with both gender and race. Thus, the adolescent Nel, the passive one of the pair, fantasizes "lying on a flowered bed, tangled in her own hair, waiting for some fiery prince" (*S*, 51). Nel's body will later become subourned to reproductive functions; her thighs' fullness will become another measure of absence when they no longer contain Jude, whose departure renders them instead a metonym for limited mobility, for walking up and down in empty rooms (*S*, 111). Trapped in the cultural myths surrounding marriage and motherhood, Nel's final domestic containment, with its ironic inversion of true mobility, seems nonetheless foreordained.

Sula, on the other hand, is all mobility.[9] Yet the "slim figure in blue" who glides out Nel's door "with just a hint of a strut, down the path toward the road" (*S*, 85)—who can ten years later boast to her grandmother Eva, "I got my mind. And what goes on in it. Which is to say, I got me" (*S*, 143)—is also to be found saying on her deathbed, "I didn't mean anything. I never meant anything" (*S*, 147). Indeed, she dies haunted by two memories of disintegration: The first is the death of her mother, the second the death of Chicken Little.

It is interesting that Morrison conceived of Nel and Sula as the separated halves of one person because this conception points to Plato's original myth of sexual division, as well as to Lacan's later claim that sexual differentiation within the womb is the rupture that inaugurates all succeeding ones that will serve to constitute the subject in language as always experiencing loss and desire. Nel and Sula's identifications with each other recall these and later mirror-stage ruptures where the alien image seen in the mirror by the infant is internalized, but remains alien. In the case of the black female subject, however, the totalizing image that allows the infant to misrecognize herself as complete is complicated by the mother's role in conveying to her child the cultural values that reinforce the negation of that image. In a sense the black face in the mirror is thus doubly alienated. While it is easier to see Nel as the recipient of identity from the spirited and undomesticated Sula, it is probably Sula who requires the more stable identity of Nel to hold on to any sense of herself. In fact, Sula is described as clinging to Nel "as the closest thing to both an other and a self" (*S*, 119).

Sula's sense of lack seems at first glance to contradict the arrogance that she inherits from Eva and the self-indulgence that marks her as Hannah's. But her narcissism seems compensatory, writ large with object loss. The narrator describes her as having "no center, no speck around which to grow" (S, 119); she is "restless," a drifter, "an artist with no art form," with a "craving for the other half of her equation" (S, 121). But her confidence, her daring, and her "gift for metaphor" belie a frightened woman who as a child held off a gang of youths by cutting off the tip of her finger—who "mutilated herself, to protect herself" (S, 101).

Morrison expands on Sula's struggle with absence and desire by raising questions of seeing and watching, suggesting that the look is often involved with Sula's acts of aggression.[10] She enjoys, for example, watching "a person's face change rapidly" (S, 119), just as she enjoys watching her mother burn: "I *wanted* her to keep on jerking like that, to keep on dancing" (S, 147). Scopophilia—"pleasure in looking"— is a drive that empowers the looker, but does not cause the looker to be threatened. It ensures that the subject remains distanced from the object viewed, assuring her of some boundary stability. Lacan says of the scopic drive, "it is this drive that most completely eludes the term castration."[11]

Sula can perhaps best be understood by way of three striking images of "ornately planned" absence, which Morrison introduces and with which she attempts to escape from language, conjoining empty spaces with mobility. The first involves the grandmother Eva and the amputated leg. Sula may have been the daughter of an indifferent mother (the narrator describes both Nel and Sula as "daughters of distant mothers" [S, 52]), yet Sula's problems with mirroring may derive in part from an altogether absent father (in contrast to Nel's), but also from her grandmother Eva. With her god-like powers of naming and her creation and control of her sprawling and fluid household, Eva seems to have no small part in the construction of Sula's identity. Yet it is difficult to imagine a more compelling maternal configuration of protection and annhilation. It is also clear that Sula has always been aware of Eva's destruction of Plum. Therefore, her fear of her grandmother and her later need to have Eva committed (contained) are understandable.

But Morrison most forcefully evokes infantile fantasies of castration in her representation of the signifying powers beyond language in the image of Eva's lost leg. Sula reveals as much when, upon her return home after ten years of wandering, she confronts Eva with the unthinkable—mention of the missing leg: "Just 'cause you was bad enough to cut off your own leg you think you got a right to kick everybody with the stump" (S, 92–93). Because her injury represents castration, not only as it operates culturally within the black world, but also as it resonates on psychic levels to remind her children of what might be described as repressed pre-mirror stage fantasies, Eva suggests something of Freud's phallic mother, the mother of pre-oedipal fantasy, but with a difference. For Eva's "castration" is not disavowed, but is uncannily revealed by Eva herself.

The "lost" leg is allowed to refer to another of those missing gaps in the narrative whose effect we nonetheless feel, but because Eva allows no stories to be told about the leg, she, in effect, controls the discourse on absence. Eva is thus able to create out of nothing a narrative, her own story of origins. In the frightening stories Eva tells to the children, the leg becomes endowed with uncanny mobility, ("how the leg got up by itself one day and walked on off" [*S*, 30]). And while the remaining leg is described as "magnificent," a fetish in one sense, it does not disavow absence, for Eva does nothing to "disguise the empty place on her left side" (*S*, 31). While one leg remains "in view," what is also in view is "the long fall of space below her left thigh" (*S*, 31). Thus, Eva seems a contradiction in terms, withdrawn to her upper floor, yet highly mobile there as she rides about in her "large child's wagon," silent over her life, yet gifted with the power to name, and hence to create, the dewys and Tar Baby, to birth and nurture Plum—and to kill him. She seems to represent a place between creation and destruction, silence and words. Thus, the stump that kicks Sula is the very reality of the void.

The second ornately planned absence that Morrison constructs involves the death of Chicken Little, an incident that is textualized by way of actions that the girls perform together without words. These actions, while only tangential to Chicken Little's death, involve their flight to the woods where each participates in the digging of a hole. Contemplating "the wildness that had come upon them so suddenly" (*S*, 57–58), the girls begin digging a hole in oddly complementary patterns of behavior—Nel using a thick twig to dig while Sula traces "intricate patterns." As the hole becomes wider and deeper, it is transformed into a burying ground where sticks, butts of cigarettes, and other "small defiling things" are covered over. A number of critics have seen in this cooperative activity a good deal of aggression, which foreshadows the accidental drowning of Chicken Little,[12] yet it also seems to suggest the textualizing of the *semiotique*, behavior that is non-verbal and grounded in drives, that the girls unconsciously feel and wordlessly act out in their tracings.

When Sula accidentally releases Chicken Little and he sails out into the lake and disappears, leaving "a closed place in the water," they have simply offered up for themselves another reading of absence. When the crazed Shadrack, who has witnessed the scene, speaks to the distraught Sula, he can say only one word: *always*, which, operating as a unary signifier, is empty of signification, a way in which Sula "hears" absence.[13] Furthermore, when they attend Chicken Little's funeral, both girls understand that "only the coffin would lie in the earth; the bubbly laughter and the press of fingers in the palm would stay aboveground forever" (*S*, 66), that is, sound and touch leave traces that persist and interfere with conscious, verbalized processes.

Sula's life thereafter is structured without a center, and, indeed, the centrifugal movements that Morrison so often textualizes can be seen in Sula's own "long fall of space." Morrison links this powerful castration image once again to Sula's lack of a stabilized center. After her breakup with Nel, she metaphorizes her old friend and the townspeople as spiders who dangle "from dark dry places . . . more terrified of the free fall than the snake's breath below" (S, 120). In spite of this image of devouring maternity that Sula recognizes, she opts for the free fall, which "required—demanded—invention: a thing to do with the wings, a way of holding the legs and most of all a full surrender to the downward flight" (S, 120).

That her fall is best experienced in sex seems to involve her need for a special, almost mystical encounter with self-obliteration, which Morrison characterizes as a quest for sadness. But sex for Sula appears as even more recognizably narcissistic, related to the problematics of selfhood. Beyond the joy of sex, which has always been its most highly valued feeling for her, sex is where she experiences a center that is at first characterized as "particles of strength" which gather in her "like steel shavings drawn to a spacious magnetic center, forming a tight cluster that nothing . . . could break" (S, 123). But then the center does give way, and it is at that point that Sula experiences a nothingness beyond language, beyond even sound. This spiralling descent, constructed as a vortex and signifying the end of desire and hence death, must be quoted in its entirety:

But the cluster did break, fall apart, and in her panic to hold it together she leaped from the edge into soundlessness and went down howling, howling in a stinging awareness of the endings of things: an eye of sorrow in the midst of all that hurricane rage of joy. There, in the center of that silence was not eternity but the death of time and a loneliness so profound the word itself had no meaning. (S, 123)

Remarkable in the way it recovers unconscous infantile fantasies of annhilation, this passage is replayed in a later scene where a much older Nel recovers her awareness of the lost object inexpressible in language, but imaged in a similar spiralling configuration. Nel's discovery of loss comes with her visit to Eva and her remembering of the death of Chicken Little. Eva brings about a kind of awakening in Nel, described as "a bright space" that "opened in her head and memory seeped into it" (S, 169). Linked to the "closed space" of Chicken Little's death, a closed space that does not conceal the void, this space is filled with the absence of Sula. But this absence can be retrieved only when Nel acknowledges her complicity in the death of Chicken Little. Thus, in the final pages of the novel Nel is depicted running not only from Eva and her uncanny knowledge, but also toward the graveyard where the Peaces lie buried. She reads the names of Plum, Hannah, Sula, and Pearl as a chant: "PEACE 1895–1921, PEACE

1890–1922, PEACE 1910–1940, PEACE 1892–1959" (*S*, 171), and observes, "they were not dead people. . . . they were words. Not even words. Wishes, longings" (*S*, 171).

As Nel stands in the graveyard, reading the headstones as, again, a kind of *semiotique*, she evokes not absence, but presence beyond words. At this point Nel's anger at Eva also recedes, and in its place rises "her very own howl"—the lament for her own pain, the cry that at the leaving of Jude she has been unable to summon, but that now arises in the configuration of another spiral—"a fine cry—loud and long—" that has "no bottom" and "no top, just circles and circles of sorrow" (*S*, 174). Thus, the holes carved from the ground of their afternoon beside the river, worked until "the two holes were one and the same" (*S*, 58), are replicated in another non-linguistic configuration: in the spiralling howls by means of which each articulates absence—castration as the loss of (an)other.[14]

BELOVED: THE LONELINESS THAT ROAMS

In *Meridian*, as we have seen, both Walker and her protagonist escape the constraints of the slave narrative through the appropriation of Native American myth. In *Beloved*, however, Morrison not only insists on retelling it, but also creates for it a form that both validates the experience and transforms it. *Beloved* is, therefore, difficult to characterize generically; it is a slave narrative, a ghost story, a history, even a *Bildungsroman*; it also draws on myth, especially African myth, and for some it falls under the heading of magical realism.[15] Jean Wyatt sees the novel as an articulation of a new female quest where "the reproductive feats of the female body" are given prominence.[16]

Perhaps it is all of these things. In any event, it is a novel in which mobility is textualized in a number of ways similar to those I have been discussing in relation to *Sula*. Often in *Beloved* Morrison makes use of the same centrifugal movement she has utilized in earlier works; yet in this novel of "leavings," centrifugal movement occupies an especially important place, giving *Beloved* an inverted kind of mobility, due in large part to the institution of slavery that ensured that blacks were "moved around like checkers," were "hanged, . . . rented out, loaned out, bought up, brought back, stored up, mortgaged, won, stolen or seized" (*B*, 23). In more specific terms slavery meant the studding of male slaves, the sexual abuse of both females and males, and the erasure of all familial identity and ties through the selling of children. In other words, Morrison represents slaves as the moveable objects they were, thereby suggesting that any black appropriation of mobility in the postemancipation years was going to be of a problematic kind.

Morrison also makes it clear that even when they cease to be fugitives in those years, her characters do not cease to run. Leavings that begin with the escape of Sethe and Paul D from Sweet Home are ongoing. Paul D has wandered for eighteen years, and in spite of his re-entry into Sethe's life in 1873—present time in the novel—he is, in reality, always leaving, forced by the ghost out of Sethe's bed and into the storeroom, then to the cold house, and, finally, because of Sethe's story, out of her life altogether (although he attempts to regard his final leave-taking as "an exit and not an escape" (B, 165). Leaving for Baby Suggs has meant the loss of all her children, including Sethe's husband Halle, while for Sethe the flight of her two young sons and the death of Baby Suggs are the most significant disappearances and the ones by means of which we, as readers, are introduced to the narrative.

Mobility also comes to signify many kinds of physical and emotional crippling for the women of 124. Baby Suggs is permanently crippled and walks "like a three-legged dog" (B, 139), and Sethe's "blasted feet" constitute one of the dominant marks of her escape from Sweet Home (B, 249). Sethe's daughter Denver can be recognized as emotionally crippled, since she never ventures beyond the perameters of the yard. Even worse is the fact that although Sethe and Paul D successfully escape Sweet Home, they fail to escape from subsequent enslaving situations, not the least of which is an enslavement to their own pasts.

In terms of language Morrison, whose writing seems to favor metonym over metaphor, represents this crippling in the metonym of feet as another form of fragmentation, thereby linking mobility to castration and the problem of subjectivity for her characters. In some instances, feet appear linked to metaphor, as, for example, when Paul D is described as a "walking man," whose feet nonetheless determine his status, since "one step off the ground" transforms him from a "Sweet Home man" into a trespasser and a piece of property (B, 125). Thus "walking on two feet" comes to mean "standing still" (B, 29). When he comes under the baleful influence of Beloved, Paul is "moved" by her in both literal and metaphoric terms, and, in rendering up his subjectivity, is no longer able to "command his feet" (B, 126), now rendered metonymically. Sixo, the most rebellious (and the most "African") of the Garner slaves, is a genuine walking man, who, in his ventures beyond the grounds of Sweet Home, becomes the most knowledgeable; however, his feet are burned away as he dies the most agonizing death of all the Garner men.

While Sethe's feet are described in more literal terms, when her own feet are the subject of the narration, feet also function metonymically in terms of her subjectivity. In the more literal sense her feet are damaged in the escape, metaphorized by Amy as "dead." Indeed, her flight from Sweet Home is accomplished more on her knees than on her feet. But ultimately her escape represents her first and last use of feet. Having resolved never to "move" again after her flight from Sweet Home, the word detaches itself from her and her own movements, and comes to represent the more horrific aspects of slavery. For example, her feet take flight in dreams, roaming outside 124, taking her finally to the "beautiful trees" where the "little legs barely visible in the leaves" are vividly imagined (*B*, 39). Finally, feet bring to mind schoolteacher who defines her as animal, a memory that returns in all its pain when Paul D, after learning of the murder of her child, tells her by way of accusation, "you've got two feet . . . not four" (*B*, 165). In Lacanian terms, metonomy, functioning as a displacement, allows for the greater psychic investment of another term to be transferred to the metonym, which then takes on the affect of the missing signifier, creating a desire that involves mnemic traces of that which has been repressed.[17] Here feet would appear to operate as a metonym for Sethe, especially because she is unable to deal with a loss involving the body of the mother, a loss that, at least until the arrival of the ghost, is unconscious.[18]

Nevertheless, in spite of the prominence of images of dismemberment mentioned above, a possible center is to be found in the role of the grandmother, Baby Suggs, whose story, remembered by Sethe, is placed—appropriately—in the center of the text. While Baby Suggs's life at Sweet Home has marked her with absence, a "sadness . . . at her center, the desolated center where the self that was no self made its home" (*B*, 140), she discovers on her first day of freedom the beat of her own heart, a center that again suggests a metonymic rather than a metaphoric function, since as a recovered body part, it directs us to an awareness of the many lost parts that dominate this novel, parts that are echoed in the "scattering" of the people. Self-naming further confirms this tentative movement. Descending from the wagon of Mr. Garner on that day, she also effects the erasure of the name inscribed on her bill of sale and replaces it with the last name of her husband, claiming also for her first name Baby—the name *he* has given her.

This act of self-naming initiates for Baby Suggs a hope that familial and communal centers can be established that can help to reunify the lost and the absent. "We scattered," Baby thinks, "but maybe not for long" (*B*, 143). And although this hope is to be dashed, she does offer up a gesture of centeredness that momentarily draws the community together. It is created—literally conjured—in the clearing where Baby preaches. Her "call"—which brings the men out of the woods to dance, the women to weep, and the children to laugh—transforms disparate groupings of people and a mixture of activities —all connected to the heart—into an energized hub where movement ceases momentarily to be synonymous with dispersion: "It started that way: laughing children, dancing men, crying women and then it got mixed up. Women stopped crying and danced; men sat down and cried; children danced, women laughed, children cried . . ." (*B*, 88). In the silence that follows their exhaustion, Baby Suggs offers "her great big heart" and establishes a viable, if transitory, center that is, in turn, confirmed in an almost ritualized manner by the great feast that miraculously materializes later at 124, after which 124 becomes the community "way station" (*B*, 163) that further bonds the community.

Yet while Morrison appears to indict the community itself for the failure of any center to hold—since it is their failure to warn the Suggs family of the arrival of the white men that is, in part, responsible for the events that follow—other ingredients of the novel suggest that the absence of community cohesiveness is directly attributable to the constitution of the African American subject within the world of slavery. For in this world the original separation is played out differently in infancy because of the problematic paternal signifier that the white world stands for and is also repeated in later boundary problems that continue to involve the white world.

Thus, boundary confusion—between past and present, living and dead, the individual and the collective, as well as between white and black—begins with the actual setting of Morrison's text, namely, with the community that exists on the outskirts of Cincinnati in the time spanning 1850 to 1873. Since Ohio is a free state and neighboring Kentucky across the river is a slave state, she appears to evoke unambiguous spaces into which and out of which the characters can move.[19] But all spaces are dangerous for slaves, as Sweet Home demonstrates. Presented as a special enclave of enlightened slavery practices, it quickly turns lethal with the arrival of schoolteacher, causing Sethe to wonder later "if Hell was a pretty place too" (B, 6).

Nevertheless, both Baby Suggs and Sethe, having accepted the Ohio River as an unambiguous dividing line between the slave and the free worlds, also accept the parameters of their yard as space possessed by them alone. When the whites cross that boundary to claim Sethe and her children as fugitives, both Baby Suggs and Sethe are changed forever. Answering Stamp Paid's criticism that Sethe has murdered her child, Baby Suggs stands by her daughter-in-law on the basis of boundaries: "They came in my yard," she tells Stamp (B, 179). This argument, repeated twice, represents the desperate, yet futile, resistence of Sethe to such invasions by the white world. Aware of this ongoing threat, both Baby Suggs and Sethe become increasingly withdrawn, and the spaces that they can preserve from invasion also shrink.[20] Baby Suggs abandons her clearing—itself an emblem of expansive and inclusive space—to pass her final days in the keeping room. Sethe also undergoes a critical withdrawal, first behind the walls of 124 and finally into a single room, declaring, "this little place by a window is what I want" (B, 272).

Indeed, this legacy of withdrawal is passed to Denver, who refuses to venture beyond the yard. Dimly aware of a cause-effect relationship between her mother's dreadful act and the outside world, she learns to watch for signs and comes to conclude that "Whatever it is, it comes from outside this house, outside the yard, and it can come right on in the yard if it wants to. So I never leave this house and I watch over the yard, so it can't happen again and my mother won't have to kill me too." (B, 205). This failure of boundaries to contain and protect thus echoes the subtle intermixing of maternal nurturance and destruction, and serves to dominate Denver's consciousness.

However, Morrison's interest in spaces and their boundaries involves the impossibility not only of keeping separate the good and bad, the beautiful and horrific, but also of keeping the past from invading the present. In another sense then, boundary confusion has a temporal as well as a spatial component that returns us again to the uncanny. One way in which Morrison represents the unwelcome return of the repressed (what Freud described, we recall, as "the phantasy of intra-uterine existence" [*SE*, 17: 244]), so threatening to the subject, can be seen in the passage in which Sethe is forced to tell her story of the murder of her infant to Paul D. This passage suggests that because the annihilation of the subject is an "actuality" that also operates beyond, or below, the level of language for both Sethe and Denver, the story is truly "unspeakable." Urged by Paul D to put her story into words at last, Sethe can only respond non-verbally, by means of movement. As he sits at her table, Paul is forced to follow Sethe's spinning movements "round and round the room. Past the jelly cupboard, past the window, past the front door, another window" (*B*, 159). Although "the wheel" never stops, Sethe's story remains elusive, and Paul hears only bits and pieces of what she says, not only because she circles the subject, but also because, as he puts it, the sound of her voice is "too near" and her words are "like having a child whisper into your ear so close you could feel its lips form the words you couldn't make out because they were too close" (*B*, 161).

What Paul's trope of the whispering child manifests is the genuine, yet unacknowledged, anxiety that the "unspeakable" nonetheless evokes for both of them. I would argue then that Paul's "whispering child" operates as a displacement that attempts to deny the frightening aspects of the maternal. For Sethe's voice is not like a child's, but the mother's, and evokes infancy and the pre-specular infant's first fragmented impressions of its world. The vocal component of pre-linguistic experience that emphasizes the connections between body and textuality is best described once again by Kristeva's concept of the *semiotique*, but especially by that aspect she designates as the *semiotic chora*. It is, in her words, "analogous only to vocal and kinetic rhythm,"[21] emphasizing sound, and because it it eludes the classifications of interiority or exteriority, it is particularly invasive.[22] Thus, what Paul perceives is that which causes material to be censored, that which has been familiar, but has become linked to what is now alien, the truly *unheimlich*, once again the real castrating powers of the Mother. Thus, Morrison's text successfully constructs representations of lack always present in the process of symbolic substitution, a problem that Sethe, too, is able to address: "Sethe knew that the circle she was making around the room, him, the subject, would remain one. That she could never close in, pin it down" (*B*, 163).

But the murder of her "crawling already?" baby daughter (whose name cannot be spoken either) must be understood in the context of Sethe's own troubled maternal history, which, although "unspeakable," is nonetheless an informing condition of her consciousness. This history is related to her not by her own mother, but by the one-armed Nan, a mother surrogate, who has nursed the small Sethe while her mother does forced labor in the rice fields. What emerges from Sethe's maternal history are memories of nurturing presences that are recalled in a language Sethe no longer "knows," but that are accompanied by numerous images of dismemberment and fragmentation—to be read on the bodies of the one-armed Nan and of Sethe's own mother, branded beneath her breast with a cross and circle. Indeed, the references linking Sethe to "re-memory" also suggest another linkage to Lacan's hypothetical *rememoration*, which directs attention not to the content of memories, but to the charting of a subject's unconscious history as it comes to be repeated in daily life.[23]

As in the case of Paul D's whispering child, this history resonates with the *chora*, the sonorous maternal envelope that encloses the infant in body, gesture, and voice and, representing what lives on of the primordial mother, remains "one of the permanent scenes of subjectivity, not so much superseded as covered over and denied by succeeding spatial developments."[24] But this envelope of sound is one of affect, for, as mentioned earlier, the Lacanian pre-specular infant—assimilating its world in a hallucinatory and fragmented manner, and out of what Ellie Ragland-Sullivan describes as a "piecemeal system, a network of fragments and part objects"[25]—also initially perceives the mother's bodily territories as its own and also takes for its own certain portions of her body, not only the voice, but also the gaze and the breast, body parts that Lacan described as *petits objets à*—objects with a little otherness. The loss of these objects is experienced by the infant as an amputation.

These concepts suggest the severity of Sethe's deprivation, for clearly an experience of castration is linked to the mother's withdrawn gaze, a loss that is established in Sethe's memory of her mother as "a particular back . . . a cloth hat" (*B*, 30). The mother's only acknowledgment of maternity, and it is an important, if highly disturbing, one for Sethe, is by way of a brand. Thus, the mother's objectification in white discourse also serves to objectify her for Sethe and further mark their separation. This separation is exacerbated when, after her mother is hanged and apparently cut down only much later, Sethe fails to find even the identifying brand, now erased because of the decaying of the body. Thus, for Sethe, infantile fantasies of dismemberment are not so much repressed as they become instead part of the mirroring experience itself.

Having lost the voice, the gaze, and the breast at far too early a stage, Sethe's existence as a subject is constituted of absences, holes in the self, that have not been covered over by the substitutive effects of language—hence their "unspeakability." For example, her eyes do not seem to engage in a mirroring. To Paul she is the girl with the "iron eyes," eyes that "did not reflect firelight," "punched out eyes" (*B*, 9). While the normative mirror-stage infant introjects a fixed, albeit external, form—an ideal ego by way of the mirroring process, a problematic "capture of the self" at best—Sethe has been denied that identificatory process, and Morrison seems to render the holes in her self as eyes that only absorb, that have no bottom to them.

Another lost object of Morrison's text is the breast, as is suggested by Sethe's concern with the theft of her milk (*B*, 17), which is clearly regarded as a part of her own body and therefore as a part of her self. It is not much of a connective leap to see that if the voice, the gaze, and the breast are parts of the infant's lost territory, the adult might experience the same sense of loss through the birthing of children. If the children also come to be seen as parts of the mother's body, as they are for Sethe, then it is understandable that under the threat of recapture she would have to attempt to "reincorporate" them. Her behavior on the arrival of schoolteacher suggests this need for integration: "She just flew. Collected every bit of life she had made, *all the parts of her that were precious and fine and beautiful*, and carried, pushed, dragged them through the veil, out, away, over there where no one could hurt them. Over there . . . (*B*, 163, italics mine).

The linking of the scattering of children to the self carries over into imagined events, into memory, which for Sethe involves a lack of control over presences that seem to function autonomously. She describes, for example, "a picture floating around out there, outside my head, I mean, even if I don't think it, even if I die, the picture of what I did, or knew, or saw is still out there" (*B*, 36). In the same manner, she is convinced she can protect her child "while I'm live . . . and when I ain't" (*B*, 45).

For Denver, on the other hand, mothering has been quite different, although hardly less problematic. Unlike her mother Denver has had her mother's almost exclusive attention for seventeen years. For her the mother "did not look away" (*B*, 12), a fact she becomes aware of only with the arrival of Paul D.[26] Sustained in this manner by the mother's gaze, Denver is also imaginarily obsessed with the mother's breast. Since we know that Denver's first two years were the two years that Sethe spent in prison, and further that Sethe was not separated from her nursing infant, we can assume that the bonding was indeed an intense one. Furthermore, Denver's taking of her sister's blood, along with the mother's milk, a fact that she has somehow come to learn about, is a source of both empowerment and plenitude for her, and also makes boundary problems difficult.

Denver's problems with sound suggest other difficulties that begin when, at the age of seven, she at last ventures beyond her yard to the house of Lady Jones, who introduces her to language as well as a social context. This interaction is short-lived because of two questions posed by one of the children, questions that apparently serve to articulate the unspeakable.

Interestingly Denver is disturbed not by the first question that Nelson Lord asks, namely, "Didn't your mother get locked away for murder?" but the second: "Wasn't you there with her when she went?" Although the second question may function as a diversion, the effect of the second on Denver seems disturbing, if ambiguous: "The thing that leapt up had been coiled in just such a place: a darkness, a stone and some other thing that moved by itself" (B, 104). This grouping of images seems to have less to do with the prison where Denver spent her first two years of life than with a pre-specular and repressed river of fragments, threatening early conscious-ness, that they reflect. After these words, Denver experiences "certain odd and terrifying feelings" and "monstrous and unmanageable dreams" that evoke "the thing that had been there all along" (B, 102–3). Under attack from the *chora* Denver retreats to the yard of 124 and refuses "to hear," and moves "into a silence too solid for penetration" (B, 103). This situation endures until the ghost makes its presence felt in the house. What Morrison seems to suggest here is that for Denver the original castration trauma is differently mediated. Because her mother *is* guilty of infanticide, there is less distancing from the real.

Indeed, in many ways Denver seems caught in a liminal state—between the imaginary and the symbolic, between infantile plenitude and narcis-sism (as seen in her need to hear stories only about herself, for example), even between mergence and separation, a situation not surprising given the circumstances of her birth. Born of a fugitive slave in a sinking boat on the border between slave and free territory in the presence of a homeless white girl, Denver indeed seems a child of no place, of in-between-ness. This condition also links her to the ghost, who is also connected with a river in accordance with African beliefs regarding the existence of spirit places.[27]

In any event, it is to the ghost that we must now turn, for *Beloved* is, first of all, a ghost story. Morrison's use of a ghost may be deemed appropriate on artistic grounds—she speaks of "artistically burying" those slaves "un-buried, or at least unceremoniously buried,"[28] but beyond its artistic func-tion, the ghost operates in a number of purposefully rich and ambiguous ways. As a number of critics have noted, it functions both individually and collectively, in both personal and social contexts.[29] For example, it does appear on one level to derive from African belief systems regarding the dead ancestors as spirits, which, during the diaspora and the disappearence of any viable tribal or family life, evolved into ghost fear.[30] But Morrison's ghost is no Jamesian one. Its activities are recognized by every family member, including the newly arrived Paul D. Nor does the community doubt its existence. What the ghost represents is seen to differ, however, according to individual desire. To Sethe, Beloved is the lost "crawling already?" baby restored to her in the flesh. Denver also accepts the myste-rious young woman as her sister, but, as we would expect, her relationship to the ghost is quite different. Stamp Paid hears the "roaring" sounds from

124 and interprets them as the voices of the brutalized and murdered slaves, "the people of the broken necks, of the fire-cooked blood" (*B*, 181), the spirits of "the disremembered and unaccounted for" (*B*, 274, 275). For Paul D, the ghost is more personal—"something I'm supposed to remember" (*B*, 234). Thus, the ghost also functions as a representation of collective absence.

Also, because Morrison conceives of the life of the murdered baby as a maturing presence, a "filter" for "all those confrontations and questions that she has in that situation,"[31] the ghost appropriately evokes not only the instability of the self, but also the self as constructed upon tracings of infantile introjections of images and sounds.

I want to argue that the ghost is also associated not simply with object loss, but also with need, demand, and desire, and their accompanying transformations. Need, involving a drive toward satisfaction of the body (of hunger, say), because of primary process laws can, in the search for immediate gratification, seek out endless replacements for the original one, thus becoming demand. Thus, while this hunger may have originally been linked to nourishment, it has, as Beloved herself indicates, moved into the area of demand. When we read that "Sethe was licked, tasted, eaten by Beloved's eyes" (*B*, 57), we get a reflection not only of Sethe's own hunger for the gaze, the voice, and the breast, but also of the later stage, which includes the splitting off of the drives from the subject that occurs when the subject takes up a speaking position in language and enters the world of desire.

Sethe's gradual ability to speak, to narrate those long-repressed stories, and their accompanying desire, is also embodied in Beloved. For example, Beloved's need for food, especially sweets, is noted early on, but Sethe quickly understands that "a way to feed her" is by means of storytelling, even though the stories have been, until that time, unspeakable. Sethe initiates what will be a prolonged unburdening of stories from the past when she tells Beloved about the earrings, and she discovers pleasure in the telling: "As she began telling about the earrings, she found herself *wanting to, liking it*" (*B*, 58, italics mine). Indeed, it is the story of the earrings that causes Sethe to remember "something she had forgotten she knew" (*B*, 61)—the important bits of maternal history that she must recover to become a subject. But to enter the world of signification—the world of linguistic substitution—is to enter the world of desire, and desire is insatiable, a fact that Beloved, who is described as inventing desire, also comes to (literally) embody. Her enlargement is accompanied by the shrinking of Sethe, who, in struggling to give Beloved all the food, all the narratives, finally begins to throw up parts of herself, thereby literalizing her own sense of object loss.

For Denver, Beloved appears after her withdrawal to her "emerald closet," again linked to food. We are told, for example, that Denver's "imagination produced its own hunger and its own food" (*B*, 28), but while Sethe imagines the restoration of the lost infant, Denver yearns for the restoration of lost infantile plenitude. What she wants from the ghost is her gaze, which mirrors that of Sethe, but far more—what is "beyond appetite," that place "where hunger hadn't been discovered" (*B*, 118). In once instance she imagines for herself an interesting fantasy of dissolution as she "floats near but outside her own body, feeling vague and intense at the same time. Needing nothing. Being what there was" (*B*, 118). But Denver is a subject and thus already alienated permanently from the organic, phenomenal world. Her being has already been surrendered for meaning, for the world of signification. Thus, Denver, too, is responsive to Beloved's desire and her involvement in the signifying process, which is also suggested in the way in which Beloved alters Denver's own story.

Before Beloved, Denver has resisted or ignored any stories that did not have her in the center, but when Beloved urges her "to tell me how Sethe made you in the boat," Denver finds herself telling more than she knows. She is aware, for the first time, that the story makes her "feel like a bill was owing somewhere and she, Denver, had to pay it" (*B*, 77). Her awareness of what that debt is comes later, when she moves beyond the boundaries of her yard and must symbolically separate herself from the mother at last. But at this point she finds herself not just hearing, but also *seeing* the story. Furthermore, for the first time she identifies not with the infant Denver, but with the nineteen-year-old Sethe.

However, it is first necessary for the imaginary world that constitutes 124, a world of mirror identifications and psychotic discourses, to intensify.[32] Only then is Denver pushed into a different relationship to both the ghost and her mother, one in which she must finally enter the world of the other, at the same time gathering up language the way Sethe attempted to gather up all that she thought constituted her self. (It is in this portion of the text that Morrison constructs, through Denver's mobility, a *Bildungsroman* within the larger text.)

At first Denver feels she is about to "be swallowed up in the world beyond the porch (*B*, 243), yet while the maternal presence continues to hold her back, another maternal voice—that of Baby Suggs—that is personal, ancestral, a teller of stories of mobility that include mention of the absent father, urges her forward: "You mean I never told you nothing about Carolina? About your daddy? You don't remember nothing about how come I walk the way I do and about your mother's feet, not to speak of her back? Is that why you can't walk down those steps?" (*B*, 244). Even the crippling of the mothers has failed to prevent their mobility, and now their narratives serve to mobilize Denver. When she responds to her grandmother's voice with the argument that efforts are futile, Baby Suggs answers, "know it, and go on out the yard" (*B*, 244).

Denver's destination, the house of Lady Jones, a different kind of nurturer who has fed Denver's hunger for learning, is an important first step because she has always seen Denver with different eyes and is now in a position to help not only with actual food, but also with language. Her utterance, "Oh, baby," has a critical effect on Denver: "It was the word 'baby,' said softly with such kindness, that inaugurated [Denver's] life in the world as a woman" (*B*, 248).

But that entry into the "sweet thorny place" known as womanhood is characterized by a continuing, albeit transformed, relationship between food and language. This new relationship involves slips of paper containing the names of the neighborhood women who contribute food to the family. This trail of names forces Denver into another stage of her journey, namely, an exchange of language with increasing numbers of the community's women. Each offering, entailing as it does the return of a dish and an expression of gratitude, enables Denver to become increasingly detached from Sethe and more integrated into the community.

Finally—and it is no coincidence that the meeting occurs on one of Denver's trips to return a dish—Denver is forced to confront her old nemesis Nelson Lord. Having once put into language that which was unspeakable, Nelson Lord once again helps Denver bridge the gap between language and being. When she encounters him on this later occasion, he says, "Take care of yourself, Denver." Yet this seemingly innocuous greeting serves to signify to Denver "what language was made for"—neither divisive nor punishing, legislating in a positive way (*B*, 252). The injunction is taken literally by Denver, who can now think about "having a self to look out for and preserve." Instead of opening on a void, Nelson's words are described as opening her mind (*B*, 252). They push her ahead to the next stage of her quest, a visit to the Bodwins, where Denver's own "unspeakable" story can finally be told.

But Morrison does not leave Denver moving easily into her place in the symbolic order and its cultural trappings, for the exorcism of the ghost involves both the collective action of the community's women and *sound*. When the women gather in force to exorcise the ghost, they appear to resort to a very African use of sound to "break the back of words." Here Morrison seems to have literalized *chora* and given it a collective character, for, as the narrator tells us, "in the beginning there were no words. In the beginning was the sound, and they all knew what that sound sounded like" (*B* , 259).

What the exorcism also constitutes is a new mobility, a reversal of all the leavings that have served to represent the effects of the diaspora in personal as well as historical terms. Thus it becomes a counter to the diasporan experience, a time of gathering. Just as Baby Suggs's call had served to gather up the people, fashion them, albeit temporarily, into a community, this later call serves to unify the community once again. But for this transformation to take place, 124, once the center—now desolated center of the community—must be relieved of the overgrown presence of absence that occupies it. It is no accident that Ella, the most victimized and the most African, a rootworker ("she believed there was a root either to chew on or avoid for every ailment" [*B*, 256]), possibly a conjure woman too, inaugurates the rescue and mobilizes the thirty women. Nor is it surprising that before they can help the inhabitants of 124, they must begin with a gathering of their own memories. When they arrive at 124, their first vision "was not Denver sitting on the steps, but themselves. Younger, stronger, even as little girls lying in the grass asleep," or "young and happy, playing in Baby Suggs' yard, not feeling the envy that surfaced the next day" (*B*, 258). The acknowledgment of their own desolated centers is manifested in the "holler" that Ella begins and that the others take up, a call that reaches Sethe:

For Sethe it was as though the Clearing had come to her with all its heat and simmering leaves, where the voices of women searched for the right combination, the key, the code, the sound that broke the back of words. Building voice upon voice until they found it, and when they did it was a wave of sound wide enough to sound deep water. . . . It broke over Sethe and she trembled like the baptized in its wash. (*B*, 261)

By gathering Sethe back into the community through their collective actions, they help to reconstitute her subjectivity so that she can live as her own "best thing" (*B*, 273), without her immobilizing sense of loss.

As a corporeal emblem of the void that has, in reality, stalked the entire community, the ghost has existed both within and without consciousness, within and without language. Her tracings have been recorded in Morrison's text, but the ghost herself must be returned to the realm where she has always existed—in the spaces between words, in the repressed consciousness of those who have encountered her. She continues to be seen in uncanny ways—as when "the photograph of a close friend or relative," when looked at too long, "shifts, and something more familiar than the dear face itself moves there" (*B*, 275). She is also seen in the fading traces of footprints by the river, footprints that fit anyone and everyone. Finally, she is wind and weather, and, like language itself, can be heard only in "the spaces the long-ago singing left behind."

NOTES

1. Toni Morrison, *Sula* (New York: New American Library, 1973), 47 (hereafter cited parenthetically in the text as *S*).

2. Robert Grant, "Absence into Presence: The Thematics of Memory and 'Missing' Subjects in Toni Morrison's *Sula*," in *Critical Essays on Toni Morrison*, ed. Nellie McKay (Boston: G. K. Hall, 1988), 94. See also Margaret Homans, "'Her Very Own Howl,': The Ambiguities of Representation in Recent Women's Fiction," *Signs* 9, no. 2 (Winter 1983): 186–205; and Maureen T. Reddy, "The Tripled Plot and Center of *Sula*," *Black American Literature Forum* 22, no. 1 (Spring 1988): 29–45.

3. Toni Morrison, "Unspeakable Things Unspoken: The Afro-American Presence in American Literature," *Michigan Quarterly Review* 28 (Winter 1989): 11.

4. Also called the *semiotic chora*, both terms describe the child's first disorganized impression of space (which involves the mother's body as well). This archaic state exists in the unconscious and works on the symbolic rather in the manner of dreams. It is something that all discourse moves "with and against" (Julia Kristeva, *Revolution in Poetic Language*, trans. Margaret Waller, [New York: Columbia University Press, 1984], 26). Yet because it involves the subject as both infant and adult, it represents, in Kaja Silverman's words, the "'place' where the subject is both generated and annihilated, the site where it both assumes a pulsional or rhythmic consistency and is dissolved as a psychic or social coherence" (*The Acoustic Mirror: The Female Voice in Psychoanalysis and Cinema* [Bloomington: Indiana University Press, 1988], 103).

5. I think it is important to emphasize at this point Morrison's interest in and use of African myth, history, and belief systems. Because of their importance to her work, any such culture-specific theories as those involving semiotics and psychoanalysis must be applied only with this kind of disclaimer. Still, because Morrison's own heritage is both Western (especially Classical) and African, and because hers is a theoretically sophisticated consciousness, I (along with a growing number of other critics) seem unable to enter her texts, especially *Beloved*, without bringing some of these ideas to bear on my readings. For studies with a psychoanalytic focus, see especially Jean Wyatt, "Giving Body to the Word: The Maternal Symbolic in Toni Morrison's *Beloved*," *PMLA* 108, no. 3 (May 1993): 474–88; see also Barbara Schapiro, "The Bonds of Love and the Boundaries of Self in Toni Morrison's *Beloved*," *Contemporary Literature* 32, no. 1 (Spring 1991): 194–210; and Deborah Horvitz, "Nameless Ghosts: Possession and Dispossession in *Beloved*," *Studies in American Fiction* 17 (Autumn 1989): 157–67.

6. Henry Louis Gates, Jr., *The Signifying Monkey: A Theory of African-American Literary Criticism* (New York: Oxford University Press, 1988), 49–50, points out that just as homonyms depend on "absent presence," the homonym *signifyin(g)* is a "shadowy revision of the white term" and is part of a larger "parallel discursive universe."

7. Toni Morrison, *Beloved* (New York: New American Library, 1987), 159. (hereafter cited parenthetically in the text as *B*).

8. Psychosis is considered by Lacanians to be a language problem and, as such, also describes a problem that the subject has in relation to the cultural Other. The existence of a weakened paternal signifier, one of the conditions for psychosis, would seem especially troublesome for the male African American subject; hence, Shadrack suggests an individual who has attempted to disavow the paternal signifier and to constitute a different world for himself. Willy Apollon, "Psychoanalytic Treatment of Psychosis," in *Lacan and the Subject of Language*, ed. Ellie Ragland-Sullivan and Mark Bracher (New York: Routledge, 1991), 120.

9. In an interview with Robert B. Stepto, "'Intimate Things in Place': A Conversation with Toni Morrison," in *The Third Woman: Minority Women Writers in the United States*, ed. Dexter Fisher (New York: Houghton Mifflin, 1980), 180, Morrison comments on Sula's "masculinity" as follows: "She will do the kinds of things that normally only men do, which is why she's so strange. She really behaves like a man. She picks up a man, drops a man, the same way a man picks up a woman, drops a woman. And that's her thing. She's masculine in that sense."

10. See Edward Guerrero, "Tracking 'the Look' in the Novels of Toni Morrison," *Black American Literature Forum* 24, no. 4 (Winter 1990): 762, argues for the look as belonging to the "dominant, racially oppressive society which constitutes whiteness as the norm" and internalized by Morrison's characters. He reads Sula's "watching" as sadistic voyeurism.

11. Jacques Lacan, "The Split between the Eye and the Gaze, in *The Four Fundamental Concepts of Psycho-Analysis*, trans. Alan Sheridan and ed. Jacques-Alain Miller (New York: W. W. Norton, 1978), 78.

12. Homans, "'Her Very Own Howl,'" sees the act as an "exploration of the violence of heterosexuality" (193).

13. According to Kaja Silverman, *The Subject of Semiotics* (New York: Oxford University Press, 1983), 170, a unary signifier has no "linguistic system nor a discourse to support it" because it is non-referential. Apollon, "Psychoanalytic Treatment of Psychosis," 121, observes the tendency of the psychotic to "unchain" voices that, detached from language, offer further evidence of "a crack in the way the unconscious subject relates himself to the Other in the symbolic," and also of a lack of a supporting truth "as a guarantee for the human search for happiness in social ties." Shadrack's utterance to Sula suggests an effort that in some sense succeeds because Sula "reads" meaning into it.

14. Homans, "'Her Very Own Howl,'" 192, describes this language as an "unborrowed woman's language," which fails to articulate: "The cry perfectly exemplifies the paradox of separatism in language: what finally expresses her woman-identified self is of necessity nonrepresentational" (193). But such language might also be described as representing the archaic language that occurs without parole, a "language" in which Morrison seems especially interested in all her work, especially *Beloved*.

15. Morrison herself does not like the term and comments that "my own use of enchantment simply comes because that's the way the world was for me and for the black people that I know. In addition to the very shrewd, down-to-earth, efficient way in which they did things and survived things, there was this other knowledge, or perception, always discredited but nevertheless there" (Christina Davis, "Interview with Toni Morrison," *Présence Africaine* 1st Quarterly [1988]: 144). Brenda K. Marshall, *Teaching the Postmodern* (New York: Routledge, 1992), 185, makes the point that "magic realism," as opposed to "real magic," implies that "realism is once again asserted as the thing itself; magic is simply the modifier that butts up against, pushes, nudges, and perhaps shakes the noun."

16. Wyatt, "Giving Body to the Word: 475.

17. Operating under the influence of primary process laws, where psychic intensity is transferred from the unacceptable object, metonomy operates as the acceptable term. Under secondary process laws, metonomy operates to saturate the text with desire, which here becomes projected onto a chain of objects, each an inadequate substitute.

18. For example, when Sethe recovers—on the semiotic level—a memory of the (always not present) mother, she imagines her whole and dancing with others slaves: "Oh but when they danced . . . the men as well as the ma'ams, *one of whom was certainly her own*. They shifted shapes and became something other. Some unchained, demanding other whose feet knew her pulse better than she did" (*B*, 31, italics mine).

19. Morrison's comments to Claudia Tate, *Black Women Writers at Work* (New York: Continuum, 1983), 119, suggest that the significance of Ohio has centered on contradiction and boundary confusion: "The northern part of the state had underground stations and a history of black people escaping into Canada, but the southern part of the state is as much Kentucky as there is, complete with cross burnings. Ohio is a curious juxtaposition of what was ideal in this country and what was base."

20. Morrison has said of the "outside" world: "Outdoors was the real terror of life. . . . if you are put out, you go somewhere else; if you are outdoors, there is no place to go" (Cathleen Medwick, "People Are Talking About . . . ," *Vogue*, April 1981, 289).

21. Kristeva, *Revolution in Poetic Language*, 26, also explains that the *chora* "precedes figuration." It is "a modality of significance in which the linguistic sign is not yet articulated as the absence of an object and as the distinction between real and symbolic."

22. Silverman, *The Acoustic Mirror*, 79.

23. Shari Benstock, *Textualizing the Feminine: On the Limits of Genre* (Norman: University of Oklahoma Press, 1991), 168.

24. Silverman, *The Acoustic Mirror*, 105–6.

25. Ellie Ragland-Sullivan, *Jacques Lacan and the Philosophy of Psychoanalysis* (Urbana: University of Illinois Press, 1987), 296.

26. Despite the death of Baby Suggs and the flight of her two brothers, what Denver describes as "all that leaving," Denver also allows as how "none of that had mattered as long as her mother did not look away" (*B*, 12).

27. Carol E. Schmudde, "The Haunting of 124," *African American Review* 26, no. 3 (Fall 1992), 410, notes that watery boundaries in African myth are set between worlds of the living and the dead.

28. Gloria Naylor and Toni Morrison, "A Conversation," *Southern Review* 21 (July 1985): 585.

29. Wyatt, "Giving Body to the Word," 479; Horvitz, "Nameless Ghosts," 162, comments that Beloved "exists in several places and has more than one voice," that she has the voice of the woman on the slave ship and the voices of Denver and Sethe; Karla C. Holloway, "*Beloved*: A Spiritual," *Callaloo* 13, no. 3 (Summer 1990), 522, sees her in historical terms as "a confrontation of a killing history and a disabling present"; Linda Krumholz, "The Ghosts of Slavery: Historical Recovery in Toni Morrison's *Beloved*," *African American Review* 26, no. 3 (Fall 1992), 395–408, sees it in more positive terms as representing "suffering and guilt," but also "the power and beauty of the past," finally "everyone's ghost" (400).

30. Donald W. Hogg, *Jamaican Religions: A Study in Variations* (Ann Arbor, Mich.: UMI Press, 1967), 59–70.

31. Naylor and Morrison, "A Conversation," 585.

32. "Psychosis" is a troublesome term to bring up in this context because what would constitute hallucinatory material to the "scientific" world would reduce the richness of a novel like *Beloved* and attempt to naturalize the non-realistic phenomena. But psychosis for Lacan consisted of the foreclosure of the paternal signifier. That is, the paternal signifier, the legislative, punishing, culturally linked agent that intervenes between mother and child, is challenged within the symbolic order.

The result is a negation of the Other, the consignment of the subject to an existence in an imaginary relationship only.

In such an imaginary relationship the *je* that represents the subject of meaning and speech is overcome by the *moi*, Lacan's term for the non-verbal, unstable subject of the imaginary. For the women of 124 the world is an imaginary one as reflected in the repetition and pronomial confusion of their discourses ("You are mine/You are mine/You are mine" [*B*, 217]).

7

Escaping the Categories of Sex: Mobility and Lesbian Writing

> It is strange, however, how often we find that the wish for masculinity
> has been retained in the unconscious and from out of its state of
> repression, exercises a disturbing influence.
>
> —Sigmund Freud,
> "Analyses Terminable and Interminable"

> "Lesbianism is the only concept I know of which is beyond the catego-
> ries of sex."
>
> —Monique Wittig
> "One Is Not Born a Woman"

Throughout this study I have deemed it important to include Sigmund
Freud's own scripting of female psychosexual development as a prominant
example of narrative that immobilizes women. In response to the lesbian,
however, the Freudian script acknowledges an awareness of female mobility, but nevertheless defines it as inappropriate and "masculine." While the
two writers I discuss here—Luce Irigaray and Monique Wittig—both disavow the Freudian scripting of the lesbian, their quarrels with Freud are
along somewhat different lines, while their textual responses to lesbian
subjectivity are creative, radical, sometimes disturbing, and usually contro-
versial. Yet both writers offer discourses marked with mobility and a
commensurate desire to escape from the maternal presence. Before examining some of the works of these two writers, it might be helpful to
summarize some of Freud's work on the subject.

In his 1931 paper "Female Sexuality," Freud posited three lines of development by means of which girls made their journeys toward a feminine
state. The first "leads to a general revulsion from sexuality" resulting in a

woman who is neurotic; only by way of a "very circuitous" path—Freud's third path—does the girl "reach her final female attitude" on normalcy (*SE* 21:230). What he designates as the second path produces the homosexual woman, whose development is not characterized by repression at all, but who, because of her refusal to surrender clitoral activity and to acknowledge the "unwelcome fact" of her castration, possesses a "masculinity complex" (*SE* 23:130). This is derived not simply from infantile sexuality, but also from problems in the oedipal stage—a disappointment in the father, which, in turn, caused the girl's regression to infantile sexuality. Freud's emphasis seems to fall on the point that without entry into the oedipal stage, the girl would not experience this "neurosis." In other words, he explains female homosexuality not as an attraction between two women, but as a neurosis in which the girl believes herself to be a man, identifying with the father or with a phallic mother. When faced with the question of why all girls disappointed in their fathers do not regress in the above manner, Freud escapes into biology: "We can only suppose that it is a constitutional factor, a greater amount of activity such as is ordinarily characteristic of a male" ("Femininity," *SE*, 22:130). At this point in her development, he concludes, the girl successfully avoids "the wave of passivity" that is her due.

Sarah Kofman has observed that Freud has difficulty keeping his paths separate, especially when discussing the normal and the neurotic. In "Female Sexuality," for example, the hysteric becomes the focus of a discussion of normal femininity (*SE*, 21:239).[1] We might argue that Freud's boundary confusion involves the hysteric and the homosexual as well if we recall his most famous case study of hysteria (whose subject is Dora), which has buried in it a story of homosexuality. Written in 1900 and published in 1905, Freud's famous "Fragment of an Analysis of a Case of Hysteria"[2] has received a lot of critical attention because Freud's own narration raises questions not only about the neutrality of the psychiatrist, but also about the act of reading and the nature of femininity itself.[3] Yet another, earlier case, "The Psychogenesis of a Case of Homosexuality in a Woman" (1922), although written much later, also reveals Freud's problems with femininity. Indeed, it is interesting to compare his study of the lesbian in "Psychogenesis" with the earlier work on Dora, whose lesbianism is treated only on the literal margins of his text.[4]

The backgrounds of both women are similar; both are eighteen when they are "handed over" by their fathers to Freud for treatment. Both are described by Freud as beautiful. Both are also notable for their intellectual gifts (Freud's lesbian patient is "clever" [*SE*, 18:147] and "exceedingly shrewd" [*SE*, 18:159–60], and he comments on her "lucid objectivity" [*SE*, 18:159]). The lesbian as a child was "a spirited girl, always ready for romping and fighting" (*SE*, 18:169). Both cases reveal problematic gender roles. The fathers of both girls are dominant and successful, and initiated the treatments. The mothers of both girls seem to be of little interest to

Freud, who views both as neurotic; Dora's mother is afflicted with "house-wife's psychosis," and the mother of the young lesbian has also "suffered for some years from neurotic troubles" (*SE*, 18:149). He is far more inter-ested, however, in the older brothers with whom the girls compete and also in what Freud calls the "mother substitutes," women usually older than the girls by ten years or so who serve as confidantes.

However, there are differences. Dora is considered the hysteric, trapped in a claustrophobic family situation and forced to negotiate her way be-tween her father and Herr K. The lesbian, however, pursues her female friend actively and openly and seems to enjoy angering her father. Unlike Dora, the lesbian is not regarded as "in any way ill" (*SE*, 18:150). While Dora is the one to break off the analysis with Freud, it is Freud who breaks off analysis with the lesbian. [5]

What apparently disturbs Freud is the lesbian's ability to control his investigation and to thwart him. Behind a surface willingness to undertake treatment for her parents' sake, the girl is perceived to harbor "defiance and revenge" (*SE*, 18:163). Instead of offering up her own "mutilated relics" like those from Dora's past, the lesbian patient appears to be withholding her "secrets." While she appears unresisting, Freud suspects that she is not being influenced, that there is instead a hidden "boundary line" barring him. Unaccustomed to being on the margins himself, Freud resists seeing this boundary problem as his own and insists instead that it is evidence of the girl's neurosis; that is, the girl does not keep him out so much as she keeps her neurosis in.

Finally, Freud is forced to confront what he does not know and admits that "the amount of information about her seems meager enough, nor can I guarantee that it is complete" (*SE*, 18:155). One reason his information is incomplete is because he has broken off the analysis. Nevertheless, he blames the girl (and homosexuals in general), rationalizing that the analysis has "yielded an anamnesis not much more reliable than the other anamne-ses of homosexuals, which there is good cause to question" (*SE*, 18:155).

Had the girl been a hysteric, she might have presented "better opportu-nities for investigation of the history of her childhood" (*SE*, 18:155), but without so much as "one hysterical symptom" to go on, Freud can only discuss the revival of her infantile oedipal situation and conclude that her desire to be revenged on her father is the basis of her homosexuality. Particularly disturbing to him is the fact that the girl not only participates "actively" in the analysis, but also possesses an emotional tranquility that Freud describes in rather interesting language: "Once when I expounded to her a specially important part of the theory, one touching her nearly, she replied in an inimitable tone, "How very interesting," as though she were a *grand dame* being taken over a museum and glancing through her lorgnon at objects to which she was completely indifferent" (*SE*, 18:163). The formi-dable archaeologist of the "Fragment," comparing himself to "those discoverers of good fortune" who "bring to the light of day after their long burial the priceless though mutilated relics of antiquity," appears offended by this unmoved viewer who can look upon his relics as uninteresting museum pieces. Furthermore, the elaborate simile, including a reference to the lesbian as a *grand dame*, indicates his repeated tendency to escape into French when called on to supply a word for a woman. Furthermore, throughout "Psychogenesis" he refers to her love object as a *cocotte* and as a *demi mondaine*, again revealing through language that femaleness, and perhaps especially homosexual femaleness, is something alien.

In any case, having reduced the significance of the girl's love object by fixing her as a common prostitute from a lower world, Freud seems intent on denying the lesbian relationship altogether. His reluctance to confront female homosexuality can be hinted at in the way in which he downplays its reality. He argues, for example, that his patient is genitally chaste, that she has avoided opportunities for "genuine" homosexual relationships, even though he has stated in the early pages of his paper that the girl's relationship with the present lover has been an intimate one. He also claims that the girl's homosexuality was initiated by her mother's pregnancy when the girl was sixteen, even though her history revealed several earlier infatuations, which suggest that it was not disappointment over the father that is the cause of her orientation.

Most problematic for feminist critics—and especially lesbians—is Freud's consistent determination to see female homosexuality in masculine terms. This tendency is evident in Freud's attempt to exaggerate the role of the patient's brother and to suggest that her desire is for him: "Her lady's slender figure, severe beauty, and downright manner reminded her of the brother who was a little older than herself. Her latest choice corresponded, therefore, not only to her feminine, but also to her masculine ideal" (*SE*, 18:156). In sum, Freud needs to keep the female homosexual masculinized, aligned with male desire. The girl's activity/desire cannot be a norm, but must operate only as a masculine masquerade. Only during her active phallic stage can she be a "little man" and live in "a masculine way" (*SE*, 22:126).

Irigaray indicts "Psychogenesis" as a "phallic instinctual script" that is ultimately about *male* homosexuality because object choice is determined by masculine desire—either for the so-called phallic mother (since the mother must be phallicized to remove castration fears) or for the man. Allowing that many homosexual women "can recognize themselves in this story or could at least try to find their bearings in it," Irigaray complains that, in reality, it obliterates female homosexuality, leaving it "travestied—transvestized— and withdrawn from interpretation," since for Freud the entire concept was "incomprehensible," finally "inadmissable" (*Speculum*, 101).[6]

Lacanian theory and the implication of his phallocentric arguments have been frustrating for Irigaray, among others. She argues that this theory naturalizes a system where phallic values are imposed on a perception that is already part of the system. She resists the notion that the girl must perceive herself as not having a penis, since such an assumption privileges sight over the other senses and forces the girl to see herself through the eyes of the boy. Even Jacques Lacan's description of the female homosexual as existing in relation to what is lacking in her appears disturbingly blind to female desire.[7] And although Lacan also differentiates between the imaginary motive of the male homosexual, which reveals the need to preserve the phallus, and the imaginary motive of the female, he does not elucidate the difference very satisfactorily, since he still presumes that women become fetishes and take up positions as men. And while he notes another difference in the "delirious style" of the male homosexual, and the "naturalness" with which homosexual women "appeal to their qualities of being men," he leaves female desire unexplained.[8]

Even if we recognize castration as represented most significantly in the mother and not in the girl, the girl is still left with what has to be a different response to this imaginary image. What that response may be remains a point of debate. It is argued that females are more likely to experience nostalgia, desire linked to deprivation. Ellie Ragland-Sullivan, also emphasizing loss, argues that the daughter is more closely linked to the castration scene. While she acknowledges the fact that "heterosexual normalcy grows out of an acceptance of the social interpretation of the castration drama," Ragland-Sullivan sees female homosexuality more in terms of denial.[9]

Nevertheless, Ragland-Sullivan's concept of a "double castration" suggests that while castration is felt as a primary effect of the real, it is also experienced as a secondary effect in the form of myths that operate on both imaginary and symbolic levels to explain that same real effect.[10] This extension of Lacan's theories helps to clarify the nature of the primordial trauma and to move us beyond a literal or personalistic castration, but it does not help us to respond to the idea that normative female sexuality signifies acceptance of social myths, while lesbianism signifies denial. On the other hand, despite the problematic connotations of denial and the tendency to link that denial with masculinity, so-called normative female sexuality is accompanied by a number of disturbing effects—depression, hysteria, passive aggression—that do not offer much of a way out of the impasse. It may be argued that lesbian denial may take a different tack than that of the normative male who attempts to feel the trauma of primary castration. Or the lesbian may exist more comfortably with lack, even exploit it textually, a question I want to raise in connection to Wittig's *The Lesbian Body*.[11]

Some recent lesbian writing seems to position itself at the point where female desire can be re-examined and textualized, a place where a radically different inscripting of that desire can occur. Of course, both lesbianism and writing about lesbianism have a long history of repression, which has interacted with what Wittig regards as a primary manifestation of lesbian desire: a resistance to the norm, a defiance of the patriarchal symbolic order.[12] Elaine Marks characterizes such defiance as a resistance to the domestication of women's sexuality.[13] Consequently, lesbian writing is often recognized as having a reactive component, much as psychoanalysis seems to recognize denial in the lesbian. Catherine R. Stimpson, in her well-known study of the lesbian novel in English, isolates in lesbian novels two "repetitive patterns": one that she designates as the "novel of damnation," represented by Radclyffe Hall's *The Well of Loneliness*, and the second as the "enabling escape," best represented perhaps by Rita Mae Brown's *Rubyfruit Jungle*.[14] But even the enabling escape is reactive, and it may be true that much lesbian writing cannot escape reaction and defiance. Nevertheless, the writings of both Irigaray and Wittig offer textual escap(e)ades of an unusual order.

Irigaray is more interested in discovering a female imaginary, in getting beyond woman as absence, as *vide* or *trou*. She also conceives of a symbolic in which categories of clitoris-vagina, active-passive can be escaped, arguing that women must find the signifiers of their own desires in the female body. She calls for the resistance of the denigration of the desire for the self-same (*Speculum*, 102).

This desire is given poetic expression in "When Our Lips Speak Together," which is at once a declaration of escape from patriarchal "enclosures, patterns, distinctions and opposites" and a demand for freedom from "their categories," from what "paralyzes us, petrifies us, immobilizes us."[15] For Irigaray, it is heterosexuality that immobilizes women: "If they say 'come,' then you may go forward.... Measure your steps according to their need—or lack of need—for their own image. One or two steps, no more, without exuberance or turbulence. Otherwise you will smash everything" ("Lips," 71). Heterosexual love possesses women's bodies, but denies desire: "Our pleasure is trapped in their system" ("Lips," 74). But what mobilizes, what goes beyond social norms, can be found in language and physicality. A particular point of attack is Claude Levi-Straus's argument that women are objects of exchange. Writing against this view, Irigaray creates a speaker who can invoke another space where there are "no walls, the clearing no enclosure" nor is there containment "within their language" ("Lips," 73).

Indeed, Irigaray's speaker, intent on denying castration as the female condition, affirms instead a depth that "does not mean a chasm," which is represented by "the density of our body" ("Lips," 75). She accuses the oppressive culture of creating woman as absence, and her narrator points to the encoding of fragmentation, a designation of woman as virgin and non-virgin, a representation of woman's body as wound in order to establish her status as property. "We are not voids," the speaker declares, "embracing lack, needing to be filled." Claiming instead that "our 'all' intermingles. Without breaks or gaps," Irigaray's speaker declares that for the lovers of the self-same "there is no abyss" ("Lips," 75).

Fluidities, always valorized over solids in Irigaray's work, fill, rather than cover, gaps and in this text become both form and content. Blood is not to be related to a virginal condition, is not a dried (solid) smear that is emblematic of a wound confirming possession, but retains its liquidity and circulates between the two lovers. Through the linguistic and bodily establishment of fluids, exchange occurs on a very different level where "our pleasure consists of moving and being moved by each other, endlessly" ("Lips," 73).

The motion that keeps the lovers "in a flux that never congeals or solidifies" assures the absence of boundaries, and the current that flows between the lovers is compared to rivers that "have no permanent banks; this body, no fixed borders" ("Lips," 76–77). In sum, the boundary dissolution that Irigaray proposes seems to test, to dare the imaginary experience that is both fusion and fragmentation, as if it were not only desirable, but also survivable.

It is also remarkable for representing what Carolyn Burke describes as "a quest for an ideological space in which to 'speak female' (parler femme). . . . [Irigaray's] text is a process of discovery and an exploration through language of the connections between female sexuality and the expression of meaning."[16]

One of Irigaray's intriguingly disruptive strategies (in which she follows Wittig) is her choice of a speaker(s) who is both je/tu, who is never the masculinized and abstracted on who is both other and self, self and other. Articulating a denial of patriarchal exchange systems that make the other the object, the speaker here is simultaneously both subject and object, uttering a multiplicity of songs.

Like Morrison, Irigaray also privileges metonyms, as the title of this piece demonstrates.[17] This preference for the kind of language that structures contiguity, combinations, and contexts indicates once again her interest in avoiding volume and fixity, best linked to the substitutive language of metaphor.[18] Lips that speak thus connect linguistic utterance with the language of the body, for as the speaker notes, "if we don't find our body's language, its gestures will be too few to accompany our story" ("Lips," 76). Again, lips perform a different exchange, simultaneously opening and closing; lips "say" together; lips of one mouth operate in a fluid exchange; lips between two mouths share language and fluids: "open or closed, for one never excludes the other, our lips say that both love each other" ("Lips," 72). This exchange is set against a masculine discourse that can only utter the word that is "correct, enclosed, wrapped around its meaning . . . without a crack, faultless" ("Lips," 72). Such utterances are used as a pretense to deny lack, whereas Irigaray's speaker can speak "from your/my lips several songs, several ways of saying" that "echo each other" ("Lips," 72).

Yet the gaps exist—in the text, with its multiple interruptions and changes of direction, and in the address to the absent mother. But we perceive such gaps as less determined, even view them as other-than-lack because mobility alters presence of absence here. And while the original separation trauma represented by the mother is inescapable for either gender, it is at least allowed to surface in Irigaray's text.

At one point in "When Our Lips Speak Together," the speaker exhorts the reader to "get out of their language. Go back through all the names they gave you" ("Lips," 69). Wittig makes similar statements in her works. Like Irigaray, she regards language itself as a source of women's enslavement. Unlike Irigaray, she removes herself from psychoanalytic questions and assumptions, and warns her readers against "traffickers in the unconscious."[19] Language, she says, "casts sheaves of reality upon the social body, stamping it and violently shaping it."[20] For her the war takes place in the area of personal pronouns, which, she says, "engineer gender all through language" ("Mark," 5). While personal pronouns are "gender bearers" only in the third person, and therefore seem to be uninvolved in structuring gender, they do not do away with the fact that once the speaker (in French) has intervened, a suspension of grammatical form occurs: The *je* marks the past participles and adjectives as feminine, thereby making the speaker's sex "public"; thus, the woman is forced "to proclaim [her sex] in her speech . . . to appear in language under her proper physical form and not under the abstract form which every male locutor has the unquestioned right to use" ("Mark," 5). To escape this grounding in the concrete while males capture the abstract world, Wittig, in *Les Guérillères*, uses the rare *elles* pronoun. Unlike *ils*, which is also assumed to be "one," *elles* "never stands for a general and is never bearer of a universal point of view."[21]

Indeed, defining gender as "the enforcement of sex in language," Wittig attempts, in her creative works, to escape gender altogether. Certainly for her, gender has no basis in what is perceived to be "natural"; women are not a natural group, she argues, for what naturalizes them is "the social phenomena which express our oppression."[22] The female sex is a political group and, as such, can be overthrown. To that end Wittig's subjects are *lesbian*, a term that she uses to refer to a subject who is "something else, a not-woman, a not-man" ("One," 49). Lesbianism then is what is outside masculine and feminine, what is outside sexuality as well, that which raises to importance "another dimension of the human" ("Paradigm," 117). Nonetheless, sexuality is not thereby denigrated; Wittig, rather like Irigaray, views sexuality as "an exercise of subjectivity that involves the search for pleasure and the creation of a unique being" ("Paradigm," 119).

Wittig's theories enable her to create texts that display a remarkable energy, derived in part from the fact that lesbian texts have historically been repressed in the patriarchal culture's war against the lesbian. Because lesbian discourse has been relegated to the margins of both cultural and textual domains, lesbian textuality comes to constitute escaped material—all the more powerful for its suppression—and as such it disrupts and overturns. Mobility is a key ingredient in such texts. Its presence points to the recovery of the body as active and liberated from its entrapment in image. Nor is the body represented as parts. The body is herewith rescued from patriarchal pronouncements about its lack, and to that end the vulva is valorized not in metaphoric terms, but in metonymic ones.

For example, in *Les Guérillères* Wittig's subjects engage in a hoop game, which enacts the configuration of the vulva and its energy, but also through its symbolism the game denies any association of the vulva with lack or fixity. In this game the women use hoops of varying colors. Territory is marked out in colors as well, as are the women who comprise large teams. As a machine sends the hoops rotating into the air, the women try to catch them while remaining in their respective territories. The impossibility of the game's object seems a given. But in the action of the ascending hoops, described as "an immense spiral," as well as in the tumultuous disarray of the players, fixity is transcended, and in its place movement, which is figured as a rising and revolving circle, is used to energize the group.[23]

More important is Wittig's attempt to liberate the body from its imprisonment in reproductive functions. She argues that heterosexuality is responsible for the valorization of maternity because it is a culture "designed to justify the whole system of social domination based on the obligatory reproductive function of women and the appropriation of that reproduction" ("Paradigm," 115). To address this concern, Wittig re-creates the story of the Fall, making mothers and amazons the active agents: "During the Golden Age, everyone in the terrestrial garden was called amazon. Mothers were not distinct from daughters. . . . They hunted together. They gathered together and they wandered together." (*LPMD*, 108). However, history brings change, and with the advent of the cities, mobility is lost, and the mother becomes split off from the amazon: "There came a time when some daughters and some mothers did not like wandering anymore. . . . They began to stay in the cities and most often they watched their abdomens grow" (*LPMD*, 108).

In *Les Guérillères*, reclamation of the amazonian myth becomes one way of recovering the vulva and of abolishing its representation as lack. While the amazons are not mentioned as Wittig's battling subjects, their stories and the warriors they celebrate link them to the amazon tradition, which, for Wittig, was not a matriarchal, but a lesbian, society. In her *Lesbian Peoples' Material for a Dictionary* Wittig describes her amazonian "companion lovers" as subjects whose activities included "living together, loving, celebrating one another, playing in a time when work was still a game"; but these companion lovers suffered banishment in later times when an amazon became regarded as "she who does not assume her destiny," after which she became one of the "violent ones" who "fought to defend harmony" (*LPMD*, 5).

Wittig would seem to discover (or recover) the presence of amazon in a remarkable number of places, but it is also true that their stories have been so appropriated, distorted, and obscured by patriarchal mythographers that amazons are inevitably depicted as involved with (and subordinate to) male heroes and always conquered. They are recounted as doing battle with Dionysus, Bellerophon, and Heracles, and Theseus was supposed to have captured Queen Antiope as booty and to have thereby caused her sister Orethyia to go to war against Attica. However, marching her armies through Thrace, Thessaly, and Boeotia, Orethyia is said to have reached even the outskirts of Athens, after which she was driven from Attica by Theseus (who later had Antiope killed in order that he could marry Phaedre).24 Another amazon, Hippolyte, was supposedly so attracted to Heracles that she offered him her magic girdle and was killed for her generosity.

Other myths speak of the amazons' descent through the mothers (a kind of narrative that encouraged Robert Graves to view them as remnants of a matriarchal system), of their domestication of males who were forced to do the housework and all the menial chores, and of their crippling of their male infants.25 However, what the patriarchal retelling of the amazonian myths conveys is that women could be captured as booty; that while they might oppose themselves to males on occasion, their resistance was short-lived; that eventually they succumbed to male attractiveness and became domesticated. One noteworthy feature of the amazon, as presented in classical myths, involves their existence on the margins of Greek civilization, suggesting that the Greek consciousness associated them with unknown, hence threatening, places. Their presence in Libya, Asia Minor, and Albania— along with the apocryphal tale of their invasion of Attica—points to the difficulty that the Hellenic people had with earlier goddess-worshipping societies.

In any case Wittig calls her amazon text an epic, arguing for the appropriateness of this form because *Les Guérillères* is an undomesticated text mobilized by its turn to the oral tradition—to storytelling and to song that celebrate the actions and ideals of these people. As a consciously undomesticated people Wittig's subjects inhabit very different spaces from those that are culturally and historically allotted to women. Preferring open air, they exist instead along the riverbanks, upon the hillsides, in the meadows: "They say they have broken with the tradition of inside and outside, that the factories have each knocked down one of their walls, that offices have been installed in the open air, on the esplanades, in the rice fields" (*G*, 131). Even more sheltered spaces do not house isolated women, but are cavelike, each likened, somewhat paradoxically, to both the egg and the sarcophagus, where "several can stay, signing, gesticulating, sleeping."26 Again, space that evokes womb and tomb is also the place of activity that is valorized by

Wittig's marchers, and their use of voice, body, and the sleep experience redefines "total idleness" as "the highest delight" (*LPMD*, 143).

Many forms of movement are depicted in *Les Guérillères*, the dominant form of which is the march. But the subjects also hunt, climb trees to gather fruit, and dance (many references are made to stamping the ground [*G*, 28, 39, 53, 61, 93, 98]). Sound also functions as a form of mobility, and shouting and laughter are elevated to important activities as well. Indeed, laughter becomes a potent weapon that is used to destroy patriarchal structures and the myths that have been used to fix women. In one scene, women's laughter is shown to be the force that can destroy patriarchal textual structures—the body of fixed representations of women (*G*, 92).

In a sense this futuristic novel goes beyond escape, articulating neither retreat nor evasion, but overthrow. This term—meaning to upset, to conquer, to end—suggests the radical nature of the work as well as its violence, ingredients that have troubled some readers. Nevertheless, Wittig's warfare is always intended to occur in the realm of language. Thus, escape for Wittig involves some provocative approaches to narrative structure—especially in the disruption of linear plot sequences— along with the destruction and reconstitution of the kind of mythic material that has been the basis of imprisoning abstractions of lesbian subjecthood. The result of Wittig's strategies is an often fragmented work whose structure allows her access to the gaps in which she professes to write and out of which she can create a different kind of textual unity, one that depends on collective subjectivity and the restoration of the body.

One form of "action overthrow" (*geste renversement*) is to be found in the recovery of the lesbian subjects' collective story. In part this story emerges, albeit incompletely, in the feminaries, which appear to function as a textual mediation positioned between a new text for a new place that cannot, however, be reached without this important older material.[27] Where the feminaries seem to fail is in their retention of symbols for the female body, even those that evoke powerful and hence positive goddess figures. Nonetheless, symbolism involves substitution, which, in its turn, covers absence, and it is precisely this absence that Wittig wants to recover. Thus, while the feminaries are regarded by the subjects as no longer being particularly useful (*G*, 49), it is also acknowledged that they have been a link to the past, a key to the older, recondite legends, and, more important, they have given "pride of place to the symbols of the circle, the circumference, the ring, the O, the zero, the sphere" (*G*, 45). This *pride of place* refers not only to the position of Wittig's lesbian subjects, but also to the valorization of the vulva. While the circle appears to operate as a symbol, and therefore must ultimately be dispensed with, the vulva needs to be textualized in order for its substitutive function to be recognized and overturned. To that end Wittig inscribes the vulva in the most obvious way, namely, by centering the O on three pages within the text. Placed in this manner, Wittig's O, circle, or zero becomes what "you invent to imprison them and overthrow them" (*G*, 114). Serving as an emblem, it nonetheless suggests the dynamic structure of the text, better represented in the hoop game and in the symbol of the spiral, but also seen in the active resistance of the subjects.

One clue to Wittig's strategies for inscribing the vulva can be found on the final page of upper-cased text. These special passages have been interspersed with the poetic segments of the work and, suggestive of the epic roll call, have consisted of women's names. However, the absence of commas between the names denies sequentiality, while the equivalence of letters denies another hierarchical process and the absence of patronyms denies reproductive history. But a last poetic fragment, coming after the recitation of names, announces itself as "VIOLENCE FROM THE WHITE-NESS," as a text "WRITTEN BY DEFAULT," one that rejects "THE DESIG-NATED TEXT" of patriarchy with its fragmenting symbols. Against this text Wittig invokes "LACUNAE LACUNAE/AGAINST TEXTS/AGAINST MEANING/WHICH IS TO WRITE VIOLENCE/OUTSIDE THE TEXT/IN ANOTHER WRITING/THREATENING MENAC-ING/MARGINS SPACES INTERVALS/WITHOUT PAUSE/ACTION OVERTHROW" (*G*, 143).

Gathering up suppressed lesbian history, which has been allowed existence only on the margins, Wittig introduces a body of writing from other spaces, ones that were thought to be empty—lacunae that become the sources of a new textual subjectivity based on the restoration of substance to the gaps. These are the spaces to be written in, but what is written there is the absent body that Wittig's text will attempt to restore. The following passage suggests the material to be used:

Whatever they have *not* laid hands on, whatever they have *not* pounced on like many-eyed birds of prey, does *not* appear in the language you speak. This is apparent precisely in the intervals that your masters have *not* been able to fill with their words of proprietors and possessors, this can be found in the gaps, in all that which is *not* a continuation of their discourse. (*G*, 114, italics mine)

Wittig's use of the negative is also part of writing in the gap. Just as *lesbian* is *not-man* and *not-woman*, her text is *not-written* in a gendered context. Her writing in the gap will instead evoke the vulva, the absent organ that can separate itself from its subordination to the womb and to the reproductive functions that have nothing to do with *jouissance* or desire.

This different emphasis explains the structuring of the novel by zero: "at this stage of the march one must interrupt the calculations and begin again at zero," the narrator tells us (*G*, 64). Zero is especially significant because it has long stood as a symbol for censorship. Stimpson observes that even the term *lesbian* was formerly not to be used; not to utter the word was to remain free from some "punitive power"; culture, she argues, "becomes the legatee of linguistic zeros, the blank pages encrypted in tombs [which] critics will never excavate."[28] In Wittig's novel, movements replicate the vulva and are consciously cyclical and circular; the paths the women follow go toward a center that is always in motion, whose circumference is, however, "nowhere" (G, 69). Thus, the zero comes to represent the energizing center not as metaphor, but as metonomy.

It is this energizing center that is suggested in the feminaries, in the myths and fairy tales which the women know, but from which they feel removed. It is stated that the feminaries supply the women with many terms that can substitute for the vulva, but that these terms are not needed, since women "as possessors of vulvas . . . are familiar with their characteristics" (G, 31) and do not need a linguistic substitute. Nonetheless, Wittig's "bearers of fables" are honored and important to the amazonian culture because of a mobility that they possess, which enables them to "recount . . . the metamorphoses of words from one place to another" (LPMD, 166). The fact that these bearers of fables cannot recount those metamorphoses without creating their own is Wittig's point. Their role is to engage in the interaction of meaning with reality and, in so doing, to assure "the avoidance of fixed meanings" (P, 166).

Important to Wittig's text is the unrecognized material relating to the vulva that myths and fairy tales reveal. For example, the siren no longer appears as a temptress figure luring men to their doom. She is represented without her dangerous or destructive aspect as a singer of a song that, as a "continuous O," speaks to lesbian subjects, recalling, once again, Wittig's O/zero/circle configuration pointing ultimately to the vulva (G, 14). The Aztec goddess Cihuacoatl, revered more for her warrior qualities than her reproductive functions, is linked to her worshippers/daughters through her strength; Amaterasu, the Japanese sun goddess, confirms the sun and not the earth as the domain of women. Since the sky gods in patriarchal cultures were always male, while the female goddesses—if they were recognized at all—were linked to earth, Wittig's strategy here is to recover the goddesses' association with the mobility of upper air and with the active natures of the sky gods, who stood in contrast to the static earth symbolism that bound women to images of grotto, cave, and cleft.

Instead of representing the vulva in terms of darkness and obscurity, Wittig makes the vulva something that *can* be seen. In her new world the female genitalia become mirrors that catch and reflect the sun: "The women say that they expose their genitals so that the sun may be reflected therein as in a mirror. They say that they retain its brilliance. They say that the pubic hair is like a spider's web that captures the rays. They are seen running with great strides." (G, 19). The mirror in which the women have been imprisoned, where they cannot move, where "limbs gain no adhesion" (G, 30), is reclaimed as a weapon enabling the subjects to imitate Amaterasu, who uses a mirror to catch the sun's rays and to blind her enemies.

In another amazonian tale Eve is returned to the garden, having regained both her mobility and her goddess status. The serpent motif also undergoes a transformation. No longer are snakes connected with the *vagina dentata*, the devouring womb, but rather they are transformed into headdresses with "hortitative" abilities that include the impartation of wisdom and advice. Such snakes as these are able to give to Eve a crownlike aura, which harkens back to the sun and the "blazing genital" (*G*, 53), whose symbol is the circle.

The fairy tale of Snow White and Rose Red also escapes the dichotomous strategies of the patriarchal story where each stands respectively for purity and passion. In this feminary story Snow White is pursued through the forest by Rose Red, whose laughter and anger are evoked to deny Snow White's claim to ancestors (Snow White is too distilled to resemble a goddess). The confrontation between the two destroys their frozen stances as opposites. Snow White recovers her anger (and a bit of red), along with Rose Red's empowering stick, while her sister, no longer red, sleeps the positive sleep of a companion lover, transformed into "a stout root, pink as a pink rose" (*G*, 48).

Thus, "ACTION OVERTHROW" aptly reveals the strategic purposes behind the women's mobility and places the vulva in the center of the women's warfare. Regarded as sacred vessels in ancient myth because of the mystery of the female body processes, including the creation of blood and milk (not to mention children), women, as analogues for the vegetative cycles of earth, *were* their wombs and hence sacred vessels. For Wittig, however, the womb must be denied power, either to direct women's lives or to immobilize them, and her speaker proclaims in the final pages of the text, "the vessels are upright, the vessels have acquired legs. The sacred vessels are on the move" (*G*, 142).

In *The Lesbian Body* Wittig continues to address the mythic dominance of the reproductive functions over the vulva and undertakes to re-create—or to invent—a variant of the ancient Eleusinian mysteries.[29] These rites are not referred to directly in *The Lesbian Body*. However, Wittig certainly evokes them in her "ceremony of the vulvas lost and found,"[30] a rite that not only introduces mobility by means of an important metaphor—the butterfly— but also points to the real *heurisis* of mother and daughter as being one in which the lesbian body is healed of its exiled condition and can exercise mobility in its own island space. However, conscious of female entrapment in metaphor, Wittig takes care to undermine the metaphor's substitutive function. Thus, in the ceremony of the vulvas lost and found the associational function of the butterflies with the vulva is carefully marked: "The vulvas are represented by blue yellow green black violet red butterflies, their bodies are the clitorises, their wings are labia, their fluttering represents the throbbing of the vulvas" (*B*, 136).

In other ways *The Lesbian Body* appears to controvert the interest in body integrity so important to the earlier text, for this more recent work appears instead to celebrate dismemberment, or at least a disturbing sadomasochistic kind of love relationship. While *Les Guérillères* may be recognizable as a kind of epic, *The Lesbian Body* is not so easily identifiable, a situation to be expected given Wittig's interest in new forms. Thus, here her interest involves the creation of a new body of texts and a text of the female body,[31] a text that, according to Wittig, has "lesbianism as its theme" (*B*, 9). It is a particularly disturbing text because of the prevalence of rending, tearing, flagellation, evisceration, and cannibalism, acts that appear to describe—on one level—the relationship of the two lovers who are both the subjects and the objects of desire. An example of their lovemaking: "*I* begin with the tips of your fingers, *I* chew the phalanges *I* crunch the metacarpals the carpals, *I* slaver at your wrists. . . . *I* tear away the biceps from the humerus, *I* devour it, *I* eat m/y fill of you m/y so delectable one" (*B*, 121).

The violence of Wittig's text, so disturbing to many feminists, has been explained—probably not to everyone's satisfaction—as "an attack against the mystique of passivity."[32] But part of our difficulty in reading this text devolves from our assumptions of categories like subject and object. Hence, to read the text as a discourse about subjectivity "beyond the categories of sex" is more helpful. Martha Noel Evans argues that the violence is necessary because, as she puts it, "as male traditions are undone, so also is the female self constructed by and in those traditions." [33]

Once again, the violence extends to the question of pronouns. Wittig's j/e (rendered *I* in the English translation), is an attempt to capture the dilemma of the woman writer alienated from the *je*, which makes her male. As Wittig explains it in her introduction to the English translation, "*J/e* is the symbol of the lived rending experience which is *m/y* writing" (*B*, 10). On the other hand, Wittig also argues that the *j/e* is not *I* destroyed: "It is an *I* become so powerful that it can attack the order of heterosexuality in texts . . . and lesbianize them" ("Mark," 11). What Wittig means by the term involves a destruction of the Western patriarchal fiction of the self, what Patrick McGee describes as "the authority of the male masculine universal" that assumes an ontological existence, whereas it is, in reality, "ontologically empty"; he contines, "by writing this universal feminine subject, Wittig destroys the metaphysical content of the masculine universal and reduces the 'universal' itself to a purely linguistic and material effect."[34]

The fragmentation achieved in the work, moving from the pronouns out into the rest of the text, gives us as readers a very unstable sense of positioning, places us, with the lesbian protagonists, disturbingly close to absence. What is most remarkable about this sliding position of the reader and the text is that as the text projects lack, it also generates a remarkable mobility that appears to sustain us in it.

In spite of its disturbing content, we soon discover a text dominated by movement.[35] This movement appears in its most obvious form in the numerous descent motifs beginning on the first page where the speaker evokes for herself and her lover a "gehenna," an underworld—the archetypal place of dismemberment and death.[36] In Wittig's work, however, the lovers descend into one another, sometimes violently, by touch and tearing, sometimes by gaze, or, as in these more innocuous lines, by voice: "Your voice invades m/e further still, it descends like a tendril to the bottom of m/y stomach" (B, 107).

It might be helpful to recall here that in the archetypal journeys upon which Wittig draws, the purpose of the descent was transformation. In Jungian terms the descent (always regarded as a male prerogative) involved a symbolic entry into the body of the mother. In this space the male quester, if he could survive dismemberment, would, in effect, have succeeded in giving birth to himself and, as a consequence of this achievement, would become a hero. But this version of the archetypal descent obviously focuses on the actions of the male and, worse, appropriates the actions of the mother so that her body processes are not only imitated, but also thereby rendered less odious and dangerous. Wittig, on the other hand, takes this myth in very different directions, applying it in one instance to the story of Orpheus and Eurydice. But in her "lesbianized" version, Eurydice, trailing her Orpheus up from the underworld, is given a voice and the ability to describe her rite of passage in relentlessly accurate images of decay, from "the stink of m/y bowels" to the "purulence of m/y eyes m/y nose m/y vulva the caries of m/y teeth the fermentation of m/y vital organs the colour of m/y rotten-ripe muscles" (B, 19–20). Despite the condition of the narrator, however, the rescuing lover, singing with victorious voice the joy of m/y recovery (B, 19–20), transforms the hellish journey into one of re-memberment.

In a later scene, where the speaker imitates the actions of Isis, much attention is again paid to body parts—a foot, the neck, head, ears (B, 79)—but, again, the recovery of the lover's "scattered fragments" is emphasized, and there is an active and energized engagement with re-membering, as the speaker replicates the ancient ritual: "I begin a violent dance around your body, m/y heels dig into the ground, I arrange your hair . . . I Isis the all-powerful I decree you live as in the past Osiris m/y most cherished m/y most enfeebled" (B, 80). In the original myths, such reclamations are less vividly rendered, but also less successful. Osiris never recovers his phallus; Orpheus (ultimately beheaded himself) looks back and loses Eurydice to the underworld. Wittig's lesbianized versions emphasize the body and its less pleasant processes and states of decay, and yet her intent may be to recover, through this radical kind of writing, the older purpose of such initiation stories, namely, the facing of horror induced by absence.

Another kind of re-membering occurs in a poem that depicts the dancing of the goddesses on a hillside. The speaker, watching the companion lovers who are also gathered there, recognizes within the group the faces of goddesses who have been released from their captivity in patriarchal myths. "I know them all by their names," the speaker claims. Having studied them in library books, she is also able to "list their attributes"; yet such a listing is not capable of bringing them to life. The texts in which the goddesses have been imprisoned have repressed their energy and, along with it, their mobility and their playfulness, qualities that have become dominant as they caper on the hillside with their worshippers. The speaker, noting a reality that contrasts with the textual representations of the goddesses, concludes, "*I* am not sorry that their severity should have remained attached to the books, since they are here before m/e so totally devoid of it" (*B*, 69). Thus, Wittig constructs a scene that brings together past and present, mixing human and divine in a rhapsodic metamorphosis, which also recalls one of the original purposes of ritual as noted by Mircea Eliade, namely, the need to effect the healing of the community by evoking the myths by which it was created, by escaping from "profane" time into liturgical, or sacred time, in order to re-enact the original scene of creation.[37] Thus, while Wittig mutes the reproductive functions of her goddesses, she does not let us lose sight of their larger relationship to the creative processes.

While it may be apparent from these examples that Wittig's creation of textual mobility involves an escape from the patriarchal renderings of certain mythic narratives in order that their earlier, pre-patriarchal stories may be recaptured, this need to escape myth does not fully account for the presence of dismemberment and violence on which the writing of the lesbian body seems to rely. A fuller examination of dismemberment seems needed here, which itself involves a descent—past mythic narrative to the ritual actions out of which such narrative emerged. Ritual concretizes myth; it is a doing instead of a telling, and while it operates on the symbolic level, it suggests a deeper reliance on the imaginary and also on the real. For ritual actions are performed according to perceptions about both the body and the cosmos and are directed in the most basic ways toward survival. Furthermore, since Wittig's aim is to expose language as empty of ontological reality, and full only in terms of its materiality, these narrative strategies succeed in filling language according to body processes that have always governed ritual and myth, its later linguistic derivatives. Therefore, the relationship of the body to cosmos describes a collective body and a relationship based on a sense of reciprocity—of taking and giving back. Yet it is also the individual human body's metabolic processes, projected onto the vegetative patterns of growth and decay, that structure ritual.

Theodor H. Gaster, attempting to demystify myth by emphasizing its functional nature, recognizes two basic processes—emptying (*kenosis*) and filling (*plerosis*)—and four basic rites that derive from them: purgation and mortification (involving emptying) and invigoration and jubilation (involving filling).[38] These dynamic processes of emptying and filling, which look back to ingestion and elimination, are the structure of the lesbian lovers' relationship. It is also significant that neither process can exist alone, nor does either occur sequentially as much as simultaneously. Thus, Wittig's attempt to link the lesbian body to the inevitable dynamic of bodily processes derives from her desire to approach the problem of exchange.

Sometimes the dynamics of emptying and filling take place on the alimentary level where the speaker announces, "*I* set about eating you . . . m/y tongue inserts itself in the auricle, it touches the antihelix, m/y teeth seek the lobe, they begin to gnaw at it, m/y tongue gets into your canal." But in the next instant, the opposite action commences. As the speaker fills herself on the lover's body, she finds herself inside the loved one, and it is the filler/devourer who is consumed: . . . . "*I* look out at you from inside yourself, *I* lose m/yself, *I* go astray, *I* am poisoned by you who nourish me" (*B*, 24). Finally, both processes seem to be taking place simultaneously.

Sometimes the emptying process is rendered as bloodletting. Once this bloodletting is undertaken by the speaker, and once it is experienced by her: "You are exsanguinated," the speaker declares, "all your blood torn forcibly from your limbs issues violently from groins carotid arms temples legs ankles" (*B*, 20). Yet this emptying process becomes transformed once again into a filling: "Each drop of your blood each spurt from your arteries striking m/y arteries vibrates throughout me" (*B*, 20). Later it is the speaker who is "bled dry" by her "abominable mistress" (*B*, 126).

Such alimentary images suggest the importance of taste, yet all the senses are put to highly mobilized, even aggressive use. Touch becomes tearing, rending, penetrating, but such actions are highly mobile as well, as the following passage shows: "Your hand followed by your arm have entered into my throat, you traverse my larynx, you arrive at my lungs" (*B*, 98). Smells—even those of decay—represent another kind of ingestion and are often positive. In one harvesting activity, for example, perfumes are gathered from the flowers. Sound is also associated with movement: "Your every movement produces a harmony of sounds" (*B*, 29), the speaker announces, likening her companion lover to Eve with her singing serpent headdress. Indeed, singing and laughter are approved forms of expression as well as important means of disruption."[39] These means of expression are neither moderate nor modulated, and as Wittig explains in her definition of *outcry*, "The companion lovers vociferate, they cry out at the top of their voices, they howl, they storm," often with no other purpose than to "pass the time" (*LPMD*, 120). It is also deemed appropriate to invoke Sappho "in a very loud voice" (*B*, 57), and even companion lovers can sometimes be heard uttering "shrieking maledictions" at each other (*B*, 60). At other times the voice can be "hateful . . . pursuing m/e tracking m/e down losing m/e undoing m/e finishing m/e off" (*B*, 108).

Sight, although momentarily imprisoning, becomes another active agent, mobilized, even aggressive. In one instant the body of the love object becomes metamorphosed into a thousand eyes so that the speaker must describe herself as surrounded by "the brilliance" of her companion's "multiple eyes" (B, 133). First made drowsy, but then resistent, the speaker undergoes an invasion: "Moving away from you I can see all the eyes of your body are fixed attentively on the different autonomous parts of m/y body. . . . M/y muscles affected suddenly convulse. . . . M/y entire body is riddled by your gaze. It immobilizes m/e" (B, 134).

Disintegration, reintegration, contraction, and expansion also describe the kind of mobility that Wittig's companion lovers undertake. Some of the most emotionally rendered passages describe a quintessential dissolution that involves images of rising and falling. For example, in one poem the lovers "create a pressure. . . . a change of atmosphere," which begins the lover's ascent, after which "a slow movement commences, an eddy develops, a current becomes apparent. You drift off suddenly, you sway from side to side, you are uplifted" (B, 100). The descents are just as violent: "I fall, I fall, I drag you down in this fall this hissing spiral, speak to m/e accursed adored eddying maelstrom torment of pleasure" (B, 50).

Wittig's inscription of the lesbian body sometimes requires an immersion in the elements. While the ancient female principle associated woman only with earth and water, Wittig associates her with air and fire as well, thus bringing all elements into an engagement with the female body, both literally and symbolically. The speaker's fiery disintegration is frequent and violent ("I melt, I disintegrate, I am burnt up" (B, 162); it is also graphic: "M/y muscles begin to roast, the fire smoulders in places, ravages in others, it is fanned by your feverish movements, it attacks m/y flesh everywhere" (B, 162). In another place the lover, whose fingertips "are sheathed in supple mirrors," ignite the narrator's body in a conflagration that continues until "our blackened skulls clash together" (B, 119). Wind in its creative and destructive forms becomes analogous to the body's dismantling processes. In one dismembering scene the lovers' bodies become perforated, after which "the first current of air" invades their muscles, quickly becoming "a squall within you and within m/e simultaneously," and culminating at last in a storm "so violent that it precipitates us against one another, it brings us down, it flattens us" (B, 108–9).

Nor does Wittig neglect women's ancient connections to earth and water, which are also related to the body and its activities. One poem represents the lover becoming part of the field: "I walk over the black earth," the speaker tells us, and "under the soles of m/y feet I see your eyeballs there, I have embedded them somewhat. . . . Your whole body is in fragments here. . . . Your body is spread still warm bleeding over the entire surface of the ploughed field" (B, 113). Once again, however, the restoration process quickly begins: "I gather you up piece by piece, I reassemble you" (B, 113).

While water is often associated with processes of dissolution, it can also be a sustaining element. Swimming in "a black liquid mass," the speaker finds herself carried out to sea (*B*, 124). Threatened by the movements of passing predators and the invasion of sea sounds, she is nonetheless determined to seek her lover "in the dark of the sea and the dark of the night which *I* cannot distinguish" (*B*, 124). In this archetypal night sea journey, where water becomes hard to differentiate from air, and finally from the body itself, the speaker finds her lover only by submitting to the waves: "The water enters by m/y mouth m/y lungs. *I* cannot spit it all out again, as the pressure grows m/y intestines m/y stomach are invaded. . . . m/y belly splits apart, the water enters and leaves m/e" (*B*, 125). Again, it is not so much by dominance as it is by means of an exchange of dominance and submission that the endless varieties of fusion and dissolution can take place.

In reality, *The Lesbian Body*, despite its violent images, is as much about re-memberment as it is about its opposite, both of which are necessary for the mobility that is the real, that has been lost through the selective and fetishistic use of the body in gendered discourse. Indeed, it is only in moments of suspended action, in immobility, that the lesbian subjects experience fear, as in the following passage where the speaker anguishes over her immobilized lover: "*I* watch you, *I* watch you, *I* cannot refrain from crying out your face has become inert. . . . at last you collapse, *I* am seized through with anguish, *I* shriek, *I* weep, *I* shake you, you do not stir" (*B*, 65).

Thus, in both these texts, Wittig creates the lesbian experience out of movement, the recovery of desire, through a new scripting of the body. It has been argued, however, that Wittig has trapped herself. Resistent to her book-burning episode in *Les Guérillères*, Margaret Homans argues that Wittig cannot thereby create a new language; she can only succeed in erecting a new fable.[40] It is also possible to question Wittig's escape from psychoanalysis, to question whether an emphasis on the importance of politics and social structures over psychoanalytic theory constitutes an adequate response to the questions that psychoanalysis raises, questions that are dealt with more creatively by Irigaray and with less distortion by Julia Kristeva.

Perhaps in her textual inventiveness Wittig does respond to questions about lack-in-being and castration. For example, her persistent and continuous dismembering and reconstruction of her companion lovers, during which they undertake ongoing exchanges—of fluids, of identities, of elements—reveals Wittig's textual engagement in a radical exchange that is often dangerous, even violent, but sometimes exhilarating. Most important, these exchanges preclude fixity and render substitution suspect. Finally, what these dismembering processes appear to assert can best be described using the old gestalt psychology bromide that the whole—or (w)hole—is more than the sum of its parts. For Wittig dares to examine and attempt to textualize the void for which women are supposed to stand, even as she accepts desire in its aggressive manifestations, neither repressing violence nor turning desire into passive aggression in an attempt to demonstrate the textual possibilities of living with absence.

NOTES

1. Sarah Kofman, *The Enigma of Woman: Women in Freud's Writings*, trans. Catherine Porter (Ithaca, N.Y.: Cornell University Press, 1985), 191, explains that "because Freud establishes only a difference in degree between the normal and the pathological, the entire portion of the text that appears to deal with just one of the directions the girl's development may take after the discovery of her castration, the neurotic direction, deals at the same time with normal development."

2. Sigmund Freud, *Dora: An Analysis of a Case of Hysteria*, trans. Philip Rieff (New York: Collier, 1971).

3. Beyond the disturbing story of a young woman who strives to free herself from becoming an object of exchange in a tangled family relationship, Freud's narrative reveals his persistent blindness to his own countertransference, a limitation that has been used to explain his lack of interest in the relationship of Dora to other women and his delayed recognition of the "homosexual current" in Dora's life.

4. Much has been written about Dora, whose situation as contained within Freud's narrative makes for fascinating reading and ongoing speculation. See especially the essays in *In Dora's Case: Freud—Hysteria—Feminism*, ed. Charles Bernheimer and Claire Kahane (New York: Columbia University Press, 1985). See also Mary Jacobus, "Dora and the Pregnant Madonna," in *Reading Woman: Essays in Feminist Criticism* (Ithaca, N.Y.: Cornell University Press, 1986), 170–93; and Hélène Cixous, "Portrait de Dora," trans. Sarah Burd, *Diacritics* 13, no. 1 (Spring 1983): 2–32.

5. Whereas in the case of Dora Freud fails to account for countertransference (where the personal history and ideology of the analyst enter into the dialectic), in the case of the lesbian he denies the possibility of any positive transference. Freud only allows himself to experience negative transference in that he accuses the patient of having "transferred to me the sweeping repudiation of men which had dominated her ever since the disappointment she had suffered from her father" (*SE*, 18:164). See also Jacques Lacan, "Intervention on Transference," in *Feminine Sexuality: Jacques Lacan and the École Freudienne*, ed. Juliet Mitchell and Jacqueline Rose (New York: W. W. Norton, 1985), 67.

6. Luce Irigaray, *Speculum of the Other Woman*, trans. Gillian C. Gill (Ithaca, N.Y.: Cornell University Press, 1985), 101.

7. Lacan, "Intervention on Transference," 96.

8. Ibid., 97,

9. Ellie Ragland-Sullivan, *Jacques Lacan and the Philosophy of Psychoanalysis* (Urbana: University of Illinois Press, 1987), 186.

10. Ibid., 297.

11. Ibid., 289–99. Ragland-Sullivan expresses pessimism about changing a psychic structure that is in place by the age of five, but ponders the possibility of modifying the symbolic order.

12. Monique Wittig, "Paradigm," in *Homosexualities and French Literature*, ed. George Stambolian and Elaine Marks (Ithaca, N.Y.: Cornell University Press, 1979), hereafter cited in the text as "Paradigm." Wittig declares that homosexuality is "the desire for one's own sex. But it is also the desire for something else that is not connoted. This desire is resistance to the norm" (114).

13. Elaine Marks, "Lesbian Intertextuality," in *Homosexualities and French Literature*, ed. George Stambolian and Elaine Marks (Ithaca: Cornell University Press, 1979), 367, 372.

14. Catherine R. Stimpson, *Where the Meanings Are: Feminism and Cultural Spaces* (New York: Methuen, 1988), 98. For another interesting study of lesbian fiction, see Gillian Whitlock, "'Everything Is Out of Place': Radclyffe Hall and the Lesbian Literary Tradition," *Feminist Studies* 13, no. 3 (Fall 1987): 555–82.

15. Luce Irigaray, "When Our Lips Speak Together," trans. Carolyn Burke, *Signs* 6, no. 1 (1980): 75 (hereafter cited in the text as "Lips").

16. Carolyn Burke, "Introduction to Luce Irigaray's 'When Our Lips Speak Together,'" *Signs* 6, no. 1 (1980): 67.

17. Stimpson, *Where the Meanings Are*, 99, notes the "vast metonymic responsibility of the kiss" in lesbian encodings of the body.

18. See "The 'Mechanics' of Fluids," in *This Sex Which Is Not One*, trans. Catherine Porter (Ithaca: Cornell University Press, 1985), 106–18; and "Volume-Fluidity," in *Speculum*, 227–40.

19. Monique Wittig and Sande Zeig, *Lesbian Peoples' Material for a Dictionary* (1976; reprint, New York: Avon, 1979), 157 (hereafter cited parenthetically in the text as *LPMD*). Wittig does not deny the unconscious, but cautions "if you have one, all the more reason to be careful of the traffickers of the unconscious."

20. Monique Wittig, "The Mark of Gender," *Feminist Issues* 5, no. 2 (Fall 1985): 4 (hereafter cited parenthetically in the text as "Mark").

21. However, Wittig has expressed chagrin over the English translation of *Les Guérillères* because the translator has replaced *elles* with "the women." The latter appears "obsessively" throughout the text and undermines Wittig's attempt to "investigate the point of view of the *elles*," to make them absolute subject, to function as an "assault" on the reader with the intent not of feminizing the world, but of reducing the power of *ils* to stand as the abstract and absolute ("Mark," 9).

22. Monique Wittig, "One Is Not Born a Woman," *Feminist Issues* 1, no. 2 (Winter 1981): 48 (hereafter cited parenthetically in the text as "One").

22. Monique Wittig, *Les Guérillères*, trans. David LeVay (1969; reprint, Boston: Beacon Press, 1971), 60 (hereafter cited parenthetically in the text as *G*).

24. In another myth Antiope is represented as the jealous abandoned woman. Robert Graves, *The Greek Myths* (Harmondsworth, Middlesex: Penguin, 1955), 2:131, links amazonian battles to setbacks in the matriarchal systems he sees as dominating pre-Hellenic Greece and Asia Minor. He argues that the amazons are, in reality, moon priestesses connected to goddess worship.

25. Graves, 1:355, regards as "fantastic" the story that the amazons, whose name means "without breasts," were believed to remove one breast in order to more accurately aim their bows and arrows. He traces the word to an Armenian term meaning "moon women" and claims that the story of the attack on Athens was derived from icons that depicted pre-Hellenic priestesses of Athens. He also

states that there probably were armed priestesses dwelling at one time at Effaces, a Minoan colony.

26. Wittig (*LPMD*), 143) transforms "sleep" into a transitive verb: "to sleep someone means both to sleep beside her and to sleep the love of her. Sleeping someone takes precedence over many other activities." The Sleeping Beauty is no longer the immobilized princess, but becomes "a companion lover who is forgetful of her clitoris."

27. Erika Ostrovsky, *A Constant Journey: The Fiction of Monique Wittig* (Carbondale: Southern Illinois University Press, 1991), 56, notes that *feminaires* is a neologism that can be linked to *bestaires*, or bestiaries, those texts of exotic animals that are also "a reminder of the age-old, derogatory association of women and animals."

28. Stimpson, *Where the Meanings Are*, 99. Stimpson also observes that zero in Hindu is *sifr*, or empty space, and came to represent another number system, one that was used subversively.

29. Martha Noel Evans, *Masks of Tradition: Women and the Politics of Writing in Twentieth-Century France* (Ithaca, N.Y.: Cornell University Press, 1987), 188, also sees vestiges of this appropriately unrecorded rite in Wittig's text. Mythographers have thought the rite to be pre-patriarchal (pre-Hellenic) and to involve the descent of the daughter into the underworld, followed by her return and reunion with her grieving mother. The later redactions of the Demeter-Kore myths reflect this ancient rite of passage, but the rape of Kore by Hades and the mediating role of Zeus mark them as later versions. Wittig views the Demeter-Kore myth as a record of the split between mother and daughter, and hence between the lesbian people, with the result that some were forced into exile—the amazons to live in the countryside, the mothers to live in the cities.

30. Monique Wittig, *The Lesbian Body*, trans. David LeVay (1973; reprint, Boston: Beacon Press, 1986), 135 (hereafter cited parenthetically in the text as *B*).

31. Ostrovsky, *A Constant Journey*, 71.

32. Diane Griffin Crowder, "Amazons and Mothers: Monique Wittig and Hélène Cixous and Theories of Women's Writing," *Contemporary Literature* 24, no. 2 (1983): 122. See also Namascar Shaktini, "Displacing the Phallic Subject: Wittig's Lesbian Writing," *Signs* 8, no. 1 (Autumn 1982): 29–44.

33. Evans, *Masks of Tradition*, 185. See Evans's reading of Wittig, 185–219.

34. Patrick McGee, *Telling the Other: The Question of Value in Modern and Postcolonial Writing* (Ithaca, N.Y.: Cornell University Press, 1992), 190.

35. Evans, *Masks of Tradition*, 188, suggests that because of our inability to ascertain where we are or where the subjects are, the work becomes "itself a movement."

35. Gehenna is in a valley near Jerusalem—a dumping ground where fires burned constantly to ward off disease. It comes later to stand for a place of torment, and in the New Testament texts it becomes synonymous with hell.

37. Mircea Eliade, *The Sacred and the Profane*, trans. William R. Trask (New York: Harcourt, Brace and World, 1959), 68–113.

38. Theodor H. Gaster, *Thespis: Ritual, Myth, and Drama in the Ancient Near East* (New York: Harper, 1950), 23. Gaster identifies mortification rites as having to do with abstinence and states of suspended animation, while purgation rites involve purification (with the aid of fire and water) and focus on the ridding of the

community of disease and evil. Invigoration concerns itself with ritual combats and fertility rites; jubilation refers to such events as communal feasts (26–49). Wittig's focus on the communal activity of the women suggests that such social processes as ritual are intended to have a valid function in her texts.

39. See Marleen S. Barr, "'Laughing in a Liberating Defiance': *Egalia's Daughters* and Feminist Tendentious Humor," in *Discontented Discourses: Feminism/Textual Intervention/Psychoanalysis*, ed. Marleen S. Barr and Richard Feldstein (Urbana: University of Illinois Press, 1989), on feminist laughter as not only an "undefined and untapped category," but also "a psychological and social event, a powerful defense—a powerful weapon" (97).

40. Margaret Homans, "'Her Very Own Howl': The Ambiguities of Representation in Recent Women's Fiction," *Signs* 9, no. 2 (Winter 1983): 190.

8

Conclusion

In her recent study of contemporary women writers, Gayle Greene laments the passing of feminist fiction. Pointing to a postfeminist backlash that has left more recent fiction writers nostalgic—forgetful about the recent past, but content to "disremember"—she sees contemporary writers representing women's problems in terms of negotiations that they now make "for position and privilege within established institutions, families and corporations, with no sense that these institutions should themselves be changed."[1]

Greene is not alone in her concerns. Similar commentary can be heard from feminist critics trying to relate the fiction of women to that elitist, yet disavowing, group of white males that constitute the postmodernists. Proclaiming the death of the subject, the reign of (inter)textuality over truth, the classic postmodernists would hardly find Greene's feminist aims—"transforming the psychic and social structures" and "raising the consciousness and expectations of a generation"—in any way part to their agenda.[2] Indeed, such concerns would automatically ban even the most experimental of the women writers from this exclusive circle. Patricia Waugh argues similarly that, unlike the postmodernists, "feminism seeks a subjective identity, a sense of effective agency and history for women which has hitherto been denied them by the dominant culture."[3] For her, women writers, feminist or not, will continue to exist in a "contradictory relationship to both the dominant liberal conception of subjectivity and writing and the classic "postmodernist deconstruction of this liberal trajectory."[4]

The concept of *textual escap(e)ades* would, I hope, suggest its own escape from the feminist-postmodernist bind. Although a number of the works I have discussed fall conveniently within Greene's designated time period for when feminist fictions were being produced, it is also true that while I see such works less as political and social statements, I also doubt whether many serious women writers consider raising consciousness as a primary objective. I would be more apt to agree with Waugh that women writers are more confrontational, that as a marginalized groups(s), such oppositional stances are to be expected. On the other hand, such stances, when approached through the problem of mobility for women, become less rigid, more subversive perhaps, but also playful. For textual escap(e)ades has meant for me that a counterwriting is an essential ingredient of the more experimental novels that I have discussed here. Originally silenced through their exclusion from the literary canon, as well as from modes of literary production, today's women writers, unlike their timid or deferential foremothers (according to Simone deBeauvoir), can call on a number of empowering narrative strategies and styles. One feminist critic noted that "sometime in the bitter years between 1963 and 1973 . . . American women poets stopped trying to please and began to adventure 'along strange ways.'"5 The same can certainly be said for women novelists now writing.

Thus, this study has intended to draw attention to writing informed by both feminism and postmodernism, writing that may be inadequately defined by either term. The writers that I have chosen to discuss here have focused on issues of mobility, on the containment and entrapment of woman as body, as exchange object, as daughter, and, finally, as writer. Each has, in her own way, engaged in a counterwriting that has resulted in the reconstruction of conventional plots and genres; some have translated the trope of mobility into intertextual material; all have revitalized and transformed the journey into a textualizing of body space.

Such narrative strategies have foregrounded female subjectivity, especially as it involves problems of mergence and separation. I would agree with Waugh that women's writing is generally less concerned with the construction of "an isolated individual ego" than with "the construction of identity *in relationship*."6 This empowering collectivity is especially important in the work of Toni Morrison and Monique Witting. On the other hand, the postmodernist response to the death of the subject has not been ignored by these writers, although it may have a different meaning for them. For most of the writers discussed in this study, the stabilized subject has always been problematic, but rather than fetishizing their writing, they have preferred to introduce into their texts images of more permeable boundaries, of fragmentation and dismemberment, constructions of multiple selves; they have welcomed the return of the repressed, introduced non-realistic material that cannot easily be naturalized, and constructed their texts by means of multivocal subject positions; often they flaunt holes and gaps. Finally, we see in these works that it is the female body that becomes the source of textual mobility, for it is through the body that is both mother and daughter, the body too often identified in the dominant discourses as lack, that women writers find ways to free themselves from entrapment and containment.

I have chosen to bring psychoanalytic theory to bear upon my readings not only because the cultural and historical containment of women has been well documented, but also because issues of mobility involve the very constitution of the subject, male and female, and speak to questions regarding the body—and the desire that informs and energizes the discourses of us all.

NOTES

1. Gayle Greene, *Changing the Story: Feminist Fiction and the Tradition* (Bloomington: Indiana University Press, 1991), 195. See especially the chapter entitled "What Ever Happened to Feminist Fiction?"

2. Ibid., 193.

3. Patricia Waugh, *Feminine Fictions: Revisiting the Postmodern* (London and New York: Routledge, 1989), 9.

4. Ibid., 10.

5. Paula Bennett, *My Life a Loaded Gun: Female Creativity and Feminist Politics* (Boston: Beacon Press, 1986), 242.

6. Waugh, *Feminine Fictions*, 10.

Selected Bibliography

Abel, Elizabeth. "(E)Merging Identities: The Dynamics of Female Friendship in Contemporary Fiction by Women." *Signs* 6, no. 3 (Spring 1981): 413–35.

Abel, Elizabeth, Marianne Hirsch, and Elizabeth Langland, eds. *The Voyage In: Fictions of Female Development*. Hanover, N.H.: University Press of New England, 1983.

Allen, Paula Gunn. *The Sacred Hoop: Recovering the Feminine in American Indian Traditions*. Boston: Beacon Press, 1986.

Apollon, Willy. "Psychoanalytic Treatment of Psychosis." In *Lacan and the Subject of Language*, ed. Ellie Ragland-Sullivan and Mark Bracher, 116–40. New York: Routledge, 1991.

Atwood, Margaret. *Lady Oracle*. New York: Fawcett Crest, 1976.

Barr, Marleen S. "'Laughing in a Liberating Defiance': *Egalia's Daughters* and Feminist Tendentious Humor." In *Discontented Discourses: Feminism/Textual Intervention/Psychoanalysis*, ed. Marleen S. Barr and Richard Feldstein, 87–99. Urbana: University of Illinois Press, 1989.

Barthes, Roland. *The Pleasure of the Text*, trans. Richard Miller. New York: Hill and Wang, 1975.

Bassuk, Ellen L. "The Rest Cure: Repetition or Resolution of Victorian Women's Conflicts?" In *The Female Body in Western Culture: Contemporary Perspectives*, ed. Susan Rubin Suleiman, 139–51. Cambridge: Harvard University Press, 1986.

Benjamin, Jessica. "The Bonds of Love: Rational Violence and Erotic Domination." *Feminist Studies* 6, no. 1 (1980): 144–71.

Bennett, Paula. *My Life a Loaded Gun: Female Creativity and Feminist Poetics*. Boston: Beacon Press, 1986.

Benstock, Shari. *Textualizing the Feminine: On the Limits of Genre*. Norman: University of Oklahoma Press, 1991.

Berman, Jeffrey. "Sylvia Plath and the Art of Dying." *University of Hartford Studies in Literature* 10, nos. 1–3 (1978): 137– 55.

Bernheimer, Charles. "Introduction: Part One." In *In Dora's Case: Freud—Hysteria—Feminism*, ed. Charles Bernheimer and Claire Kahane, 1–18. New York: Columbia University Press, 1985.

Black Elk. *Black Elk Speaks*, ed. John G. Neihardt. New York: William Morrow, 1932.

Bourjaily, Vance. "Victoria Lucas and Elly Higginbottom." In *Ariel Ascending: Writings About Sylvia Plath*, ed. Paul Alexander. New York: Harper and Row, 1985.

Broe, Mary Lynn, and Angela Ingram, eds. *Women's Writing in Exile*. Chapel Hill: University of North Carolina Press, 1989.

Bromberg, Pamela S. "The Two Faces of the Mirror in *The Edible Woman* and *Lady Oracle*." In *Margaret Atwood: Visions and Forms*, ed. Kathryn Van Spanckeren and Jan Garden Castro, 12–23. Carbondale: Southern Illinois University Press, 1988.

Broner, E. M. *Her Mothers*. 1975. Reprint. Bloomington: Indiana University Press, 1985.

Butscher, Edward. *Sylvia Plath: Method and Madness*. New York: Seabury Press, 1976.

Chodorow, Nancy. *The Reproduction of Mothering: Psychoanalysis and the Sociology of Gender*. Berkeley: University of California Press, 1978.

Christian, Barbara. "Alice Walker: The Black Woman Artist as Wayward." In *Black Women Writers (1950–1980): A Critical Evaluation*, ed. Mari Evans, 456–77. Garden City, N.Y.: Doubleday, 1984.

———. *Black Women Novelists: The Development of a Tradition 1892–1976*. 1980. Reprint. Westport, Conn.: Greenwood Press, 1985.

Cixous, Hélène. "Castration or Decapitation?" trans. Annette Kuhn. *Signs* 7, no. 1 (Autumn 1981): 41–55.

———. "The Laugh of the Medusa," trans. Keith Cohen and Paula Cohen. *Signs* 1, no. 4 (Summer 1976): 875–93.

———. "Portrait de Dora", trans. Sarah Burd. *Diacritics* 13, no. 1 (Spring 1983): 2–32.

Cixous, Hélène, and Catherine Clément. *The Newly-Born Women*, trans. Betsy Wing. Minneapolis: University of Minnesota Press, 1986.

Crowder, Diane Griffin. "Amazons and Mothers: Monique Wittig and Hélène Cixous and Theories of Women's Writing." *Contemporary Literature* 24, no. 2 (1983): 117–44.

Daly, Mary. *Gyn/Ecology: The Metaethics of Radical Feminism*. Boston: Beacon Press, 1978.

David-Ménard, Monique. *Hysteria from Freud to Lacan: Body and Language in Psychoanalysis*, trans. Catherine Porter. Ithaca, N.Y.: Cornell University Press, 1989.

Davis, Christina. "Interview with Toni Morrison." *Présence Africaine* 1st Quarterly (1988): 141–56.

DeKoven, Marianne. *Breaking the Sequence: Women's Experimental Fiction*, ed. Ellen G. Friedman and Miriam Fuchs. Princeton, N.J.: Princeton University Press, 1989.

Doane, Mary Ann. *The Desire to Desire: The Woman's Film of the 1940s*. Bloomington: Indiana University Press, 1987.

DuPlessis, Rachel Blau. *Writing Beyond the Ending: Narrative Strategies of Twentieth-Century Women Writers*. Bloomington: Indiana University Press, 1985.

Ehrenreich, Barbara, and Deidre English. *Complaints and Disorders: The Sexual Politics of Sickness*. Old Westbury, N.Y.: Feminist Press, 1973.

Eliade, Mircea. *The Sacred and the Profane*, trans. William R. Trask. New York: Harcourt, Brace and World, 1959.

Evans, Martha Noel. *Masks of Tradition: Women and the Politics of Writing in Twentieth-Century France*. Ithaca: Cornell University Press, 1987.

Felman, Shoshana, ed. *Literature and Psychoanalysis: The Question of Reading Otherwise*. Baltimore: Johns Hopkins University Press, 1982.

Fetterly, Judith. "Reading About Reading: 'A Jury of Her Peers,' 'The Murders in the Rue Morgue,' and 'The Yellow Wallpaper.'" In *Gender and Reading: Essays on Readers, Texts and Contexts*, ed. Elizabeth A. Flynn and Patrocinio P. Schweikart, 159–64. Baltimore: Johns Hopkins University Press, 1986.

Flax, Jane. "The Conflict Between Nurturance and Autonomy in Mother-Daughter Relationships and within Feminism." *Feminist Studies* 4, no. 1 (1978): 171–89.

Freibert, Lucy M. "The Artist as Picaro: The Revelation of Margaret Atwood's *Lady Oracle*." *Canadian Literature* 92 (Spring 1982): 23–33.

French, Marilyn. Introduction to *Her Mothers*, by E. M. Broner. 1975. Reprint. Bloomington: Indiana University Press, 1985.

Freud, Sigmund. *Dora: An Analysis of a Case of Hysteria*, trans. Philip Rieff. New York: Collier, 1971.

————. *The Standard Edition of the Complete Psychological Works of Sigmund Freud*, ed. James Strachey. 24 vols. London: Hogarth Press, 1953–74.

Friedman, Ellen G., and Miriam Fuchs, eds. *Breaking the Sequence: Women's Experimental Fiction*. Princeton, N.J.: Princeton University Press, 1989.

Gallop, Jane. *The Daughter's Seduction: Feminism and Psychoanalysis*. Ithaca, N.Y.: Cornell University Press, 1986.

Gardner, Judith Kegan. "The Maternal Deathbed in Women's Fiction." *Feminist Studies* 4, no. 1 (1978): 146–65.

Gaster, Theodor H. *Thespis: Ritual, Myth, and Drama in the Ancient Near East*. New York: Harper, 1950.

Gates, Henry Louis, Jr. *The Signifying Monkey: A Theory of African-American Literary Criticism*. New York: Oxford University Press, 1988.

Gilbert, Sandra, and Susan Gubar. *The Madwoman in the Attic: The Woman Writer and the Nineteenth-Century Literary Imagination*. New Haven, Conn.: Yale University Press, 1979.

Gilman, Charlotte Perkins. *The Charlotte Perkins Gilman Reader*, ed. and with Introduction by Ann J. Lane. New York: Pantheum, 1980.

Grace, Sherrill E. *Violent Duality: A Study of Margaret Atwood*, ed. Ken Norris. Montreal: Véhicule Press, 1980.

Grant, Robert. "Absence into Presence: The Thematics of Memory and 'Missing' Subjects in Toni Morrison's *Sula*." In *Critical Essays on Toni Morrison*, ed. Nellie McKay, 90–103. Boston: G.K. Hall, 1988.

Graves, Robert, *The Greek Myths: 1, 2.* Harmondsworth, Middlesex: Penguin, 1955.

Greene, Gayle. *Changing the Story: Feminist Fiction and the Tradition.* Bloomington: Indiana University Press, 1991.

Grosz, Elizabeth. *Jacques Lacan: A Feminist Introduction.* New York: Routledge, 1990.

Hirsch, Marianne. "Review Essay: Mothers and Daughters." *Signs* 7, no. 1 (Autumn 1981): 200–22.

Hite, Molly. *The Other Side of the Story: Structures and Strategies of Contemporary Feminist Narratives.* Ithaca, N.Y. Cornell University Press, 1989.

Hogg, Donald W. *Jamaican Religions: A Study in Variations.* Ann Arbor, Mich.: UMI Press, 1967.

Holland, Norman N., and Leona F. Sherman. "Gothic Possibilities." In *Gender and Reading: Essays on Readers, Texts and Contexts,* ed. Elizabeth A. Flynn and Patricinio Schweikart, 215–33. Baltimore: Johns Hopkins University Press, 1986.

Homans, Margaret. "'Her Very Own Howl': The Ambiguities of Representation in Recent Women's Fiction." *Signs* 9, no. 2 (Winter 1983): 186–205.

Hoy, Judy. "Of Holy Writing and Priestly Voices: A Talk with Esther Broner." *Massachusetts Review* 24, no. 2 (Summer 1983): 254–69.

Hutcheon, Linda. "From Poetic to Narrative Structures: The Novels of Margaret Atwood." In *Margaret Atwood: Language, Text, and System,* ed. Sherrill E. Grace and Lorraine Weir, 17–31. Vancouver: University of British Columbia Press, 1983.

Irigaray, Luce. "And the One Doesn't Stir Without the Other," trans. Hélène Vivienne Wenzel. *Signs* 7, no. 1 (Autumn 1981): 60–67.

———. *Speculum of the Other Woman,* trans. Gillian C. Gill. Ithaca, N.Y.: Cornell University Press, 1985.

———. *This Sex Which Is Not One,* trans. Catherine Porter. Ithaca: Cornell University Press, 1985.

———. "When Our Lips Speak Together," trans. Carolyn Burke. *Signs* 6, no. 1 (1980): 67–79.

Jacobus, Mary. *Reading Woman: Essays in Feminist Criticism.* New York: Columbia University Press, 1986.

Jensen, Emily. "Margaret Atwood's *Lady Oracle*: A Modern Parable." *Essays on Canadian Writing* 33 (Fall 1986): 29–49.

Kahane, Claire. "The Gothic Mirror." In *The (M)other Tongue: Essays in Feminist Psychoanalytic Interpretation,* ed. Shirley Nelson Garner, Claire Kahane, and Madelon Sprengnether, 334–51. Ithaca, N.Y.: Cornell University Press, 1985.

Kahn, Coppélia. "The Hand That Rocks the Cradle: Recent Gender Theories and Their Implications." In *The (M)other Tongue: Essays in Feminist Psychoanalytic Interpretation,* ed. Shirley Nelson Garner, Claire Kahane, and Madelon Sprengnether, 72–88. Ithaca, N.Y.: Cornell University Press, 1985.

Kofman, Sarah. *The Enigma of Woman: Woman in Freud's Writings,* trans. Catherine Porter. Ithaca, N.Y.: Cornell University Press, 1985.

Kolodny, Annette. "A May for Rereading: Or, Gender and the Interpretation of Literary Texts." *New Literary History* 11, no. 3 (Spring 1980): 451–67.

Kristeva, Julia. *Desire in Language: A Semiotic Approach to Literature and Art*, ed. Louis S. Roudiez. New York: Columbia University Press, 1980.

_____. *The Kristeva Reader*. ed. Toril Moi. New York: Columbia University Press, 1986.

_____. *Revolution in Poetic Language*, trans. Margaret Waller. New York: Columbia University Press, 1984.

_____. "Stabat Mater." In *The Female Body in Western Culture: Contemporary Perspectives*, ed. Susan Rubin Suleiman, 99–118. Cambridge: Harvard University Press, 1986.

Krumholz, Linda. "The Ghosts of Slavery: Historical Recovery in Toni Morrison's *Beloved*." *African American Review*, 26, no. 3 (Fall 1992): 395–408.

Lacan, Jacques. *Écrits: A Selection*, trans. Alan Sheridan. New York: W. W. Norton, 1977.

_____. *The Four Fundamental Concepts of Psycho-Analysis*, trans. Alan Sheridan and ed. Jacques-Alain Miller. New York: W. W. Norton, 1978.

_____. "Intervention on Transference." In *Feminine Sexuality: Jacques Lacan and the École Freudienne*, ed. Juliet Mitchell and Jacqueline Rose, 61–73. New York: W. W. Norton, 1985.

_____. *The Seminar of Jacques Lacan. Book III, The Psychoses, 1955–1956*, ed. Jacques-Alain Miller. New York: W. W. Norton, 1993.

Lameyer, Gordon. "The Double in Sylvia Plath's *The Bell Jar*." In *Sylvia Plath: The Woman and the Work*, ed. Edward Butscher, 143–65. New York: Dodd Mead, 1977.

deLauretis, Teresa. *Alice Doesn't: Feminism, Semiotics, Cinema*. Bloomington: Indiana University Press, 1987.

Lecker, Robert. "Janus Through the Looking Glass: Atwood's First Three Novels." In *The Art of Margaret Atwood: Essays in Criticism*, ed. Arnold E. Davidson and Cathy N. Davidson, 177–203. Toronto: Anansi, 1981.

Lotman, Jurij M. "The Origin of Plot in the Light of Typology," trans. Julian Graffy. *Poetics Today* 1, nos. 1–2 (Autumn 1979).

McCombs, Judith. "Atwood's Fictive Portraits of the Artist: From Victim to Surfacer, from Oracle to Birth. *Women's Studies* 12 (1986): 69–88.

McGee, Patrick. *Telling the Other: The Question of Value in Modern and Postcolonial Writing*. Ithaca, N.Y.: Cornell University Press, 1992.

McMillan, Ann. "The Transforming Eye: *Lady Oracle* and the Gothic Tradition." In *Margaret Atwood: Visions and Forms*, ed. Kathryn Van Spanckeren and Jan Garden Castro, 48–64. Carbondale: Southern Illinois University Press, 1988.

Marshall, Brenda K. *Teaching the Postmodern: Fiction and Theory*. New York: Routledge, 1992.

Medwick, Cathleen. "People Are Talking About . . ." *Vogue*, April 1981, 289.

Meese, Elizabeth A. *Crossing the Double-Cross: The Practice of Feminist Criticism*. Chapel Hill: University of North Carolina Press, 1986.

Miller, Jacques-Alain. "Microscopia: An Introduction to the Reading of *Television*." In *Television*, trans. Denis Hollier, Rosalind Krauss, and Annette Michelson and ed. Joan Copjec, xi–xxxi. New York: W. W. Norton, 1989.

Minh-ha, Trinh T. *When the Moon Waxes Red: Representation, Gender and Cultural Politics*. New York: Routledge, 1991.

_____.*Woman, Native, Other: Writing, Postcoloniality and Feminism*. Bloomington: Indiana University Press, 1989.

Moi, Toril. "Representations of Patriarchy: Sexuality and Epistemology in Freud's Dora." In *In Dora's Case: Freud—Hysteria—Feminism*, ed. Charles Bernheimer and Claire Kahane, 181–99. New York: Columbia University Press, 1985.

Morrison, Toni. *Beloved*. New York: New American Library, 1987.

_____. *Sula*. New York: New American Library, 1973.

_____. "Unspeakable Things Unspoken: The Afro-American Presence in American Literature." *Michigan Quarterly Review* 28 (Winter 1989):1–34.

Naylor, Gloria, and Toni Morrison. "A Conversation." *Southern Review* 21 (July 1985): 567–93.

Neumann, Erich. *The Great Mother*, trans. Ralph Manheim. Princeton, N.J.: Princeton University Press, 1963.

Plath, Sylvia. *The Bell Jar*. New York: Harper and Row, 1971. Reprint. New York: Bantam, 1971.

Poirier, Suzanne. "The Weir Mitchell Rest Cure: Doctor and Patients." *Women's Studies* 10 (1983):15–40.

Ragland-Sullivan, Ellie. *Jacques Lacan and the Philosophy of Psychoanalysis*. Urbana: University of Illinois Press, 1987.

_____. "The Sexual Masquerade: A Lacanian Theory of Sexual Difference." In *Lacan and the Subject of Language*, ed. Ellie Ragland-Sullivan and Mark Bracher, 49–80. New York: Routledge, 1991.

Reddy, Maureen T. "The Tripled Plot and Center of *Sula*." *Black American Literature Forum* 22, no. 1 (Spring 1988): 29– 45.

Rich, Adrienne. *Of Woman Born: Motherhood as Experience and Institution*. New York: W. W. Norton, 1976.

Rose, Jacqueline. "Dora: Fragment of an Analysis." In *In Dora's Case: Freud—Hysteria—Feminism*, ed. Charles Bernheimer and Claire Kahane, 128–48. New York: Columbia University Press, 1985.

_____. "Introduction II." In *Feminine Sexuality: Jacques Lacan and the École Freudiènne*, ed. Juliet Mitchell and Jacqueline Rose, 27–57. New York: W. W. Norton, 1981.

Rosenberg, Jerome H. *Margaret Atwood*. Boston: Twayne, 1984.

Rubenstein, Roberta. *Boundaries of the Self: Gender, Culture, Fiction*. Urbana: University of Illinois Press, 1987.

Sadoff, Dianne F. "Black Matrilineage: The Case of Alice Walker and Zora Neale Hurston." *Signs* 11, no. 1 (Autumn 1985): 4–26.

Scarberry, Susan J. "Grandmother Spider's Lifeline." In *Studies in American Indian Literature: Critical Essays and Course Designs*, ed. Paula Gunn Allen, 100–107. New York: Modern Language Association of America, 1983.

Schmudde, Carol E. "The Haunting of 124." *African American Review* 26, no. 3 (Fall 1992): 409–16.

Schwartz, Murray M., and Christopher Bollas. "The Absence at the Center: Sylvia Plath and Suicide." *Criticism* 18 (1976): 147–72.

Silverman, Kaja. *The Acoustic Mirror: The Female Voice in Psychoanalysis and Cinema*. Bloomington: Indiana University Press, 1988.

_____. *The Subject of Semiotics*. New York: Oxford University Press, 1983.

Stanton, Domna C. "Difference on Trial: A Critique of the Maternal Metaphor in Cixous, Irigaray, and Kristeva." In *The Poetics of Gender*, ed. Nancy K. Miller, 157–82. New York: Columbia University Press, 1986.

Stepto, Robert B. "'Intimate Things in Place': A Conversation with Toni Morrison." In *The Third Woman: Minority Women Writers in the United States*, ed. Dexter Fisher, 167–82. New York: Houghton Mifflin, 1980.

Stimpson, Catherine R. *Where the Meanings Are: Feminism and Cultural Spaces*. New York: Methuen, 1988.

Suleiman, Susan Rubin. *The Female Body in Western Culture: Contemporary Perspectives*. Cambridge: Harvard University Press, 1986.

Tate, Claudia. *Black Women Writers at Work*. New York: Continuum, 1983.

Treichler, Paula A. "Escaping the Sentence: Diagnosis as Discourse in 'The Yellow Wallpaper.'" In *Feminist Issues in Literary Scholarship*, ed. Shari Benstock, 62–78. Bloomington: Indiana University Press, 1987.

Wagner, Linda W. "Plath's *The Bell Jar* as Female *Bildungsroman*." *Women's Studies* 12 (1986): 55–68.

Walker, Alice. *The Color Purple*. New York: Washington Square Press, 1982.

_____. *In Search of Our Mothers' Gardens*. New York: Harcourt, Brace, Jovanovich, 1983.

_____. *Living by the Word: Selected Writings—1973–1987*. New York: Harcourt, Brace, Jovanovich, 1988.

_____ *Meridian*. New York: Washington Square Press, 1976.

Watts, Alan W. *Myth and Ritual in Christianity*. Boston: Beacon Press, 1968.

Whitlock, Gillian. "'Everything is Out of Place': Radclyffe Hall and the Lesbian Literary Tradition." *Feminist Studies* 13, no. 3 (Fall 1987): 555–82.

Wittig, Monique. *Les Guérillères*. Trans. David LeVay. 1969. Reprint. Boston: Beacon Press, 1971.

_____. *The Lesbian Body*. trans. David LeVay. 1973. Reprint. Boston: Beacon Press, 1986.

_____. "The Mark of Gender." *Feminist Issues* 5, no. 2 (Fall 1985): 3–12.

_____. "One Is Not Born a Woman." *Feminist Issues* 1, no. 2 (Winter 1981): 47–54.

_____. "Paradigm." In *Homosexualities and French Literature*, ed. George Stambolian and Elaine Marks, 114–21. Ithaca, N.Y.: Cornell University Press, 1979.

Wittig, Monique, and Sande Zeig. *Lesbian Peoples' Material for a Dictionary*. 1976. Reprint. New York: Avon, 1979.

Wood, Ann Douglas. "'The Fashionable Diseases': Women's Complaints and Their Treatment in Nineteenth-Century America." In *Clio's Consciousness Raised*, ed. Mary S. Hartman and Lois Banner, 1–22. New York: Harper Colophon, 1974.

Woolf, Virginia. *A Room of One's Own*. New York: Harcourt, Brace and World, 1929.

Wyatt, Jean. "Giving Body to the Word: The Maternal Symbolic in Toni Morrison's *Beloved*." *PMLA* 108, no. 3 (May 1993): 474–88.

Yaeger, Patricia. *Honey-Mad Women: Emancipatory Strategies in Women's Writing*. New York: Columbia University Press, 1988.

Ywahoo, Dhyani. *Voices of Our Ancestors*. Boston: Shambala, 1987.

Index

About the Author

LINDSEY TUCKER is currently Associate Professor of English at the University of Miami. She is the author of *Stephen and Bloom at Life's Feast* (1984), and the editor of *Critical Essays on Iris Murdoch* (1992). She writes widely on contemporary women writers.

ISBN 0-313-29156-X

9 780313 291562

90000>

EAN

HARDCOVER BAR CODE